GAY, STRAIGHT, AND THE REASON WHY

GAY, STRAIGHT,
and the
REASON WHY

THE SCIENCE OF SEXUAL ORIENTATION

SIMON LeVAY

OXFORD
UNIVERSITY PRESS

OXFORD
UNIVERSITY PRESS

Oxford University Press is a department of the University of Oxford.
It furthers the University's objective of excellence in research, scholarship,
and education by publishing worldwide.

Oxford   New York
Auckland   Cape Town   Dar es Salaam   Hong Kong   Karachi
Kuala Lumpur   Madrid   Melbourne   Mexico City   Nairobi
New Delhi   Shanghai   Taipei   Toronto

With offices in
Argentina   Austria   Brazil   Chile   Czech Republic   France   Greece
Guatemala   Hungary   Italy   Japan   Poland   Portugal   Singapore
South Korea   Switzerland   Thailand   Turkey   Ukraine   Vietnam

Oxford is a registered trade mark of Oxford University Press
in the UK and certain other countries.

Published in the United States of America by
Oxford University Press
198 Madison Avenue, New York, NY 10016

Library of Congress Cataloging-in-Publication Data
LeVay, Simon.
Gay, straight, and the reason why: the science of sexual orientation/Simon LeVay.
p. cm.
Includes bibliographical references and index.
ISBN 978-0-19-973767-3 (hardcover); 978-0-19-993158-3 (paperback)
1. Sexual orientation. 2. Sex (Psychology)
3. Sex (Biology) I. Title.
BF692.L476 2010
155.3—DC22
2009049210

9 8 7 6 5 4 3

Printed in the United States of America on acid-free paper

CONTENTS

NINE

THE BODY 221

TEN

THE OLDER-BROTHER EFFECT 247

ELEVEN

CONCLUSIONS 271

INTRODUCTION

In August 1991, when I was a neuroscientist working at the Salk Institute for Biological Studies in San Diego, I published a short research paper in the journal *Science*. The article was titled "A difference in hypothalamic structure between heterosexual and homosexual men." It attracted a great deal of interest from the media, the general public, and the scientific community, and it helped trigger a wave of new research into an age-old question: What makes people straight or gay?

The *hypothalamus** is a small region at the base of the brain that helps regulate several of our instinctual drives, including

---

* Most technical terms are italicized at first mention and are defined in the Glossary, starting on page 297.

our sex drive. In my study, I took specimens of the hypothalamus from men and women who had died and were undergoing autopsy. About half of the men were gay. I focused on a region at the front of the hypothalamus that is known to be involved in regulating the sexual behaviors typically shown by males. Within this region lies a rice-grain-sized collection of nerve cells named *INAH3*, which is usually larger in men than in women. I confirmed this basic sex difference. In addition, however, I found that INAH3 was significantly smaller, on average, in the gay men than in the straight men. In fact, there was no difference in size between INAH3 in the gay men and the women in my sample. I interpreted this finding as a clue that biological processes of brain development may influence a man's sexual orientation.

I was certainly not the first person to have thought about sexual orientation from a biological perspective. A hundred years ago, a German physician and sex researcher, Magnus Hirschfeld, proposed that brain development followed different paths in fetuses destined to become gay adults and those destined to become straight. Just a year before I published my study, a Dutch group reported that another cluster of cells in the hypothalamus, the *suprachiasmatic nucleus*, also differed in size between gay and straight men. And, during the mid 1980s, psychiatrist Richard Pillard of Boston University had reported evidence that homosexuality clustered in certain families, raising the possibility that genes running in those families might be influencing the sexual orientation of family members.

But my report differed in significant respects from most earlier ones. For one thing, by studying a brain region that is known to help regulate our sexuality I was, perhaps, cutting closer to the heart of the matter than earlier studies had done. Also, many of the earlier studies had talked about homosexuality as if it was an abnormality or problem, while heterosexuality was something so normal that it barely needed to be mentioned. The Dutch researchers, for example, had titled their study "An enlarged suprachiasmatic nucleus in homosexual men"—as if gay men had some kind of pathological swelling or tumor in that part of their brains. I doubt that the Dutch researchers actually thought about the matter in that way. Still, by titling their study as they did they fostered a point of view that has been all too prevalent over the years—a point of view that could be summarized in the question: What's wrong with gay people?

There's nothing wrong with gay people. I'm gay myself, and happy to be so. There are some differences between us and the rest of humanity, certainly, as I'll discuss in this book. Some of these differences are trivial, and some may influence people's lives in interesting ways, making being gay or straight more than just a matter of "who we love." But pathology doesn't come into it.

Whatever the exact reason, my 1991 study received a lot more attention from the media, and from the public at large, than had earlier studies. On the day of publication, most of the leading U.S. newspapers carried front-page stories about it. Because I was home-town talent, the *San Diego Union-Tribune* actually gave my report top billing, relegating what was probably a more significant news item on that day—the collapse of the Soviet Union—to a humbler position on the page.

Gay people reacted more favorably to my report than they had done to earlier studies. Some gay academics did exhibit a certain hostility—I recall psychologist John De Cecco of San Francisco State University denouncing it as "another example of medical homophobia" in a television interview. More commonly, though, gay people told me that my finding validated their own sense of being "born gay" or being intrinsically different from straight people. This they perceived as a good thing, because people with anti-gay attitudes often portray homosexuality as a lifestyle or a choice that people make—and by implication a bad choice.

My own position is this: The scientific knowledge currently available does bolster the idea that gays and lesbians are distinct "kinds" of people who are entitled to protection from discrimination, especially by governments, rather in the same way that racial minorities are. But I also believe that there would be plenty of reasons why gay people should be accepted and valued by society, even if being gay were proven to be an outright choice.

I wrote extensively about the social implications of this kind of research in my earlier book, *Queer Science*,[†] so I will not revisit that theme here, except for a few closing remarks. Rather, my intent in the present book is simply to give some idea of where the science stands today, 19 years after my *Science* paper appeared.

---

† Endnotes begin on page 309, and consist of literature references only.

That paper was followed by a welter of new research. Not by myself, because I left my position at the Salk Institute in 1992. Since then, I have occupied myself as a writer and teacher, but I have maintained a close interest in the field that I had worked in. Much of the new research has been done by a younger generation of scientists—neuroscientists, endocrinologists, geneticists, and cognitive psychologists—in laboratories across the United States, in Canada, Britain, and several European countries.

My study, and the publicity it generated, helped trigger much of this new work, but it certainly wasn't the whole inspiration. Richard Pillard, for example, along with psychologist Michael Bailey of Northwestern University, published an important genetic study on sexual orientation in late 1991, just a few months after my *Science* paper appeared. Their study had been completed before my paper came out and was in no way influenced by it. Pillard and Bailey's work led to further studies by their own research groups, and it helped draw molecular geneticists and other specialists into the field.

Taken together, the multitude of research studies published since 1991 have greatly strengthened the idea that biological factors play a significant role in the development of sexual orientation—in both men and in women. More than that, they tend to bolster a particular kind of biological theory. This is the idea that the origins of sexual orientation are to be sought in the interactions between sex hormones and the developing brain. These interactions are what predispose our developing minds toward some degree of "masculinity" or "femininity." In other words, this theory places sexual orientation within the larger framework of *gender*—the collection of psychological traits that differ between the male and female sexes—but gender as seen from a very biological perspective.

The idea that the interaction between sex hormones and the fetal brain might be an important factor in the development of sexual orientation is not new. In fact, Magnus Hirschfeld suggested as much in the early 20th century. But now there is evidence, and that evidence is what much of this book is about.

The first chapter of the book discusses the meaning of terms like *sexual orientation, homosexual, bisexual, heterosexual, gay,* and *straight,* and it reviews what we know about the prevalence of different sexual orientations, both in contemporary Western society and across cultures and historical periods. It also examines how stable a person's sexual orientation is over her or his lifetime. My conclusion from this review will be that sexual orientation is indeed a fairly stable aspect of human nature, and that straight, gay, and bisexual people have existed across many, perhaps all, cultures. This suggests that biological factors common to all humanity could be responsible for the emergence of individuals with different sexual orientations. Nevertheless, this review also makes clear that we need to think somewhat differently about sexual orientation in men and in women, and that cultural forces greatly influence how homosexuality is expressed in different societies and across the span of history. There are limits, in other words, to what we may hope to explain with biological ideas.

The second chapter is a brief review of *nonbiological* theories of sexual orientation. These include traditional Freudian theories that focus on parent–child relationships, as well as behaviorist ideas that see a person's sexual orientation as the end-product of a learning process. The chapter will also consider the idea, espoused by some Christian conservatives as well as by a few gay activists, that a person's sexual orientation is the result of a conscious and voluntary choice. I'll conclude that all such theories fail to adequately explain the diversity in people's sexual orientation. This failure makes the search for biological factors all the more compelling.

Chapter 3 lays out the skeleton of a biological theory of sexual orientation. It describes what we know about other aspects of sexual development and how they are regulated: by a cascade-like sequence of interactions between genes, sex hormones, and the cells of the developing body and brain. These processes don't go forward in complete isolation from the outside world—there is the potential for interactions between internal biological programs and environmental factors, and such interactions likely increase as development goes on. As a result of genetic differences between individuals, as well as the random variability of biological processes and perhaps feedback effects from the environment, these biological processes go forward differently in different individuals, leading to diversity in sexual orientation. I lay out how these ideas will be tested in the remaining chapters of the book.

Chapter 4 asks: Are there differences between gay and straight people when they are still children—that is, before their sexual orientation becomes apparent to themselves or others?

The answer is: Yes, there are. Retrospective studies, as well as prospective studies that follow children through to adulthood, are in agreement: Children who eventually become gay are different, at least on average, from those who become straight. *Pre-gay* children are, to a variable extent, atypical or nonconformist in a number of gender-related traits, meaning that these traits are shifted toward the norms for the other sex, as compared with children who grow up to become straight. The differences are not necessarily as marked as some popular stereotypes would suggest. Still, they do indicate that sexual orientation is influenced by factors operating early in life. And because there is evidence that biological factors influence these gendered childhood traits, the finding that pre-gay children are gender-nonconformist in these traits is very consistent with a biological model of sexual orientation.

What about adulthood? Even though many gender-nonconformist children grow up into gay adults, they often become more gender-conformist in the process. Nevertheless, as will be discussed in Chapter 5, psychologists have amassed a great deal of evidence about psychological differences between gay and straight adults. Most, although not all, of these differences concern traits that typically differ between men and women, and the differences are usually such that gay people are shifted toward the other sex, compared with heterosexual individuals of their own sex. It is difficult to explain these shifts in gay people as the *result* of being gay. Rather, it seems likely that they reflect differences in the early sexual development of the brain, differences that affect a "package" of gendered psychological traits including sexual orientation.

Chapter 6 investigates the role of sex hormones in the development of sexual orientation. I review experiments in which researchers have artificially manipulated the sex hormone levels of animals during development. This manipulation can cause animals that would otherwise have become heterosexual to mate preferentially with animals of their own sex. Although such experiments cannot be undertaken in humans, there are "experiments of nature" that accomplish something similar. There are also observations on certain anatomical markers, such as finger lengths, that say something about the hormonal environment to which gay and straight people were exposed before birth. From these studies we can conclude that, in humans as in animals, a whole variety of gendered traits including sexual orientation are influenced by sex hormone levels during development. The strength of this influence, however, is still somewhat uncertain.

In Chapter 7, I discuss the evidence that a person's genetic endowment influences her or his ultimate sexual orientation. Much of this evidence comes from family and twin studies: These studies indicate that *genes* exert a significant, although not all-dominating influence on sexual orientation. Many efforts are being made to track down the actual genes involved, but the results so far are only suggestive. There is one species, the fruit fly *Drosophila melanogaster*, in which the genetics of sexual orientation has already been elucidated in considerable detail. I briefly review this work in order to give an idea of what could possibly be achieved in humans in the future. Lastly, I consider how it might be that genes predisposing to homosexuality persist in the population even though gay people have relatively few children. It turns out that robust mechanisms are capable of keeping such genes in circulation.

In Chapter 8, I turn to my own area of expertise, the brain. Several studies, including my own study on INAH3, point to structural differences between the brains of gay and straight men. Similar differences have been recently described in one animal species—sheep—in which individual males prefer to mate exclusively with females or with other males. The brains of gay people don't just look different from those of straight people; they function differently, too. The chapter will review a range of functional studies, including one that reports on different activity patterns in the hypothalamus of gay and straight people when these people are exposed to odors that are thought to act as human *sex pheromones* (chemical signals produced by one individual that influence the sexual behavior of another).

The bodies of gay and straight people are not obviously different—if they were, telling them apart would be much easier than it is. Still, as Chapter 9 will describe, there have been reports of subtle anatomical differences. These include differences in the proportions of the limbs and trunk. Some studies have reported that the bodies of gay men and women are less symmetrical than those of their straight peers, but closer analysis throws some doubt on this claim. There do seem to be differences in the lateralization (or sidedness) of brain structure and function.

There are also subtle but objectively detectable differences in unconscious behaviors such as walking style and voice quality. Recognizing these subtleties is the basis of *gaydar*—the sometimes fallible sense of whether a person one meets is gay or straight.

Chapter 10 discusses an intriguing finding by a Canadian research group: A boy's birth order in his family affects his likelihood of becoming a gay man. This effect of birth order is quite small, but it has been observed in many different populations. Birth order effects are usually explained in terms of the different ways that parents treat early-born and later-born children, but the Canadian researchers have produced evidence that the cause in this case is something quite different, namely biological interactions between pregnant women and their fetuses.

The final chapter represents my attempt to draw the various lines of evidence together into a coherent theory of sexual orientation. I will argue that the same processes that are involved in the biological development of our bodies and brains as male or female are also involved in the development of sexual orientation. Nevertheless, I also emphasize our inability to explain in any precise way why any particular individual becomes gay or straight, let alone bisexual. Much remains to be discovered, and I point to various promising directions for future research.

ONE

WHAT IS SEXUAL ORIENTATION?

exual orientation has to do with the sex of our preferred sex partners. More specifically, it is the trait that predisposes us to experience sexual attraction to people of the same sex as ourselves (*homosexual, gay,* or *lesbian**), to persons of the other sex (*heterosexual* or *straight*), or to both sexes (*bisexual*). In this chapter, I explore the implications of this definition.

---

* I use "homosexual" and "gay" interchangeably, but the two terms have different connotations. "Homosexual" has the flavor of a label applied *to* a set of people; "gay" is the self-chosen identifier that has largely replaced it. I also used "gay woman" and "lesbian" interchangeably; some other writers have drawn distinctions between the two terms or have entirely rejected the term "gay" as applied to women.

CRITERIA FOR SEXUAL ORIENTATION

We usually judge sexual orientation based on a person's sexual *attraction* to men and to women—that is, on her or his *feelings*—as expressed in answers to direct questions such as "Are you sexually attracted to men, to women, or to both men and women?" The question doesn't refer to the interviewees' feelings of sexual attraction at the very instant of being asked, of course, but to their tendency or predisposition to experience such feelings over some extended period of time, perhaps over their entire adult life.

In some studies, such as the pioneering work of Alfred Kinsey in the 1940s and 1950s, sexual *behavior* has been taken into account—that is, the extent to which a person actually has sexual contacts with men or women. The problem with that approach is that sexual behavior is influenced by many factors that have nothing to do with one's basic sexual feelings and that are changeable over time. Is a woman in prison a lesbian simply because she has sex with the women she is locked up with? Probably not. Is a man straight simply because he follows his church's teaching to "be fruitful and multiply"? Probably not.

The factors that influence the choice of actual sex partners include the availability of partners, the person's moral sense, the desire to conform or have children, curiosity, financial incentives (e.g., prostitution), and so on. It's true that, on occasion, actions may speak louder than words—as for example when a self-declared heterosexual man is observed seeking sexual contacts in men's toilets. Still, by and large, we do best to listen to what people tell us about their sexual feelings.

Sexual attraction may not be a single, unitary phenomenon. There is *physical attraction*, meaning the desire to engage in actual sexual contact, and *romantic* or *emotional attraction*, which is a desire for psychological union that need not always be expressed in sexual contact.

Romantic attraction shades off into forms of close friendship that are not explicitly sexual. In 18th-century Europe, for example, it was quite common for "heterosexual" men to write letters to each other so laden with intimate sentiments as to leave a modern reader in no doubt that the two men were passionately in love. "My dear Heinrich," wrote the novelist Jean Paul to his friend Friedrich Heinrich Jacobi, "do tell me once again when the opportunity occurs that you love me. Like the young girl I want to hear that repeated, if not trillions then millions of times . . . " And Jacobi replied in kind: "I feel that exactly the same as you, that a friend should love his friend as the woman loves the man, the lover the loved one."[1] Yet both of these men married women, and there is no particular reason to think that either of them desired to have sexual contacts with men.

It's very possible that some such men would have been bisexual or gay in a more liberated environment. But it's also relevant that, in those times, there was little awareness or discussion of homosexuality. In that atmosphere, heterosexual men and women may have been freer than they are today to feel and express intimacy with persons of the same sex—there was simply no suspicion that such intimacy represented a sexual bond. At any rate, because of the "fuzzy edges" of romantic attraction, many researchers consider physical attraction to be the more reliable criterion for sexual orientation.

As another alternative to feelings or behavior, researchers sometimes use *arousal* as a criterion for sexual orientation. Sexual arousal means "being turned on" sexually: It is the temporary state of excitement that a person may experience in the presence of an attractive partner or while viewing erotic images, or while imagining or engaging in actual sexual contacts. One way to measure arousal is to monitor *genital responses* in the laboratory. For men, this can involve a device placed around the penis that measures the degree and rate of penile erection during, say, the viewing of erotic images. For women, it can involve an analogous device that measures color changes in the wall of the vagina as it becomes engorged with blood during sexual excitement. Such genital arousal phenomena are probably closely related to physical attraction, in men at least, and measuring them may circumvent any reluctance of the person to speak frankly about his or her feelings. For that reason, genital measures are sometimes used to assay the sexual feelings of child molesters. Monitoring genital arousal is too time-consuming and intrusive to be of widespread use in sex research, but I will mention a few studies that use these techniques.

An inner, psychological state of sexual arousal precedes and accompanies genital arousal, or may occur without any genital arousal. Some researchers ask subjects to estimate their degree of sexual arousal while viewing various kinds of potentially arousing images or videos—by pushing or pulling a lever, for example. Others have attempted to access psychological arousal by the use of functional brain imaging techniques, and I will describe their findings in Chapter 8. In theory, perhaps, a subject's sexual orientation could be assessed by such techniques in the absence of any cooperation on his or her part. The efficacy of brain scanners as "lie detectors" is unproven, however, and the attempt to use scanners for this purpose is ethically questionable.

In short, the low-tech method of assessing people's sexual orientation—simply asking them about their feelings of sexual attraction to men and to women—is the best method for most purposes.

SEXUAL ORIENTATION IN MEN AND WOMEN

As sketched in Figure I.I, we can think about sexual orientation in men and women in two alternative ways. The usual terminology of sexual orientation—heterosexual, bisexual, and homosexual—emphasizes the equivalence of sexual orientation in the two sexes. In both men and women, heterosexuality means attraction to the other sex, homosexuality means attraction to the same sex, and bisexuality means attraction to both sexes. This usage makes sense culturally, because in both sexes, heterosexuals are the majority, the people who are commonly perceived

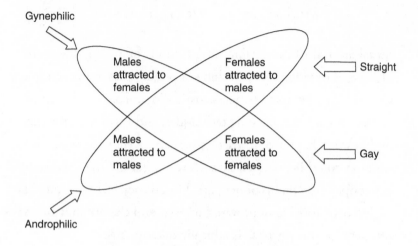

Figure I.I Alternative conceptions of sexual orientation.

as "normal," and in both sexes, homosexuals (and perhaps bisexuals) are a small and often stigmatized minority.

But does this usage make sense when we are trying to understand causation? In other words, should we be looking for similar causes that propel both men and women toward heterosexuality, and similar causes that propel both men and women toward homosexuality?

One can certainly construct developmental models that work the same way in both sexes. Here are a couple of hypothetical examples. In one, we could imagine that the development of heterosexuality involves a psychological process in early life by which we first establish a sense of our own sex as male or female, and then exclude people of this sex from the realm of attractive sex partners. Thus, we are left with people of the other sex as potential objects of attraction. Both male and female homosexuality, in this model, could result when children identify themselves as belonging to the other sex than the one to which they belong anatomically. In a second, equally hypothetical model one could suggest that heterosexuality results from a "conformist" trait that causes both men and women to accept the cultural norms for their sex, while homosexuality results from a "rebellious" trait that causes both males and females to reject those norms. In either model, a single process or trait would explain the development of homosexuality in both sexes.

In contrast with such ideas, one can also emphasize the equivalence of heterosexuality in men and homosexuality in women—because, after all, both are defined by sexual attraction to *women*. Similarly, heterosexuality in women is in a sense equivalent to homosexuality in men—both are defined by sexual attraction to *men*. Sex researchers sometimes use special terms when they want to emphasize this way of looking at things: *gynephilic* (woman-loving) when referring to straight men and gay women, and *androphilic* (man-loving) when referring to straight women and gay men.[†]

[†] The terms androphilic and gynephilic are usually understood to mean attraction specifically to *adult* males or females, whereas homosexual and heterosexual define attraction to same- or opposite-sex persons without regard to those persons' age. This distinction is not particularly relevant to the theme of this book, which does not focus on sexual attraction to children.

It's just as easy to construct developmental models that fit in with this point of view. For example, one could speculate that a certain gene mediates sexual attraction to the look, voice, smell, or behavior of women, and that this gene is switched on in straight men and gay women, but switched off (or absent) in straight women and gay men. And vice versa for a gene mediating attraction to the look, voice, smell, or behavior of men. Another hypothetical model of this kind might invoke the rewarding effect of sexual pleasure as a causal agent, so that (regardless of one's own sex), one becomes permanently oriented toward the sex of the partner with whom one first has sex. Thus, people who initially happen to have sex with females become gynephilic (straight men and gay women), and those who initially have sex with males become androphilic (straight women and gay men). I hasten to add that I don't actually believe this model, but it is one that has been put forward in the past to explain the development of sexual orientation, particularly homosexuality, as we'll see in Chapter 2.

It's also possible to construct hybrid models that incorporate elements of both kinds of models just described. But the general point is this: We need to be careful not to assume that the same processes necessarily cause homosexuality (or heterosexuality) in both sexes. It is quite possible that a single factor might promote homosexuality in one sex and heterosexuality in the other—or indeed that the factors influencing sexual orientation are completely unrelated in the two sexes.

STABILITY OF SEXUAL ORIENTATION

Calling it a *trait* implies that sexual orientation is stable over time. Obviously, most of us believe that sexual orientation is stable, because we use terms like "a lesbian" or "a straight man" to describe individuals. This usage wouldn't make much sense unless sexual orientation was a reasonably durable attribute.

It's the stability of our *attractions* that we're discussing here. If we considered actual *behavior*, then volatility would be the rule for plenty of people. On the basis of her behavior, actress Anne Heche has switched sexual orientation at least twice—once in 1997 when she took up with Ellen DeGeneres, and again 3 years later when she abandoned that relationship and started dating cameraman Coleman Laffoon. But without interviewing Heche about her feelings it's impossible to make any judgment about what happened to the underlying direction of her sexual attractions over that period.

Surprisingly few studies have actually followed people over time to see whether their sexual orientation remains the same or changes. In one report published in 2003, researchers at the University of Otago in New Zealand took advantage of a long-itudinal study of men and women who were all born in the same town in 1972 and 1973.[2] These people were interviewed about their sexuality when they were 21 years old, and again when they were 26. At the age of 21, 443 of the 448 men in the study (99%) reported exclusive or near-exclusive attraction to women. Of these "heterosexual" men, only three (less than 1%) reported any significant attraction to men at the age of 26. Similarly, of the 430 women, 422 (98%) reported exclusive or near-exclusive attraction to men, and of these "heterosexual" women only six (1.4%) reported significant attraction to women at the age of 26. In other words, an initial heterosexual orientation was nearly always stable over a period of 5 years. Of the five men who were "non-heterosexual" (bisexual or homosexual) at age 21, four remained so at age 26. Of the eight non-heterosexual women, however, only three remained so 5 years later.

This latter finding could be taken to suggest that the sexual orientation of non-heterosexual young women is quite unstable, but the sample size was too small to draw any firm conclusion. Another study, by psychologist Lisa Diamond of the University of Utah, focused specifically on 89 young women whose sexual attractions were non-heterosexual at the start of the study.[3] When reinterviewed 10 years later, all but eight of these women were still non-heterosexual. There were often more subtle shifts within the broad category of "non-heterosexual," however, and there were more changes in the *labels* that the women applied to themselves than in the actual direction of their attractions.

It seems fair to conclude from these and other studies that people's basic sexual orientation doesn't commonly undergo major shifts. This is in line with most people's perception that it's appropriate to label people as straight, bisexual, or gay/lesbian. Nevertheless, many women are capable of experiencing sexual attractions other than those predicted by their underlying sexual orientation.

It does sometimes happen that men and women "come out" as gay or lesbian later in life—in their 40s, 50s, or even later—often after many years of heterosexual marriage. I have met quite a number of such people, and in discussing their life histories with them I have been struck by a major difference between the sexes. The men regularly say that that they were aware of same-sex attraction throughout their adult lives. They did not act on it (or did act, but were not open about it), and may not even have considered themselves gay, for a variety of reasons such as shame, religious teaching, or the desire to have a conventional family. U.S. Congressman Robert Bauman, who was married to a woman for two decades before coming out as gay, gave this account to historian Eric Marcus:

> It was nearly 20 years later that my wife and priest confronted me. I was already a congressman by this time, drinking heavily, involved with hustlers, and in and out of gay bars. . . . All through this period I was thoroughly convinced that I wasn't gay. I wasn't a homosexual. I couldn't be a person like that. People wonder how I could have convinced myself of that, but from an early age it was a matter of building certain walls within my mind. . . . [I]t took almost 3 years of religious and psychiatric counseling for me to acknowledge that I was gay.[4]

The women give much more diverse accounts, but quite commonly they will say that they were completely unaware of sexual attraction to women until they met a specific woman or went through a significant life event, such as divorce, later in life. Here's how comedian Carol Leifer put it in an online interview:

> [I]t was like my life threw me a surprise party. I really didn't have any clue, and in fact, had very good physical relationships with men. It was around when I turned 40 that I had this really intense desire to have an affair with a woman. It just kind of overtook me, kind of like when you feel like you're on a mission.[5]

Thus, my informal impression is that, at the level of conscious awareness of sexual attraction, some women but few men gravitate toward an authentically new homosexual orientation late in life.

There has been a long-running debate about whether gay people who want to become heterosexual can do so through some kind of intervention. Methods that have been promoted as helping people achieve this goal include psychoanalysis, other forms of psychotherapy, and religion-based group programs.[6] The majority viewpoint among mental-health professionals is that this so-called *conversion therapy* has little chance of success and can cause significant harm by reinforcing the gay person's negative self-image.[7] Still, one study, by Columbia University psychiatrist Robert Spitzer, did identify 200 individuals who told him that they had experienced a significant shift from homosexuality toward heterosexuality as a result of conversion therapy.[8] Women reported such change more often than men, but few individuals of either sex said that they had completely lost their same-sex attraction.

I interpret Spitzer's study to mean that at least a few highly motivated gay people can be helped to engage in and derive some degree of pleasure from heterosexual relationships, and to pay less attention to their homosexual feelings. This should hardly come as a surprise, since we know that many gay people were hetero-sexually married and had children before coming out as gay. But much more useful than conversion therapy, in my opinion, is therapy aimed at overcoming the self-hatred that causes some gay people to want to become straight in the first place. Psychoanalyst Richard Isay has provided useful insights in this area.[9]

PREVALENCE OF DIFFERENT ORIENTATIONS

Alfred Kinsey invented a seven-category scale of sexual orienta-tion running from 0 (exclusive heterosexuality) to 6 (exclusive homosexuality), with the intervening numbers representing var-ious degrees of bisexuality. This is the famous *Kinsey scale.* Contemporary researchers often use fewer categories—five or even three. In the case of three categories, they are often defined as "heterosexual," meaning exclusive or near-exclusive attraction to the other sex; "bisexual," meaning significant attraction to both sexes; and "homosexual," meaning exclusive or near-exclu-sive attraction to one's own sex.

The distribution of sexual orientations in the population has been studied by means of large-scale random-sample surveys that have been conducted in the United States, Britain, Australia, and Canada.[10] Fairly typical are the findings of a U.S. study conducted in the early 1990s.[11] In this study, 96.4% of men and 98.3% of women reported heterosexual (only or mostly opposite-sex) attraction; 0.6% of men and 0.8% of women reported bisexual attraction; and 3.1% of men and 0.9% of women reported homosexual (only or mostly same-sex) attraction. These data are plotted graphically in Figure I.2.

Although the numbers vary somewhat, most studies agree on several points. First, heterosexuality is far and away the most common orientation among both men and women. Second, with regard to non-heterosexual people, there is a difference between the sexes. Most non-heterosexual men are homosexual; few say that they are roughly equally attracted to both sexes. Non-heterosexual women, on the other hand, report bisexual

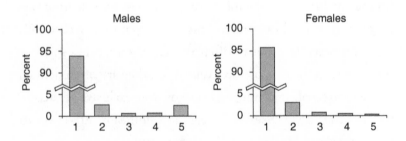

Figure I.2 Distribution of sexual orientations for males and females, based on data from Laumann et al. (1994). Group 1: attracted to opposite sex only; Group 2: mostly to opposite sex; Group 3: to both sexes; Group 4: mostly to same sex; Group 5: to same sex only.

or homosexual attraction in roughly comparable numbers: There is no clear dip in the curve between heterosexuality and homosexuality, as there is with men. In fact, some studies report greater numbers of bisexual women than homosexual women.

Some critics have argued that these national surveys are unreliable.[12] They might under-report the prevalence of gay people, and perhaps bisexual people too, because respondents are unwilling to acknowledge same-sex attraction—a trait that is still stigmatized in some quarters. This may in fact be the case, and we certainly need to be cautious on this score. Still, studies that have paid particular attention to confidentiality and anonymity (by, for example, allowing subjects to supply their answers outside of the interviewer's presence, or by computer), or that have been conducted more recently (and thus in more gay-positive times), or in more gay-friendly countries than the United States, have mostly failed to come up with higher numbers of non-heterosexual people. In fact, with regard to its estimate of the prevalence of gay men (3.1%), the results of the U.S. survey just mentioned remain near the high end of the estimates in the various surveys that have been published.

Michael Bailey and his colleagues at Northwestern University (including Meredith Chivers, who is now at Queen's University in Kingston, Ontario) have studied the sexual orientation of both men and women by measuring genital arousal during the viewing of erotic videos.[13] Heterosexual and homosexual men showed genital responses that accorded with their self-declared attractions: Straight men responded to erotic videos of women, and gay men responded to erotic videos of men. Surpisingly, most men who identified as bisexual, and who reported roughly equal attraction to both sexes, did not show equivalent responses to erotic videos of men and women. Rather, they responded much more strongly to one sex—usually men—than the other. Only those "bisexual" men who had an actual history of multiple physical and romantic relationships with both men and women showed genital arousal to both the male and female erotic videos.

The researchers speculated that the majority of men who identify as bisexual actually only experience attraction and arousal to one sex but report attraction and arousal to both for some nonsexual reason. Alternatively, it may be that bisexual men sometimes experience different *kinds* of sexual attraction to men and women.[14] For example, they may be more physically attracted to men and more romantically or emotionally attracted to women. It's possible that physical attraction leads more reliably to genital arousal than does romantic attraction. Whatever the reason, the nature of bisexual attraction in men deserves further study.

The findings in women are almost the opposite of those in men.[15] *More* women are genitally aroused by both male and female videos than one would expect, including most women who say they are only sexually attracted to men. Only women who identify as bisexual or lesbian are liable to show sex-specific arousal: If they do, it is to female videos.

Richard Lippa and Travis Patterson of California State University, Fullerton, have come to a similar conclusion, based on experiments in which they showed pictures of male and female swimsuit models to self-identified heterosexual men and women.[16] The men said they were sexually attracted only to the female models, and they spent most of the available time looking at the females. The women, on the other hand, said they were sexually attracted to both the males and the females, and they spent about equal time looking at both sexes.

Although the findings in women are perplexing in their own way, they may fit in with reports that sexual orientation is more fluid in women than in men.[17] To put it crudely, most men can figure out their sexual orientation by consulting their genitals, but few women can do so. This suggests that sexual orientation is a "higher-level" phenomenon in many women than it is in men, perhaps because it is more embedded in relationship issues.

In a review of the topic, Michael Bailey has raised the question (without offering a definitive answer) of whether most women can be said to have a sexual orientation at all, as opposed to a preference for male or female partners that is driven by non-sexual motivations.[18] Regardless of the answer to this question, the reality is that women who say they are sexually attracted to women (or to both women and men) differ in a wide variety of ways from women who say they are sexually attracted only to men, as will be documented in later chapters of this book. Thus the assumption that women have a sexual orientation is, at the very least, a useful working hypothesis.

ARE THERE CATEGORIES?

On the face of it, the findings described so far suggest that sexual orientation in men can be described to a first approximation in terms of two categories—straight or gay—whereas sexual orientation in women has more of a *dimensional* quality—women are distributed in a continuum across the spectrum of sexual orientation, so that dividing them into two (or even three) categories looks more like a semantic convenience than an objective reality.

There exists a set of statistical procedures called *taxometric analysis* that can be used to assess whether a psychological trait, however dimensional it may appear in the raw data, actually has some underlying categorical structure. Steven Gangestad of the University of New Mexico, along with Michael Bailey and Nicholas Martin, applied these procedures to sexual orientation.[19] Briefly, the method involved assessing in a large dataset how sexual orientation varied with other measured traits, in this case childhood gender-nonconformity and adult masculinity or femininity. According to the analysis, two "hidden" or "latent" categories underlay the data for both men and for women. One category in each sex appeared to consist almost entirely of straight people: This category contained about 85%–88% of the men and 90%–95% of the women. The other category, containing 12%–15% of the men and 5%–10% of the women, was apparently a mix of roughly equal numbers of gay and straight people.

One possible way to interpret these data would be to say that one developmental factor (such as a gene or prenatal hormone level) directs development strongly toward heterosexuality and an alternative factor provides the *capacity* for homosexual development but doesn't rigorously *specify* it. Thus, people in whom this latter factor operates gravitate toward one orientation or the other depending on environmental conditions or even pure chance. There are other possible interpretations of the data, however, and this analytical approach has not inspired further research up to now.

SEXUAL ORIENTATION ACROSS CULTURES

Have gay and bisexual men and women existed across different cultures and historical periods? And, if so, have their relative numbers been the same as what we see in contemporary Western society?

Sociologist Fred Whitam conducted informal surveys of male sexual orientation in several less-Westernized cultures, such as Guatamala and the Philippines.[20] He concluded that, in such countries, about 5% of the male residents of large cities are gay, which roughly matches the estimated prevalence of male homosexuality in large Western cities such as London. (Large cities tend to have a higher prevalence of gay people than the national average, probably on account of the migration of gay people from rural areas to cities.[21])

With regard to historical periods, the problem is that sexual orientation was rarely conceptualized or described in the same way as it is today. The term "homosexual," for example, was first introduced in the 1860s. In earlier Western culture, most people thought of homosexuality, not as an attribute of a distinct group of people, but as a sinful or criminal behavior ("sodomy") that anyone might be tempted to engage in. To the extent that there was any recognition of a distinct group of people characterized by same-sex desire, it focused on a subset of what we would now call gay men and women, namely gay men who were extremely feminine in manner and social role, and gay women who were extremely masculine.

The term "molly," for example, was used in 18th-century London to refer to homosexual men who socialized in "molly-houses," where they affected women's dress and manners and entered into same-sex liaisons that they termed "marriages."[22] It seems likely that more conventionally gendered homosexual men existed at that time but chose to maintain their anonymity. After all, voluntarily outing oneself as a homosexual man would hardly have been an attractive option in 18th-century England, where sodomy was still a capital offense.

In some cultures, unmarried women have been sequestered and thus were invisible to men and unobtainable as sex partners. In such environments, male adolescents were often sought after as sex partners by adult men, especially by young unmarried men. Ancient Greece is a particularly well-known example—so much so that "Greek love" has long been used as a colloquial term for homosexuality.[23] A more recent example was the same-sex culture that existed in Afghanistan under the Taliban, when all women were hidden behind their *burqas*. "I like boys, but I like girls better," one Kandahar resident told the *Los Angeles Times*. "It's just that we can't see the women to see if they are beautiful. But we can see the boys, and so we can tell which of them is beautiful."[24] About half of all men in Kandahar engaged in sex with boys at one time or another, according to one local medical professor interviewed for the article.

In such cultures, the choice of adolescent boys as partners probably reflects the fact that these youths, lacking beards and adult musculature, are closer to women in appearance than are adult men. Thus, it would be quite wrong to assert that many or most men in ancient Greece or in Afghanistan were homosexual in the sense of having a strong preference for males when given the choice of sex partners. What these cultures do demonstrate is the degree to which sexual desire and sexual behavior accommodate themselves to a restricted range of options, just they do in prisons and other single-sex environments today.

Yet even in ancient Greece there was awareness that some men and women did have an authentic preference for same-sex partners. This comes across most clearly in Plato's *Symposium* (*The Drinking Party*), in which one of the participants extemporized a creation myth to explain the existence of homosexual and heterosexual men and women. Plato's account could be interpreted as the first genetic theory of sexual orientation.[‡]

In fact, two of the participants at that party, Pausanias and Agathon, were a male couple who are known to have stayed together well into their adult lives—an arrangement suggesting that these men were homosexual in the modern sense. But their long-lasting partnership seems to have been unusual. We have no way of knowing what the actual prevalence of homosexuality in the modern sense was in ancient Greece, other than that it existed.

Anthropologists have established that sexual relationships between males and between females have occurred widely in non-Western cultures. In one particularly common arrangement, boys who have been feminine since childhood may choose to adopt an adult gender role as a female or as some combination of

---

[‡] Plato put the account into the mouth of the comic playwright Aristophanes. He described how humanity originally existed as double creatures, like pairs of present-day humans stuck together. Some of these pairs consisted of two males, some of two females, and some were male–female hybrids. In punishment for their transgressions, an angry god cut them all into halves. Sexual attraction is the desire to be reunited with one's ancestral other half. Thus, the three kinds of original creatures gave rise to gay men, gay women, and heterosexual men and women, respectively. Plato may have created the story by expanding on a preexisting myth of the creation of men and women by division of a single ancestral creature; such stories existed in Egyptian (Geb and Nut), Judaic (Adam and Eve), and possibly Babylonian mythologies.

female and male; they may enter into sexual relationships or marriages with conventionally masculine men.[25] In many Native American cultures, these individuals were given specific names, such as *winkte* in the Lakota language, and they were considered to be *two-spirit people* who took on special roles in society. One Lakota man offered a "biological" explanation for the origin of *winktes.* "We think that if a woman has two little ones growing inside her, if she is going to have twins, sometimes instead of giving birth to two babies they have formed up in her womb into just one, into a half-man/half-woman kind of being."[26]

Similarly, there are accounts in various non-Western cultures of women taking on male or male/female roles and partnering with conventionally feminine women. Walter Williams cites a 16th-century account of such women living in northeastern Brazil: "They wear their hair cut in the same way as the men, and go to war with bows and arrows and pursue game, always in company with men; each has a woman to serve her, to whom she says she is married, and they treat each other and speak with each other as man and wife."[27] Explorers named Brazil's great waterway the "river of the Amazons" because of the similarity of these local women to the warrior women of Greek mythology.

Two-spirit people and amazons were clearly homosexual in the sense that they were consistently attracted to persons of the same anatomical sex as themselves. They were also what we would call *transgendered,* however, which is not the case for most contemporary gay men and women. There are some people in our society—very feminine gay men and very masculine gay women—who occupy a region of overlap between "homosexuality" and "transgenderism." A possible American example was Chastity Bono, who identified as a lesbian woman for many years but announced in 2009 that she was changing her sex to male and her first name to Chaz. The two-spirit people and amazons may be thought of as occupying that same territory.

What about the conventionally gendered individuals who partnered with two-spirit people or with amazons? Were they the counterparts of today's conventional gay men and women? Very possibly some of them were, but they were not usually recognized as anything different from regular men or women. Lakota men who entered a relationship with a *winkte*, for example, quite commonly took up with anatomical women before or after that relationship. In the distant past, when polygamy was practiced, they often had a *winkte* and a female wife at the same time. Thus, although men who partnered with *winktes* were commonly subject to some ridicule for doing so, they were not thought of as a different *kind* of person in the same way that *winktes* were. To assert that they were in fact homosexual would be to claim far more understanding of their mental lives than we in fact possess.

Thus, what we learn from different times and cultures is somewhat paradoxical. On the one hand, there is widespread evidence of homosexual relationships, as well of homosexual individuals who were more or less transgendered. But the majority of gay men and women in our own culture—those who have a secure identity as to their own anatomical sex and an enduring preference for same-sex partners—don't seem to have numerous and obvious counterparts in other cultures. And the homosexual relationships that we think of as typical today—relationships between pairs of fairly similar, like-aged, conventionally gendered men or women—seem in other cultures to have been much less common or less visible than relationships characterized by differences in age or in gender. To use the terminology applied by sociologist Stephen Murray, *age-stratified* and *gender-stratified* relationships have been the dominant forms of homosexual bonding in other cultures, while *egalitarian* relationships are the most visible form in our own.[28]

Do these differences between cultures undermine the effort to understand sexual orientation in biological terms? Probably not, for several reasons. For one thing, the differences may not be as great as they seem. Both gender-conformist and gender-nonconformist gay people may well have existed in all cultures, but with differing visibility. Just among American lesbians of the last hundred years or so, there have been marked swings between a cultural emphasis on gender-nonconformity ("diesel dykes," for example) and on gender-conformity, and between an emphasis on egalitarian relationships and on those that are gender-stratified (so-called "butch–femme" relationships).[29] Yet these swings, driven by social forces such as the women's liberation movement of the 1960s and 1970s, probably mask a more or less constant underlying reality, which is that spectra of gender diversity exist within the category of gay women and within the category of gay men. A biological theory of sexual orientation needs to explain not only why there is a link between homosexuality and a broader gender-nonconformity, but also why there is such diversity in gender-related traits among gay people. Biologists also have to acknowledge that much that is important about sexual orientation—especially the diverse ways that homosexuality and heterosexuality are conceived and acted out in different societies—lies outside of the arena of biological investigation.

TWO

Why We Need Biology

Almost everyone has some opinion about what determines sexual orientation. Usually, they frame their ideas in terms of what went wrong in the lives of gay people. Some theories are little more than old wives' tales; others present at least the semblance of scientific credibility. In this chapter, I review the principal *nonbiological* theories that have been presented over the years. Each of these theories has significant shortcomings. Collectively, their weakness spurs the search for other, *biological* explanations.

PSYCHOANALYTIC THEORIES

Most of us think of the sex drive as something that makes its first appearance at or after puberty, when raging sex hormones transform the body and mind of a meek-mannered child into that of a horny adolescent. The founder of psychoanalysis, Sigmund Freud (1856–1939), took a very different view. He proposed that the erotic instinct, or *libido* as he called it, is already fully active at birth and undergoes several radical transformations during childhood.[1] A newborn infant's libido, Freud claimed, is focused on the mouth and is satisfied by suckling at the mother's breast. Then it moves to the anus, where it is satisfied by defecation. At about 2 years of age, the libido becomes focused on the *phallus* (penis or clitoris), where it can be satisfied by masturbation.

What happens next Freud spelled out more explicitly for males than females, perhaps because the majority of his clients were men. At around the same time as the libido becomes focused on the phallus, it also begins to be directed externally, toward other people. In boys, the libido is directed toward other males, because they also possess a penis. This is, therefore, a homosexual phase, but one of which adult men (whether straight or gay) have repressed all memory.

At about 3 years of age, a boy's libido transfers to his mother. This is the famous *oedipal phase*, named for Oedipus, the character in Greek mythology who unwittingly married his own mother. The boy remains sexually fixated on his mother for 2 or 3 years.

Then his libido enters a period of latency in which it is largely inactive, to be awoken again after puberty in the form of adult heterosexuality. This is the developmental process that Freud considered normal.

Homosexuality in adult men resulted, according to Freud, from a disruption of this process. In *pre-oedipal homosexuality*, the libido failed to enter the oedipal phase, and simply remained stuck for a lifetime in the early homosexual phase. In *oedipal homosexuality*, the libido did enter the oedipal phase but failed to leave it, so the boy remained erotically fixated on his mother.

Freud placed much more emphasis on oedipal than on pre-oedipal homosexuality. And this raised a problem: Why would remaining erotically fixated on one's mother make a boy grow up to be sexually attracted to men? Wouldn't it be more likely to make him heterosexual, given that his mother was a woman?

To get around this problem, Freud proposed that the growing boy, unable to shake off his attraction to his mother but equally unable to satisfy that desire, resolves the dilemma by identifying with his mother and seeking sex partners who represent himself. In other words, when he enters sexual relationships with other men, he is psychologically reestablishing the oedipal bond, but with roles reversed.*

---

* In a later formulation, Freud proposed that homosexuality results when the boy is so identified with his mother that he seeks to take her place in her sexual relationship with his father (the so-called "negative oedipal complex"). In that model, adult homosexuality is the reenactment of the desired relationship with the father.

That left the question: What caused a boy to remain eroti-cally focused on his mother and thus to become homosexual? The reason, Freud said, was that his mother was too close-binding or even seductive, and thus prevented him from breaking away. Alternatively (or additionally), the father might be distant or hostile, generating in his son an irrational fear of castration and thus forcing him into an excessively close relationship with his mother.

In constructing this theory, Freud was probably influenced by what gay men told him about their childhood relationships with their parents. As has been documented more recently in statisti-cal studies of large numbers of subjects, gay men do indeed describe their relationships with their mothers as closer, and their relationships with their fathers as more distant or hostile, as compared with how straight men describe these relationships.[2] As with most other statements in this book, this is a statement about averages, and it's not true for everyone: There are plenty of gay men who got on famously with their fathers, and plenty of straight men who didn't. Still, the fact that this significant differ-ence exists, on average, between gay and straight men demands some explanation, and Freud provided one.

The problem is that there are other possible explanations, some of which are more plausible or straightforward than Freud's. The simplest one is that boys who become gay (pre-gay boys) and those who become straight (pre-straight boys) differ from each other in ways that parents pick up on. As pointed out by Richard Isay, if pre-gay boys have traits that fathers dislike and mothers like, then this would set up the same relationships that Freud described, but with the direction of causation reversed.[3] Rather than a mother's closeness or a father's hostility making their son gay, it would be the son's "gayness" making his mother close and his father hostile.

In Chapter 4, I'll present evidence that pre-homosexual boys do indeed differ from pre-heterosexual boys in a number of traits—traits that can be summarized with the term "gender-nonconformity." Thus, it's very plausible that some fathers might reject their pre-homosexual sons on account of what they perceive as "sissiness" or a lack of interest in the typically masculine activities that fathers often like to engage their sons in. Conversely, some mothers might actually like such traits in their sons. Even if they don't, they might become unusually protective of a son whom they see being exposed to teasing or hostility from the father or from other children.

Over the course of the 20th century, Freudian theory had a lot of its raw sexual content watered down or excised. Some later analysts, such as Carl Jung, thought of the libido as a more general motivating force within the psyche, rather than an explicitly sexual urge. And the oedipal complex became a simple desire for emotional closeness with the mother, rather than a lust for sexual intercourse with her. But that change didn't undermine the role of the mother–son bond in the development of homosexuality, in many psychiatrists' minds. "You've got to get these mothers out of the way," said UCLA psychiatrist Richard Green to a couple who feared that their gender-nonconformist son would become homosexual. He recommended that the father spend more one-on-one time with the boy.[4]

Green himself has since changed his views about the development of sexual orientation, but other therapists—especially those who purport to offer advice on preventing or "curing" homosexuality—continued to emphasize the crucial role of the oedipal complex. The late Charles Socarides, a psychoanalyst who claimed to have helped many men get the "monkey of homosexuality off their backs,"[5] attributed male homosexuality to "a lifelong persistence of the original primary feminine identification with the mother, and a consequent sense of deficiency in one's masculine identity."[6] Joseph Nicolosi, who is one of the best-known "reparative therapists" currently active, writes that "if a father wants his son to grow up straight, he has to break the mother–son bond that is proper to infancy but not in the boy's best interest afterward."[7]

What about sexual orientation in women? Freud believed that a young girl, like a boy, goes through an early oedipal fixation on her mother, but when she finds out that her mother lacks a penis she redirects her sexual desire toward her father. Thus, the girl begins to compete with her mother for her father's love. In the one case of female homosexuality that Freud described in detail, this relationship was damaged by the birth of a younger brother when the girl was 16. "It was not *she* who bore the child, but her unconsciously hated rival, her mother," wrote Freud. "Furiously resentful and embittered, she turned away from her father and from men altogether."[8] Instead, she fell in love with a woman, who (in Freud's view) represented both her (hated) mother and another brother, older than herself, whose penis had made a "strong impression" on her when she was 5 years old. Thus, it was really a bisexual relationship rather than a strictly homosexual one.

Byzantine accounts such as this one—and I've omitted most of the details—were Freud's stock in trade. They raise the question: How did Freud figure all this out, and what evidence did he present to persuade us that he was right? For the most part, there *was* no evidence: We just have to trust that Freud's insights were correct. And that's the general problem with psychoanalytical theories.[9] It's not that they've been proven wrong; it's just that there's no good reason to think they're right. In that situation, their implausibility and complexity counts against them. They're like the theory that unidentified flying objects are alien spacecraft: They could be—but why believe that theory when there's no evidence to support it and more mundane explanations exist?[10]

LEARNING THEORIES—INFLUENCE OF EARLY SEXUAL EXPERIENCES

In stark contrast to this psychoanalytic perspective, learning theorists (especially those who fall under the heading of *behaviorists*) have taken a much simpler view of the mind. In behaviorist thought, the minds of babies are pretty much blank slates, although they come supplied with the ability to form mental associations, to seek pleasurable experiences, and to avoid unpleasant ones. A person's tendency to seek male or female sex partners, from this perspective, is simply the consequence of innumerable "carrots" and "sticks" that have shaped his or her sexual feelings during childhood and adolescence.

According to a simple behaviorist theory, popular in the 1960s and 1970s, the major "carrot" influencing sexual orientation is the pleasure of sex itself, especially orgasm. If a person's first sexual contact is with a woman, he or she will desire further contacts with women; if it was with a man, he or she will desire further contacts with men. Thus, a person who starts off with no particular preference in sex partners gradually develops an engrained attraction to one sex or the other.[11] This theory has led to the idea that male homosexuality results from sexual contact with an older male—a stranger or an older brother—during childhood or adolescence.[12] Although the contact might be a one-time experience, the boy may evoke memories of it during solitary masturbation, thus strengthening its influence.[13]

According to one study, both gay men and lesbians are indeed far more likely to have had sexual contact with an older person of their own sex during childhood or adolescence, compared with heterosexual people.[14] Another study focused on males and females who had been sexually abused (usually by men) during their childhood: It found that abused males were significantly more likely than non-abused males to form homosexual partnerships in adulthood, but that abused females were not.[15]

On the face of it, such findings could be taken to support the idea that the sex of one's first sex partner influences a person's ultimate sexual orientation. For this to be true, however, we would have to assume that the children or adolescents were sexually passive targets for molestation by their elders. In reality, it is likely that many of them, especially the adolescents, already felt sexually attracted to same-sex partners. If so, they may have initiated the contacts or responded willingly to the older persons' advances. Even if not, the older persons may have picked up on cues that were indicative of the child's future sexual orientation and selected the child on that basis.

Cross-cultural evidence also speaks against the notion that the sex of a person's first sex partner influences their ultimate sexual orientation. In some non-Western cultures, such as that of the Sambia of New Guinea, all boys are required to engage in sexual contacts with older male youths for several years before they have any access to females, yet most if not all of these boys become heterosexual men.[16] Similarly, homosexual behavior is common among British children and adolescents who attend single-sex boarding schools, yet adult Britons who attended such schools are no more likely to engage in homosexual behavior than those who did not.[17]

Finally, many (probably most) young people in our own culture develop an awareness of their sexual orientation while they are still virgins, or before they have had any sexual experiences with partners of their preferred sex. These people's sexual orientation could not have been determined by the sex of their first partners.

An opposite idea has been that children who are molested are *turned off* the sex of the person who molested them, because the molestation is an unpleasant experience. For boys, this would produce an effect exactly opposite to the one just described: Boys who were molested by men would be steered toward heterosexuality, not homosexuality. This is not something that people want to hear, so the idea has been applied mostly to girls: Girls molested by men, the idea goes, become lesbian.

Ellen DeGeneres has often heard this theory. When she was a teenager, DeGeneres was molested by her stepfather. "People I've confided in about this say, 'Oh, that's why you're a lesbian,'" she told *Allure* magazine. "But I was a lesbian way before that. My earliest memories are of being a lesbian."[18]

Some lesbians *do* believe that molestation played at least some role in their becoming lesbian. Donna Rafanello interviewed 60 lesbians who, like herself, were survivors of childhood sexual abuse. The women gave very diverse accounts of how the experience of molestation related to their lesbian orientation as adults. A common view, though, was that the experience reinforced something that was already inside of them. "I'm grateful to both of my molesters for making my choice to follow my natural inclination to be a lesbian more clear-cut," said one woman. Another said: "I think I may have had a tendency to be gay, and then [the abuse] happened. So it sort of pushed me over to that side."[19] Curiously, the woman who was most emphatic that the molestation caused her homosexuality was molested by a woman, her stepsister.

Many lesbians were molested as children, and it's understandable that these women might come to believe that the experience played a role in the development of their sexual orientation. But many straight women were molested too. Sexual abuse of girls is shockingly common: One out of three girls in the United States has an experience meeting a broad definition of sexual abuse before she reaches the age of 18.[20]

If a causal relationship exists between sexual abuse by men and lesbianism, one would expect more lesbians than straight women to report having been abused. In a study that compared matched pairs of lesbian and straight women, no such difference existed.[21] Such findings undermine the idea that the experience of sexual abuse during childhood is a significant cause of homosexuality in women.

LEARNING THEORIES—GENDER LEARNING

Because so many people become aware of their sexual orientation before they have had sexual contact with their preferred partners, or before they have had any sexual experiences, theorists have looked for other ways in which people might "learn" their sexual orientations. The most commonly expressed idea is that sexual orientation develops out of a broader process of gender learning.

Gender is the set of mental and behavioral traits that differ, to a greater or lesser degree, between males and females. An example of a gendered trait shown by children is engagement in rough-and-tumble play: Boys engage in more such play than girls in most or all human cultures. (I will have more to say about childhood gender characteristics in Chapter 4, and about adult gender characteristics in Chapter 5.)

According to the *standard social science model*,[22] gender differences are learned. The learning might take place directly, for example by parents rewarding sons who engage in rough-and-tumble play and punishing daughters who do so. Alternatively, the child may take a more active role—first establishing a sense of its own sex and then participating in the acquisition of other gender characteristics through imitation of same-sex role models and other forms of social interaction.[23]

John Money, a well-known sex researcher at Johns Hopkins School of Medicine, who died in 2006, was the leading proponent of the idea that a person's sexual orientation develops as part of this process of gender learning.[24] As evidence in favor of his theory, Money cited a remarkable and ultimately tragic case history. This concerned a child named Bruce Reimer. Bruce was born a normal boy, but he suffered the destruction of his penis during a botched circumcision procedure when he was 7 months old. Money told the parents that such a young boy would not yet have acquired a definitive gender or sexual orientation. He therefore advised them to have the boy's testicles removed also, and to raise him as a girl. This they did. Over the ensuing years, Money reported that the change of gender was a great success, and that the child—its name changed to

Brenda—developed a suite of girlish characteristics and looked forward to marrying a man.

In reality, Brenda never accepted a female gender identity, hated her developing breasts, and ultimately demanded and received medical treatment to turn her back into a male. He then adopted a new name, David. As an adult man, David was sexually attracted to women, contrary to Money's prediction. Money never divulged the true story, but the facts were revealed after some detective work by sexologist Milton Diamond of the University of Hawaii[25] and by a journalist who wrote a book about the case.[26] Sadly, David Reimer eventually committed suicide.

One case history by itself should not make or break a theory. Still, there are other cases whose outcomes also refute the notion that sexual orientation develops as a part of the process of gender learning. Another boy, like Bruce Reimer, lost his penis in infancy (at 2 months of age) and was reassigned as a girl. This child did successfully adopt a female gender identity that lasted through into adulthood, but she was predominantly attracted to women and was partnered with one at the most recent follow-up.[27] This again is contrary to Money's learning theory of sexual orientation; that theory would predict that, having learned a female gender identity, she would also learn to be sexually attracted to men.

In a similar vein, medical scientists at Johns Hopkins Medical Institutions studied 14 genetic males who were reassigned as female when they were babies because they had severe congenital malformations of the pelvic area that left them without a functional penis.[28] As they grew up, most of these individuals chose to revert to the male sex, but regardless of whether they did or not, those who were old enough to report a sexual orientation said that they were sexually attracted to females. These results suggest that sexual orientation is not learned but inborn. Looking at all these cases together, it seems that gender identity may be somewhat more susceptible to social influence than is sexual orientation. Here too, however, "nature" usually trumps "nurture."

If role modeling played an important part in the development of sexual orientation, we'd expect that the sexual orientation of a child's parents would be a strong influence on that child's ultimate sexual orientation. In fact, however, the vast majority of gay people have *straight* parents. This may be an unfortunate fact, in that it deprives gay children of the support that gay parents would be most able to give them. Nevertheless, it argues against an important influence of role modeling or parental teaching in the development of sexual orientation.

Of course, some gay people are parents themselves, so what about *their* children? Do they grow up gay under the influence of parental role modeling? The answer is no, not usually. Children raised by gay parents don't differ in sexual orientation (or in any other significant characteristics) from those raised by straight parents, according to a review of numerous studies.[29*]

---

* Girls who are the biological children of lesbians may have an increased likelihood of becoming bisexual or lesbian, perhaps on account of genes running in those families—see Chapter 7.

IS IT A CHOICE?

About one-third of all Americans believe that being homosexual is a "lifestyle choice," according to a *Los Angeles Times* poll.[30] This is about the same as the fraction of Americans who think gay people are "born that way."

For some reason, no poll that I'm aware of has asked *straight* Americans what made them heterosexual. If they were asked, I doubt that more than a handful would assert that they chose to be straight. More likely, they would say something like, "It's just human nature." In other words, they would claim that they were born straight. Yet to believe that one is born straight, but that gay people chose to be gay, is to conceptualize homosexuality as some kind of willful deviation from a person's own true nature. Indeed, the belief that being gay is a choice is connected with all kinds of negative beliefs about gay people and how they should be treated.[31]

If their sexual orientation was indeed a choice, gay people should remember having made it. But, by and large, they don't. In the mid 1990s, researchers at the RAND Institute analyzed the responses of gay men and lesbians to a questionnaire in *The Advocate*, a leading gay magazine. Only 4% of gay men and 15% of lesbians said that choice had anything to do with why they were gay.[32] In contrast, 90% of the gay men and 50% of the lesbians said that they felt they were "born gay." (The women also mentioned other factors, such as childhood experiences.)

This striking difference of opinion between the general population and gay people themselves may have to do with the *level* at which people conceptualize sexual orientation. Among the general population, especially those who do not have gay friends or relatives, it seems natural to conceptualize sexual orientation at the level of people's actual sexual behavior, the communities they join, and the identities they claim for themselves. At these levels, choice certainly does play an important role.

Among gay people themselves, it seems more natural to conceptualize sexual orientation in terms of sexual attraction, because sexual attraction is the wellspring of motivation that influences (but doesn't dictate) all their behavioral choices. To a large extent then, people who argue about whether being gay is a choice or not are talking past each other. As discussed in the previous chapter, I agree with most sex researchers in taking the direction of sexual attraction as the key criterion for sexual orientation, and like most sex researchers, I doubt that people choose to experience sexual attraction to one sex or the other.

THE BIOLOGICAL ALTERNATIVE

In part, researchers have turned to biological ideas about sexual orientation because other theories have failed to provide persuasive explanations. In addition, however, biological research has advanced to the point where it can offer ideas about the development of traits that used to fall squarely within the province of psychology. *Biological psychology* (or *psychobiology*) is the name of the hybrid discipline that has grown up around these ideas.

With regard to sexual orientation, biological psychologists have made a variety of important observations:

- Homosexual behavior is common among *nonhuman animals*. In a few species, individual animals have a durable preference for same-sex partners.
- Both in childhood and during adult life, gay people differ from straight people of the same sex in a variety of mental traits that fall under the general label of *gender*.
- Evidence suggests that the levels of *sex hormones* circulating during fetal life influence these gendered traits.
- Evidence suggests that *genes* influence sexual orientation and other aspects of gender.
- Structural and functional differences exist between the *brains* of gay and straight people. To judge from animal experiments, these are caused by differences in prenatal hormone levels or in the way that the brain responds to hormones.
- Differences exist in the structure and function of the *bodies* of gay and straight people.
- *Birth order* influences sexual orientation in men, and this influence appears to operate through biological mechanisms rather than social ones.

The following chapters lay out the evidence for these statements and attempt to tie them together to form a coherent biological theory of sexual orientation.

THREE

The Outline of a Theory

Humans are animals. We cannot fully understand ourselves without acknowledging our kinship with other species and learning from what they have to teach us. Observations on nonhuman animals, and experiments that make use of them, are fundamental to human biology, and they should be fundamental to psychology and sociology too.

That's not to say that humans are the *same* as other animals. Every species is the product of its own evolutionary history and is therefore unique—otherwise it would not be a species. Humans differ markedly in bodily appearance from our closest nonhuman relatives. A chimpanzee—even wearing a tuxedo— doesn't risk being mistaken for a person. Our human minds

mark us off even more clearly from chimpanzees and other primates. We are unique in our highly developed capacities for
toolmaking, language, empathy, foresight, art, science, and spir-
ituality.[1] Some aspects of our minds and behaviors have close
parallels among nonhuman animals; others do not.

MALE AND FEMALE BRAINS

Where does our sexuality stand in this respect? Let's start with
some anatomy. Across all mammalian species, including ourselves, consistent differences exist between male and female
bodies. These differences are most obvious in the genitals and in
secondary sexual characteristics such as mammary glands
(breasts), but equally important and consistent are differences
in the internal reproductive organs: Males have testes, prostate
gland, and some other sexual glands, along with the tubing
to connect them, while females have vagina, uterus, oviducts
(fallopian tubes), and ovaries.

Although less obvious at a casual glance, there are also anatomical differences between male and female brains. A key discovery was made in the late 1970s by neuroanatomist Roger
Gorski and his colleagues at UCLA.[2] They were studying the
hypothalamus, an ancient region at the base of the brain that
plays an important role in the regulation of many basic behaviors, such as feeding and drinking, as well as reproductive behaviors. Using rats as their animal model, Gorski's group focused

on a region at the front of the hypothalamus called the *medial preoptic area*, which was known to be involved in the generation of the sexual behavior that is typically shown by male animals, such as mounting of females. Within the medial preoptic area they noticed a cluster of cells that was much larger in male than in female rats: They named this cluster the *sexually dimorphic nucleus of the preoptic area*, or *SDN-POA*. (Sexually dimorphic means differing in structure between males and females. A nucleus, in neuroanatomical parlance, means a consistently recognizable aggregate of neurons at a certain location within the brain.)

Since the time of Gorski's discovery, comparable cell groups have been described in the hypothalamus of other mammals, including primates.[3] The comparable cell group in the human hypothalamus is named INAH3, which stands for the "third interstitial nucleus of the anterior hypothalamus." INAH3 is typically about two to three times larger in men than in women.[4]

We now know that the sexual dimorphism of SDN-POA (or INAH3) represents just one of numerous sex differences in brain organization.[5] These involve not only differences in the relative sizes of brain regions in males and females, but also differences in brain connections, synaptic architecture, and the distribution and amounts of neurotransmitters (signaling molecules used in neuron-to-neuron communication) and receptors (molecules that detect and respond to neurotransmitters and hormones). Not surprisingly, then, activity patterns also differ between the brains of males and females, even when they are engaged in similar mental tasks. These differences can, for example, affect the lateralization of cerebral functions—that is, the extent to which a mental task engages one side of the brain more than the other.

Sex differences are most marked for brain circuits that are involved in sexual functions, such as the hypothalamus and some other structures in the basal forebrain that are connected with it: These include structures named the *amygdala* and the *bed nucleus of the stria terminalis*.[6] Comparing these regions in a male and female brain, an expert would have a good chance of telling which sex was which. In other regions of the brain, whose functions may not be directly concerned with sexual behavior, the differences are more subtle: It may take measurement of a considerable number of male and female brains, and the application of statistical tests to the results, to establish a sex difference. Sometimes, the differences have to do with synaptic architecture or chemistry rather than size. Nevertheless, most of the brain is "gendered" in one way or another.[7]

MALE AND FEMALE BEHAVIORS

Given these biological differences between male and female brains, it's not surprising that mental and behavioral differences exist between the sexes. Male and female animals usually show fairly robust differences in sexual behavior: Most commonly, males seek female sex partners, whereas females seek males, and the actual behaviors that male and female animals display during courtship and mating differ in stereotypical ways. A female rat, for example, will solicit sex from a male by repeatedly approaching and retreating from him while wiggling her ears in a provocative fashion. The male follows the female and attempts to mount her from the rear. The females raises her rump and moves her tail to the side, thus, exposing her genital area (the *lordosis reflex*). The male briefly penetrates the female, the pair separates, and the mating is repeated several times until the male ejaculates. Guiding these behaviors are sensory cues, such as the distinct odors, vocalizations, visible movements, and tactile stimuli generated by male and female rats. Males and females respond to these cues in distinct ways.

In addition to these sex differences in partner choice and the behavioral patterns associated with courtship and mating, male and female rats differ in a range of other behaviors, such as aggressiveness, exploratory behavior, navigation, behavior toward pups, and so on. In other words, there is a constellation of *gendered* or *sex-biased* traits in rats and other animals, some closely connected with reproduction and some less so.[8]

DEVELOPMENT OF SEX DIFFERENCES IN ANIMALS

How do these behavioral differences come about? Starting with the pioneering studies of the French endocrinologist Alfred Jost in the mid 20th century, biologists have discovered a chain of causal events that leads from genes to sexually differentiated mental or behavioral traits.

The chain begins with sex chromosomes: Male mammals, including human males, possess an X *chromosome* and a Y *chromosome*, whereas females possess two X chromosomes. The Y chromosome carries only a small number of genes, but one of them, called SRY, is a master gene that initiates male development.[9] It does so by instructing two small patches of embryonic tissue to develop into testes: These are the male reproductive glands that produce sperm and that also secrete testosterone, the principal sex hormone in males. Testosterone in turn drives the development of the rest of the body and the brain in a male-typical direction.

In females, other genes instruct those same patches of embryonic tissue to develop into ovaries: These are the female reproductive glands that produce ova and also secrete two hormones that are important in female development and physiology, estrogen and progesterone. But these hormones are not secreted in significant amounts during prenatal or early postnatal development: They only come into their own at puberty. Thus, during fetal life, the key distinction between males and females is that males have high levels of circulating testosterone and testosterone-like hormones (collectively called *androgens* or "male-makers") that are secreted by the testes, whereas female have low levels of these hormones. (The androgens that are found in female fetuses are secreted by the adrenal glands.[10])

The sex difference is not absolute, however: When researchers took blood samples from a large number of male and female human fetuses at mid pregnancy, they found a slight overlap in the testosterone levels of males and females.[11] In other words, it is not possible to identify a fetus's sex with complete certainty on the basis of a one-time testosterone measurement.

Female development is sometimes referred to as the "default" pathway, because it goes forward in the absence of a specific genetic signal derived from SRY. Nevertheless, a complex suite of genes has to operate in females to produce the ovaries and other features of female anatomy. Since males also possess all those genes, the question arises as to why males don't develop female reproductive anatomy (such as a uterus) in addition to their male anatomy. The answer is that SRY and other "downstream" genes actively repress the female developmental pathway. For example, the developing male testes produce a protein hormone called *antimüllerian hormone* (AMH) that prevents the maturation of the uterus and the oviducts.

Testosterone plays the leading role in the sexual differentiation of the brain. The evidence for this statement comes from experiments in which the levels of testosterone have been artificially manipulated.[12] With regard to SDN-POA, for example, lowering the levels of testosterone in developing rats (by castration) or blocking testosterone's effects (with chemical antagonists of testosterone) leads to the development of an SDN-POA that is smaller, and contains fewer nerve cells, than in untreated males. Conversely, *adding* testosterone to developing female rats (by injection) leads to the development of an SDN-POA that is larger, and contains more nerve cells, than in untreated females, and is about the same size as in untreated males.

Although SDN-POA is the "model system" that has been most extensively studied, these hormonal manipulations actually affect the development of many sexually differentiated systems in the brains of rats and other animals. And it is not always the case that high testosterone levels lead to *larger* structures. There is another cell group in the rat's hypothalamus, called AVPV, that is sexually dimorphic in the reverse direction: It is larger in females than males. (AVPV is involved in the regulation of the female rat's reproductive cycle.) In this case, high testosterone levels during development cause AVPV to end up *smaller*, and to contain fewer cells, than it otherwise would.[13]

Although hormonal manipulations can greatly alter the sexual development of the brain, as just described, the *timing* of these manipulations is very important. In the case of the rat's SDN-POA, the most dramatic effects are seen if testosterone is added or removed during a *critical period* of development. The critical period begins suddenly on the 18th day of fetal life (which is about 4 days before birth) and tapers off more gradually a few days or weeks after birth.[14] Castration of adult male rats has no effect on the size of SDN-POA, although it does cause some shrinkage of individual neurons within SDN-POA.[15]

What is happening during the critical period? In male rat fetuses, a surge of testosterone is secreted by the testes, beginning about the 15th day of fetal life. The surge reaches a peak on the 18th day and gradually declines thereafter, with a secondary peak immediately after birth.[16] This surge does not normally occur in females. Thus, castration of males (or the use of testosterone blockers) prevents the surge (or blocks its effects), whereas adding testosterone to females mimics the normal male surge.

The normal testosterone surge in males affects the ultimate size of sexually dimorphic cell groups such as SDN-POA and AVPV. It does so, not by influencing how many nerve cells are created, but by influencing how many die.[17] In the normal course of development, immense numbers of young neurons die without ever become functionally integrated into brain circuits. This *programmed cell death*, although seemingly wasteful, actually helps to sculpt the complex cellular architecture and connections of the mature brain.[18] In the case of SDN-POA and AVPV, about the same number of nerve cells are created in males and females, but in the course of the first few days after birth testosterone reduces the rate of cell death in SDN-POA, but accelerates the rate of cell death in AVPV.[19] Thus, SDN-POA ends up larger in males, whereas AVPV ends up larger in females. If cell death is prevented (by eliminating one of the genes responsible for it), then males and females end up with similar numbers of cells in these "sexually dimorphic" cell groups, in spite of the differences in testosterone levels.[20]

Testosterone doesn't just influence neuronal survival, however: At later stages of development it also influences the growth of neurons, their synaptic connections with other neurons, their sensitivity to hormones, and their activity patterns. In other words, this hormone has a pervasive influence on brain structure and function.

These early effects of testosterone on the rat's developing nervous system are referred to as *organizational effects*, because they influence the basic layout of neuronal systems in a more or less permanent way. Organizational effects by themselves are not sufficient for adult sexual function, however. Hormones are also necessary in adulthood to facilitate and sustain sexual behavior. These are called *activational effects*, because they "turn on" functional systems whose basic structure has developed much earlier in life. Activational effects are generally not permanent: The continued presence of hormones is required, or the behavior will cease. In male rats, for example, removal of testosterone by castration quickly extinguishes male-typical sexual behavior. In female rats, estrogen and progesterone have important activational effects, controlling the periodic onset and cessation of the rat's sexual receptivity around the estrous cycle. They do this by modifying the excitability of neurons in certain parts of the hypothalamus[21] and by causing synaptic connections to form and dissolve in a cyclical fashion.[22]

Although the concept of organizational and activational effects of sex hormones has proven useful, the distinction between the two may not always be as clear-cut as once thought.[23] For example, organizational effects may occur not merely during early development but also at puberty, when the sexual differentiation of the brain continues beyond what has been accomplished during the early developmental period.[24] And at least one sexually dimorphic brain structure has been shown to change size even in adult rodents in response to hormonal manipulations.[25] This adult plasticity apparently reflects changes in the size of neurons, however, and not their number.[26] Why some brain systems seem to be "set in concrete" after the completion of early development, while others remain somewhat malleable, is not yet understood.

Given that testosterone levels early in development have long-lasting effects on the organization of sexually dimorphic brain regions such as SDN-POA, it's hardly surprising that they also affect sexual functioning in adulthood. For example, a great deal of research has been done on the two key behaviors involved in mating by rodents: mounting (shown most commonly by males) and the lordosis reflex (shown most commonly by females).

William C. Young and his colleagues at the University of Kansas performed the key studies in the 1950s.[27] They found that female guinea pigs that were exposed to testosterone prenatally were much more likely to mount other animals in adulthood, and less likely to display lordosis when mounted, than untreated females. Conversely, males deprived of testosterone during the critical period were *less* likely to mount other animals and *more* likely to display lordosis than untreated males. In other words, the disposition to perform mounting or lordosis in adulthood is a consequence of the organizing effect of high or low testosterone levels, respectively, during early brain development.

These early findings have since been extended to other behaviors and to other species. For example, Young's graduate student Robert Goy went on to direct a many-year study of rhesus monkeys at the University of Wisconsin, starting in 1971. In rhesus monkeys, pregnancy lasts 166 days, compared with only 22 days in rats. Goy's group found evidence for several distinct "critical periods" during a rhesus monkey's fetal life, during which different aspects of sex-differentiated behavior are organized.[28]

SEXUAL PARTNER PREFERENCE IN ANIMALS

The aspect of behavior that is most relevant to the topic of this book is the preference of most animals for sexual contact with opposite-sex partners. Is this preference "organized" by sex hormones during development? The answer is yes—to a degree. If newborn female rats are briefly exposed to testosterone, for example, they will prefer female sex partners in adulthood— the opposite of the usual preference for males.[29] Conversely, male rats that are deprived of testosterone by castration around the time of birth, and then treated with female hormones in adulthood, will prefer males as sex partners.[30] Simply treating an adult male rat with female hormones has no such effect.

Similar findings have been made in a variety of other species. Female zebra finches that are treated with masculinizing hormones while still in the egg or while they are nestlings prefer to form lifelong pair bonds with other females in adulthood, rather than with males.[31] Male pigs that are castrated soon after birth and given estrogen injections in adulthood prefer to approach other males and perform sexual solicitations to them, even in the presence of potential female partners. Such behavior is not shown by male pigs that were hormonally intact in early life, even if they are castrated and given estrogens in adulthood.[32]

Still, there are some caveats that need to be expressed. For one thing, there may be interactions between these organizing effects of hormones and social factors. In the case of the zebra finches, for example, the full masculinizing effect of early hormone treatment on the partner preference of female birds only occurs if those birds are also deprived of social contact with males while they are juveniles.[33]

A second important point is that the actual hormones involved differ between species.[34] In birds, such as zebra finches, estrogen rather than testosterone is the circulating hormone that masculinizes the brain during development. In rodents and carnivores, testosterone plays a significant role,[35] but some of its actions require conversion to estrogen (by an enzyme named *aromatase*) once it enters the brain.[36] In primates, on the other hand, testosterone by itself seems to be the principal hormone: Aromatase can also convert testosterone to estrogen in the primate brain, but blocking aromatase has much less dramatic effects in primates than it does in other mammals. In humans, in fact, genetic mutations that render aromatase completely nonfunctional seem to leave male psychosexual development unaffected.[37] In other words, applying the lessons of one species to another can be tricky.

Testosterone and estrogen may not be the only hormonal players influencing the sexual differentiation of the brain during fetal life. I mentioned earlier a male-specific hormone called antimüllerian hormone (AMH) whose main role is to suppress the development of the female reproductive tract. Recently, researchers at the University of Otago in New Zealand studied genetically engineered male mice in which AMH (or its receptor) had been knocked out.[38] At least one gendered trait was affected in these animals: Whereas male mice typically explore their surroundings more than females do, the AMH-deficient males showed the lower levels of exploration typical of female mice. The Otago researchers believe that AMH normally enters the brain during prenatal or early postnatal life and contributes to male-typical development of some neuronal systems.

It is also possible that some aspects of the sexual differentiation of the brain do not depend on hormones at all. Recall that every cell in an animal's body contains a copy of that animal's entire *genome* (its complete genetic endowment) in its nucleus, including its sex chromosomes. Thus, all brain cells "know" the sex of the animal they are part of, even without exposure to any sex hormones. Do they make any use of that internal information? To answer this question, molecular geneticists have produced mice in which the "intrinsic sex" of brain cells differs from the anatomical and hormonal sex of the entire animal. Study of these animals has shown that the intrinsic sex of brain cells does indeed influence the sexual differentiation of the brain and sexually differentiated behaviors such as aggression.[39]

These effects are less dramatic than the well-established effects of sex hormones, but the fact that they can be demonstrated at all should make us cautious in attributing each and every sex difference in brain and behavior to differences in hormone levels, whether during development or in adult life.

ORIGINS OF VARIATION WITHIN EACH SEX

I've outlined what we know about the chain of events that lead, in nonhuman animals, from sex chromosomes, to early hormone exposure, to brain differentiation, and finally to differences in behavior between male and female adults. Do we know anything about what factors might modify this chain of events so as to produce a diversity of outcomes among adults of the *same* sex?

One such factor is *genetic variation* among individuals of the same sex. For example, male animals are typically more aggressive than females, but individual males differ in aggressiveness. To study the biological basis for this variability, Dutch researchers bred two strains of mice, one of which was reliably more aggressive than the other. They found that there were consistent biological differences between males of the two strains, including higher circulating testosterone levels during early development in the more aggressive mice.[40] In another study, a research group at Brigham Young University found that male rats from two different strains had different-sized SDN-POAs. The rats from the strain with the larger SDN-POAs engaged in more aggressive sexual behavior than did those from the other strain.[41] The difference between the strains seems to have been caused by genetic differences in the sensitivity of the rats' brains to sex hormones.

Another approach to studying the influence of genes on sex-differentiated behavior is to remove a particular gene of interest, using the techniques of molecular genetics. University of Virginia researchers, for example, produced female mice lacking one of the genes responsible for the animals' sensitivity to estrogen: These females did not perform lordosis under any circumstances.[42] Such artificial experiments do not necessarily explain the variability in sexual behavior within a natural population, but they do offer avenues for exploring the roots of such variability.

Another factor that probably plays a greater role than commonly realized is sheer *random variability*—variability that is not controlled by genes but that is the product of some kind of biological "dice-throwing" during development. When we consider that mammals, including humans, possess only 20,000 genes or so, and that these genes have to regulate the development of billions of brain cells and all their synaptic connections, along with the entire remainder of the body, it's obvious that brain organization cannot be genetically specified in precise detail. Rather, genetic instructions produce trends and tendencies that allow for some diversity in outcome.

Here's one example illustrating the significance of such random variability. In species in which pregnant females carry multiple fetuses at the same time—which is to say, in most mammals—both male and female fetuses are likely to be present in the same uterus, but chance dictates how many there are of each sex and how they are positioned relative to each other. In rats and mice, the uterus consists of two tube-like "horns," and the fetuses are strung out along each horn like peas in a pod. Fetuses (of either sex) that happen to be located between two males develop higher levels of testosterone in their blood than do fetuses of the same sex that lack any male neighbors.[43] That's because they pick up some testosterone that has diffused across the short space between adjacent fetuses. The extra dose of testosterone has a long-lasting effect on the size of the animals' SDN-POA and on their sexual behavior.[44] This particular effect is obviously not relevant to the majority of humans who are singletons, but there are probably numerous other ways in which nature throws dice to produce diversity in gendered traits.

Finally, *environmental factors* can influence the chain of developmental processes so as to produce variability in brain organization and gender-related behavior among animals of the same sex. Stress is one environmental factor that operates prenatally. When pregnant rats or mice are severely stressed during the critical period mentioned earlier, the stress is communicated via hormonal channels to their fetuses. As a consequence, testosterone levels in male fetuses are much lower than usual from the 18th day of pregnancy onward (i.e., during the critical period).[45] The SDN-POA of these prenatally stressed males is smaller than in unstressed males, and the animals' sexual behavior in adulthood is feminized: They are more likely to show the lordosis reflex, and when given a choice of sex partners they will prefer males.[46]

Postnatal environmental factors that can influence sexual behavior include social conditions during rearing. I mentioned one example earlier: Depriving young female zebra finches of contact with males intensifies the effects of early hormone treatment on their partner preference in adulthood. Goy's group studied the effect of single-sex group rearing on the play-sex behavior of juvenile rhesus monkeys.[47] Generally speaking, juvenile males and females display both mounting behavior (the typical sexual behavior of adult males) and presenting behavior (the posture adopted by an adult female who is soliciting a mount), but juvenile males show more mounting and juvenile females show more presenting. Depriving young monkeys of the company of opposite-sex peers, however, increased the likelihood that they would show play-sex behaviors typical of the other sex.

Another example of the effect of social conditions comes from the work of Bradley Cooke (now at Georgia State University) and colleagues. They report that rearing male rats in isolation after weaning reduces the size of a sexually dimorphic structure in their brains (a region within the amygdala) in adulthood, and also leaves them deficient in some male-typical sexual behaviors.[48] Early social isolation reduces testosterone levels in male rats.[49] These lower testosterone levels may be the reason (or part of the reason) why isolation affects the development of brain structure and sexual behavior.

Even social experiences *before* weaning may play a role in the development of sexual behavior. Psychobiologist Celia Moore, of the University of Massachusetts, found that mother rats lick their male infants more than their female infants. The increased licking experienced by males contributes to the full development of sexually dimorphic neural structures and male-typical sexual behavior in adulthood. This probably happens because the sensory experience of being licked increases testosterone secretion in rat pups.[50]

In Figure 3.1, I've sketched the bare bones of the pathway that appears to control the development of sexual partner preference, and other gendered traits, in a variety of nonhuman animals that have been studied in the laboratory. Differences in levels of circulating sex hormones—usually testosterone—during one or more critical periods of development cause the brain to develop in a more male-like or more female-like direction, and these differences influence a spectrum of gendered traits in juvenile life and adulthood, including the preference for male or female sex partners. Genetic differences, random variability, and environmental factors influence this pathway by changing early sex hormone levels, by modifying the brain's responsiveness to sex hormones, or by changing the developmental sequences that intervene between hormone detection, neuronal growth, synapse formation, neurotransmitter release, and so forth.

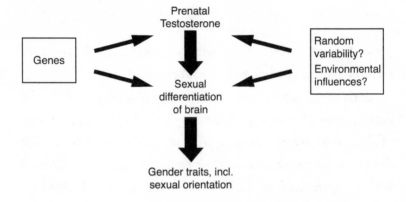

Figure 3.1 Development of sexual orientation: basic elements of a prenatal hormonal theory.

RELEVANCE TO HUMAN SEXUAL ORIENTATION

The remainder of this book is an exploration of the idea that this same causal pathway is the principal route by which humans acquire their sexual orientation. This is not a new idea. In fact, its roots can be traced back to biologically focused sex researchers of the early 20th century, such as the German gay-rights pioneer Magnus Hirschfeld and the Austrian endocrinologist Eugen Steinach.[51] In the latter part of the 20th century, the German neuroendocrinologist Günter Dörner promoted a prenatal hormonal theory of human sexual orientation, based in part on experiments in rats.[52] Other researchers have put forward similar ideas.[53]

Two things have changed in recent years. First, a great deal of new and detailed research has been done, both on humans and on experimental animals, that has helped strengthen, modify, and flesh out the theory. This new research will be presented in the following chapters.

In addition, attitudes have changed over time. Günter Dörner, for example, began his research with the point of view that homosexuality was a mental disorder that had a biological cause. He suggested a method to prevent homosexuality in men, which would be to administer extra testosterone to male fetuses who were at risk of becoming gay adults.[54] Later in his career, Dörner presented his research in a very different way: He said that it demonstrated the natural, nonpathological nature of homosexuality, and that homosexuality should therefore be deleted from the World Health Organization's list of mental disorders.[55] Dörner's change of heart paralleled a broader change in views about homosexuality in academe and among the general public over the last several decades. Although the issue of "what makes people gay" still has some social, political, and legal resonance, most researchers now view sexual orientation as worth studying simply because it is a significant aspect of the diversity that makes us human. This is how I aspire to cover the topic in the remaining chapters of this book.

SEXUAL ORIENTATION IN NATURE

Before abandoning my focus on nonhuman animals, however, it's worth taking a brief look at the question of sexual orientation in nature. What I've discussed up to this point has been, for the most part, an account of how sexual behavior, including sexual partner preference, can be influenced in laboratory animals by hormonal, genetic, or other methods. Of course, this could be read as bolstering a pathological view of homosexuality, because it takes a syringeful of drugs to produce it. That's not actually how I view the matter, because I see these interventions simply as probes into the workings of a natural process. But to get away from the laboratory and all it implies, let's take a brief look at the wider world of animal sexuality.

Sexual contacts and partnerships between animals of the same sex have been described in hundreds of species, according to an encyclopedic survey by Bruce Bagemihl.[56] Many of these descriptions are casual or anecdotal in nature; nevertheless, such behaviors have been closely studied by *ethologists* in quite a few species, ranging from birds to primates.[57]

For the most part, what has been described is not homosexuality in the sense of a durable preference for sexual contacts or relationships with same-sex partners. Rather, it is same-sex contacts by animals that also engage in heterosexual contacts, or would do so if given the chance. Thus, it could be read as illustrating a broad bisexual potential in the animal kingdom.

Sometimes, homosexual partnerships have the quality of "second-best" choices that are forced on individuals by circumstances. That seems to be true for two species of birds that have been closely studied, greylag geese (*Anser anser*) and western gulls (*Larus occidentalis*). A research group at the Konrad Lorenz

Research Station in Austria has observed a flock of free-ranging (but nonmigratory) greylag geese over many years.[58] These geese form sexual pair bonds that typically last 2 or 3 years. At any time, some fraction of the pairs in the flock consists of male–male pairs. This is related to the fact that there is usually an excess of males in the flock, because females are more frequently killed by predators. In years when the excess of males is high, the number of male–male pairs can rise to more than 20% of all pairs; in years when males and females are present in approximately equal numbers, it falls to 10% or so. The males who form these partnerships tend to be the older birds; these birds may be forced into same-sex partnerships because they are rejected by females. Male–male partnerships often break up if females become available. Although the males in a pair bond engage in sexual contact, they don't do so very amicably. Usually, both birds struggle to take the "top" position—the one adopted by the male in heterosexual matings.

According to the Austrian researchers, males who lack partners have low rank in the flock and may therefore be disadvantaged in a variety of ways, such as being pushed to the outside of the flock, where they are exposed to predation. Thus, the adaptive value of these same-sex relationships may be that they help males retain some social status. It is possible that some of the males have a lifelong preference to bond with other males, but this has not been clearly established so far.

Somewhat similar observations were made on western gulls by ecologist George Hunt and his colleagues at the University of California, Irvine.[59] During the 1970s, gull colonies on the Channel Islands off the coast of Southern California had a marked excess of females, because males were weakened by exposure to pesticides. Up to 14% of all nesting pairs during that period consisted of female–female pairs. These birds behaved very like male–female pairs, sexually and otherwise. Later, when the source of pollution was controlled and the sex ratio returned to equality, the number of female–female pairs fell dramatically.[60] Sometime in the mid-1990s I was part of a group of observers who scoured one island in search of female–female pairs, but we found none.

Female–female pairs are not necessarily nonreproductive, because individuals in these relationships frequently have sexual contacts with male partners outside of the pair bond. Thanks to such behavior, many of the female–female gull pairs successfully hatch their eggs and cooperate in raising their chicks. Thus, homosexual relationships may not be as maladaptive in evolutionary terms as they seem at first glance. It's not known whether male graylag geese who engage in male–male relationships father offspring by sex with females outside of their pair bonds.

Turning to primates, one species well known for homosexual behavior is our oversexed relative, the bonobo or pygmy chimpanzee (*Pan paniscus*). Male and female bonobos engage in frequent sexual contacts with both same-sex and opposite partners: No individuals exhibit exclusively homosexual or exclusively heterosexual behavior. Homosexual contacts (as well as many heterosexual contacts) appear to serve the purposes of conflict resolution and alliance formation, according to primatologists who have made careful observations of bonobos.[61] Female alliances in particular, which are cemented by frequent sexual contacts, have allowed females to assert greater dominance in bonobo society than is seen among other great apes.

Paul Vasey, who is an ethologist and anthropologist based at the University of Lethbridge in Canada, has focused on same-sex behavior among female Japanese macaques (*Macaca fuscata*).[62] The females observed by Vasey mounted other females on frequent occasions, in addition to engaging in sexual contacts with males. This homosexual behavior was only shown by certain geographically restricted and genetically distinct populations of Japanese macaques.[63] According to Vasey, the female–female mounting serves no evolutionarily adaptive function, such as conflict resolution or alliance formation. Rather, he suggests that females simply "discovered" the pleasurable nature of mounting in the course of mounting males—a behavior they sometimes engage in order to stimulate reluctant males into sexual activity. Because males don't always tolerate being mounted by females, the females switched to more cooperative female partners. Vasey's theory is not proven, but it does illustrate a point worth emphasizing: Not every behavior has to have an explicit value in terms of survival or reproductive success. Some behaviors are accidental by-products of other evolutionary adaptations, and are not adaptive in themselves.

Homosexuality, in the sense of a durable preference for same-sex partners, has not been widely described among nonhuman animals. One species in which it does occur, however, is that of domesticated sheep (*Ovis aries*). About 10% of rams (males) refuse to mate with ewes (females) but do readily mate with other rams.[64] Aside from their atypical partner choice, the sexual behavior of these homosexual rams is typical for rams: They go through the same series of behaviors that heterosexual rams perform when approaching and mounting females— including the characteristic head-raised, lip-curling behavior known as the *flehmen response*, which helps with the detection of sex pheromones—but they penetrate their partners anally rather than vaginally. Whether homosexual rams also occur among wild sheep is not known. A great deal of male-on-male mounting does occur in wild sheep species, however.[65]

Because rams, like men, can be rather cleanly divided into homosexual and heterosexual groups on the basis of their preference for male or female sex partners, sheep have become the focus of a research effort to explain what determines an individual ram's sexual orientation. The findings of this research will be presented in later chapters. For now, it's simply worth mentioning that the sexually dimorphic cell group in the sheep's hypothalamus—the one that is equivalent to the rat's SDN-POA—is larger in heterosexual rams than in homosexual rams.[66] This finding suggests that some aspect of the developmental pathway involving sex hormones and the brain differs between rams of different sexual orientations, in line with the ideas developed earlier in this chapter on the basis of experiments on laboratory animals.

The observation of homosexual behavior among nonhuman animals suggests that the capacity for such behavior could have evolved for a variety of different reasons, some of which have just been mentioned. Of course, these reasons could be relevant to humans too. I will revisit this issue in Chapter 7, in connection with a discussion of genetic influences on human sexual orientation.

FOUR

CHILDHOOD

This chapter and the next one lay out evidence for the idea that gay and straight people differ from each other in more than their sexual orientation. To some extent, homosexuality is part of a "package" of mental traits, many of which can be considered gender-variant or gender-nonconformist, whereas heterosexuality is part of a package of gender-typical or gender-conformist traits. This chapter discusses this idea with regard to children, and the following chapter discusses it with regard to adults.

On the face of it, this excursion into psychology is quite a departure from the biological issues discussed in the previous chapter, and it may not be immediately obvious what the topic has to do with the central theme of this book, which is how sexual orientation develops. In reality, however, there is a close connection. The idea will be put forward, partly in these two chapters and partly later in the book, that the association between sexual orientation and other gendered traits arises because all these traits differentiate under the influence of a common biological process—the sexual differentiation of the brain under the influence of sex hormones.

Obviously, this point of view carries a risk of stereotyping. As has been confirmed by many surveys over past half-century, the general population views gay men as relatively feminine and lesbians as relatively masculine.[1] These beliefs—especially when reduced to stereotypical descriptors such as "queeny" or "mannish"—have not been exactly helpful in promoting respect for gays and lesbians. They can also make it hard for men and women who don't seem to match those stereotypes to accept that they are gay, even if they are conscious of same-sex attraction or engage in homosexual behavior.

A great deal of diversity is present in the gender-related traits of gay men and of lesbians, as there is among heterosexual people too. Some gay men are so radically gender-nonconformist that they border on transexuality. In the other direction, some gay men seem indistinguishable from average heterosexual men, or even push the envelope of masculinity beyond the heterosexual norm. The converse is true for lesbians. This diversity is widely acknowledged, particularly within the gay community—by the characterization of individual lesbians as "butch" or "femme," for example—but the diversity may take the form of a contin-uum rather than distinct types.

Most researchers who have studied the mental traits associ-ated with sexual orientation have simply compared samples of gay and straight people, and have presented the results as aver-ages. Thus, the diversity *within* the categories of gay and straight people tends to get ignored. Ultimately, this could limit our understanding of the topic. It could be, for example, that gay people who are very gender-nonconformist and those who are more conventionally gendered arrive at their sexual orientations through quite different pathways, so lumping them together might muddy the picture. It is a reasonable first step, however, to compare gay and straight men, and lesbian and straight women, as if they are monolithic groups, and to see how far that approach takes us. Where relevant research exists, I will discuss differences within the categories of "gay" and "straight."

DEVELOPMENT OF GENDERED CHILDHOOD TRAITS

With regard to childhood, the topic of this chapter, it's impor-tant first of all to point out that children, like adults, have a gender: In other words, there are fairly consistent differences in the mental and behavioral characteristics of boys and girls. Here are some examples of traits that are gendered in childhood.

Boys are more active than girls, and they engage in more rough-and-tumble play.[2] Boys and girls have different toy preferences: Boys prefer toy vehicles, toy weapons, balls, and construction toys; girls have broader preferences, but tend to prefer dolls and household items such as toy kitchen implements.[3] Girls are more interested in infants than are boys.[4] Boys have better throwing accuracy but girls have better control of fine hand movements.[5] Boys do better than girls at a range of visuospatial tasks, such as targeting (throwing accuracy) and *mental rotation* (deciding whether two objects seen from different viewpoints are identical or not).[6] Girls have better verbal fluency than boys.[7] Girls are more people-oriented; boys are more thing-oriented.[8] Boys prefer the company of boys; girls prefer that of girls.[9] Girls' and boys' voices are recognizably different, even though there is no difference in the pitch of their voices before puberty.[10] All these statements are statements about averages, of course, and don't necessarily apply to individual children.

Although there is considerable agreement that childhood gender differences exist, there are diverse opinions as to how they arise. The traditional feminist perspective, which is closely related to the standard social science model mentioned in Chapter 2, attributes them principally to parental encouragement, role modeling, peer pressure, and other forms of socialization. There is little doubt that those forces do indeed have an effect. In one study, infants whose parents reinforced traditional gender-typed behavior came to exhibit more such behavior.[11] And in a very large study of 3-year-old British children, the average gender characteristics of boys and girls who had an older sibling were shifted in the direction of the sex of that sibling, presumably as a result of role modeling.[12] Even so, these socialization effects are quite small; boys with older sisters, for example, were far more masculine than any girls, even those girls who had older brothers.

A great deal of evidence suggests that biological factors play an important role in influencing children's gender development. For one thing, some of these gendered characteristics exist in nonhuman animals, where socialization effects are likely to be less strong, if they exist at all. The greater participation in rough-and-tumble play by males, for example, has been observed in the young of apes, monkeys, rodents, and other mammalian species.[13] The toy preferences of male and female monkeys are uncannily similar to those of boys and girls, even when the monkeys are tested with human children's toys that they have never seen before.[14] And juvenile female rhesus monkeys spend more time with infants than do juvenile males.[15]

Another reason for suspecting that biological factors are at work is that some of these gendered traits arise very early in life. The people/thing difference, for example, is present on the day of birth: Newborn girls prefer to look at faces, whereas newborn boys prefer to look at mechanical mobiles.[16] The male superiority in mental rotation is evident by 3–5 months of age, before socialization factors could plausibly influence this trait.[17] Differences in toy preference are evident at 3–8 months of age.[18]

Finally, there is evidence that prenatal hormones influence at least some of these gendered traits. With experimental animals, it's a fairly straightforward matter to demonstrate this. For example, the administration of testosterone to female rhesus monkeys during fetal life increases their participation in rough-and-tumble play when they are juveniles.[19] In sheep, the same treatment causes juvenile ewes to rise higher in the female dominance hierarchy than ewes who were not exposed to testosterone.[20]

In the case of humans, this kind of intentional experiment would be unethical, but something similar has occurred the form of "experiments of nature," meaning genetic conditions that affect the hormonal environment during fetal life. One such condition is congenital adrenal hyperplasia, or CAH (earlier called adrenogenital syndrome). In CAH, a genetic mutation knocks out one of the enzymes involved in the manufacture of corticosteroid hormones (hormones produced in the adrenal gland). As a by-product of this condition, the adrenal glands secrete higher-than-normal levels of androgens (testosterone-like hormones). The condition is generally recognized at birth and corrected; thus, the period of abnormal androgen exposure is mainly before birth, although the exact period and degree of exposure is not usually known.

In boys, these extra androgens do not have obvious effects, because all male fetuses are awash in testosterone. In girls, however, the effects can be quite marked. In severe cases, the girls' genitals are partially masculinized. In milder cases, in which the androgen exposure was less or occurred later in fetal life, there may be few or no abnormalities in the girl's genitals. (In recent years, it has proven possible to diagnose and treat CAH well *before* birth.)

Several groups have investigated whether CAH girls' exposure to unusually high levels of androgens has any effect on their gendered traits during childhood.[21] It does. CAH girls are, on average, more active and aggressive than unaffected girls and engage in more rough-and-tumble play. They have toy preferences similar to those of boys, are better than other girls at some visuospatial tasks such as targeting, are less interested in infant care or doll play, and are less certain that they want to be mothers when they grow up. These effects tend to be greater in girls who have the more severe forms of the condition and who therefore probably had more exposure to androgens.

Another group of girls who may experience higher-than-usual levels of testosterone before birth are those who shared a uterus with a boy—in other words, the female members of opposite-sex twin pairs. These girls might be human counterparts to the female fetuses that develop next to males in the rodent studies mentioned in the previous chapter. Whether testosterone does indeed spread in significant amounts between human fetuses is not known for sure: Direct measurements have not been reported, but some subtle anatomical measures related to finger lengths do suggest that transfer occurs[22] (see Chapter 6). Researchers who have studied gender-related traits in girls with male twin brothers have come up with mixed results: One group reported that these girls are more prone to aggression than control girls,[23] while another group failed to detect any effect on toy preferences.[24] Studies on adult women with male twin brothers have also yielded mixed results—these will be discussed in the next chapter.

Although the opposite-sex twin studies have yielded equivocal results, the CAH studies strongly suggest that prenatal androgen levels influence a variety of gender traits in childhood. Still, CAH is a special case, and the question remains: Do prenatal androgens help generate the diversity in gender characteristics among the general population of healthy girls (or boys)?

Melissa Hines and her colleagues at London's City University approached this question by measuring testosterone levels in the blood of several hundred pregnant women, and then studying the children who resulted from those pregnancies.[25] (Sampling the mothers' rather than the fetuses' blood is less than ideal, but obtaining fetal blood samples is too invasive for this kind of study. Maternal testosterone levels do give some idea of the testosterone levels to which the fetus is exposed.) Among the girls born of these pregnancies and studied at 3 years of age, gender characteristics were strongly related to maternal testosterone: The higher the testosterone levels, the more masculine were the girls' gendered traits. In contrast, these traits appeared to be unaffected by a variety of potential socialization factors, such as the presence or absence of a man in the home. More recently, Hines (along with Bonnie Auyeung, Simon Baron-Cohen, and others) has measured testosterone in amniotic fluid rather than in the mother's blood. With this improved sampling method, the researchers were able to show that higher prenatal testosterone levels were associated with more masculine play behavior, in both girls and boys.[26] Another study found that *lower* prenatal testosterone levels were associated with greater empathy at 6–8 years of age.[27]

I don't want to leave readers with the impression that everything is cut and dried, and that all findings support the simplest model, which is that high prenatal testosterone leads to masculine traits and low levels lead to feminine traits. It's not that simple. For example, although girls with CAH are better at targeting than other girls, they are not better at mental rotation, according to a study by Hines' group.[28] And CAH *boys* actually performed *worse* at mental rotation than other boys—the opposite of what one would have predicted on the basis of the simplest model. This anomalous finding was supported by another study, in which high prenatal testosterone in normal boys was related to slightly *lower* performance on a mental rotation task at 7 years of age.[29]

Such anomalous findings are no reason to abandon the general hypothesis, but they do suggest that there are complexities that need to be explored. For example, a full accounting will probably require more attention to the *timing* of testosterone exposure (mental rotation might be organized postnatally rather than prenatally, for example) and to *nonlinear effects* (meaning that testosterone might have its greatest masculinizing effect on a trait at some intermediate level, and less effect at both lower and higher levels). I will return to these issues later in the book.

CHILDHOOD TRAITS ASSOCIATED
WITH ADULT SEXUAL ORIENTATION:
RETROSPECTIVE STUDIES

Do children who become gay adults (pre-gay children) differ from children who become straight adults (pre-straight children)? There's one major obstacle to answering this question, of course, which is that neither children themselves, nor the people who nurture them or study them, can know for sure what the future sexual orientation of any particular child will be. So, how can we study the characteristics of pre-gay children and compare them with those of pre-straight children, if we don't which are which?

The most obvious and widely used method is retrospective. Adults remember their childhoods (although not infallibly), and many have provided descriptions of what they were like as children. Here, for example, are extracts from two men's published autobiographies:

> [My father] loved power tools and guns, old Cadillacs, pickup trucks, and campers. I didn't. He liked to build houses, hunt deer, and tinker with engines, and he would have enjoyed having me working and playing at his side, but while he was out in the shop painting, plumbing, or rewiring, I was lying on the living room floor, listening on the radio to Milton Cross narrate Texaco's "Saturday Morning at the Opera."

I grew up in the projects with a small group of friends, and we spent all our time thinking, talking, and playing sports. . . . [My father] taught me how to throw a curve, and he often got us bleacher seats for Red Sox games at Fenway Park. These games were the most exciting part of my youth. . . . I felt I belonged in the game. It was as if somebody had injected baseball into my veins, and from then on it was always in my blood.

Which of these two narratives was written by a gay man and which by a straight man? The answer, actually, is that *both* were written by gay men. The first was written by Mel White, the well-known gay clergyman and author.[30] The second was written by Dave Pallone, the National League baseball umpire who came out as gay after he left the sport.[31] Individual recollections by gay men, then, are quite diverse, as are those of lesbians, straight women, and straight men. Some accounts match stereotypes; some don't.

Psychiatrists who have seen many gay men in their practices do report that such men consistently speak of having been gender-nonconformist during their childhoods. Thus, Richard Isay, himself a gay man, wrote as follows:

Each of the several hundred gay men I have seen in consultation or treatment over the past 30 years has described having had one or more gender-discordant traits during childhood. Most frequently, they report a lack of interest in "rough-and-tumble" or aggressive sports; many speak of having preferred

to play with girls rather than other boys. . . . Almost all recall
that as children they felt a close bond with their mothers, with
whom they shared many interests.[32]

Reports such as this suggest that the stereotypes are correct, but
still, there is reason for caution in interpreting them. Typically,
these reports deal with gay men, not lesbians. And they may
not be representative of all gay men: Boys who are strongly
gender-nonconformist are more likely than other boys to experience anxiety and depression in adulthood,[33] and for this reason
may be more likely to end up in therapy. Finally, such studies
are not quantitative, and they lack control groups of non-gay
subjects.

To get beyond these potential problems, researchers have
interviewed large numbers of gay and straight adults about their
childhood and applied statistical tests to the results. In a 1983
study, for example, Ray Blanchard and his colleagues at Toronto's
Centre for Addiction and Mental Health used this method to
conclude that pre-gay boys are less physically aggressive than
pre-straight boys.[34] In another study from the same period,
UCLA psychologists gave questionnaires to 792 subjects—198
gay men, 198 lesbians, 198 straight men, and 198 straight
women—who were recruited from the general population.[35]
The questionnaires asked about 58 play and sports activities in
earlier and later childhood. The responses for one activity—
participation in baseball at age 5–8—are shown in Figure 4.1.

Overall, the study documented very sizeable and statistically
significant shifts in the gender-typed behaviors of pre-gay children,

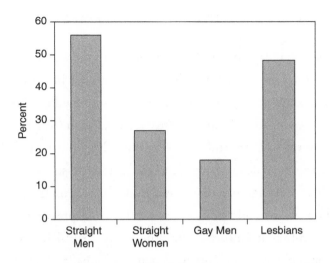

Figure 4.1 Sports participation. This bar graph shows the percentage of straight and gay men and women, interviewed around 1980, who said they played baseball between ages 5 and 8. If the study were repeated today, it might well show smaller differences, given the increased participation in sports by girls. Data from Grellert et al., 1982.

both boys and girls, compared with pre-straight children of the same sex. Pre-gay children participated less in gender-typical activities and more in gender-atypical activities. Still, not all children—whether pre-gay or pre-straight—conformed to these patterns.

In the mid 1990s, Michael Bailey and Kenneth Zucker reanalyzed the data from 41 retrospective studies of this kind.[36] They confirmed that differences exist between the gender characteristics of pre-gay and pre-straight children, always in the direction of gender-nonconformity among the pre-gay children. These differences were very sizeable and statistically significant for both pre-gay boys and pre-gay girls, but the differences were larger for boys than for girls. In other words, based on these retrospective data, gender-nonconformity in childhood is more predictive of adult homosexuality for boys than for girls.

Several further studies of this kind have been carried out since the time of Bailey and Zucker's meta-analysis, with similar results.[37] For example, one recent study focused on the question of how consistently pre-gay boys differ from pre-straight boys across different cultures.[38] For the study, several hundred gay and straight men in Turkey, Brazil, and Thailand were questioned about their childhood characteristics. The findings were very consistent: In all three cultures, pre-gay boys were less aggressive and less interested in sports than pre-straight boys. They were more likely to have associated with girls and to have participated in typical girls' activities. The study also included samples of self-identified bisexual men: These men reported childhood characteristics that were intermediate between those reported by gay and straight men, but they were generally closer to those of the straight men.

Another recent study, carried out by a Finnish group led by Katarina Alanko, focused on twins.[39] This study confirmed the association between childhood gender-nonconformity and adult homosexuality, and again found that this association, although present in both sexes, was stronger for males than for females. The study also made use of the twin paradigm to investigate genetic effects underlying the association. I'll discuss this aspect of the study in Chapter 7.

Further bolstering the findings of these studies are reports by anthropologists who have studied a variety of non-Western cultures. In most cases, these studies have focused on men who, in adulthood, take on a feminine or mixed-gender role and who partner sexually with more conventionally gendered men. As already mentioned in Chapter I, such individuals usually have a history of marked femininity during childhood.[40] The anthropological literature on women is much more limited, but to the extent that it exists, it supports the relationship between cross-gendered behavior in childhood and adult homosexuality. The Mohaves of the American West, for example, recognized a group of girls called *hwame* who "threw away their dolls" and, in adulthood, married women.[41] Because the anthropological literature focuses for the most part on homosexual adults who are gender-nonconformist or even transgendered, it leaves unclear whether there have been more conventionally gendered homosexual adults in non-Western cultures, and if so what their childhood characteristics may have been.

With all retrospective studies the potential problem is that recollections may be inaccurate. This could happen if gay adults are "looking for reasons" why they are gay or want to conform to stereotypes. It has been claimed, for example, that Radclyffe Hall, author of the 1928 lesbian classic *The Well of Loneliness*, invented a masculine childhood for herself that didn't correspond to reality.[42] Equally, straight adults might forget or be unwilling to admit to gender-nonconformist childhood characteristics if those characteristics caused them embarrassment or led to bullying.

It seems unlikely that inaccurate recollections of this kind could account for the very large and consistent differences that have been reported in the retrospective studies, but the possibility has spurred psychologists to come up with new approaches.

One novel study of this kind involved home videos.[43] Researchers from Michael Bailey's group at Northwestern University, led by Gerulf Rieger, recruited gay and straight men and women who possessed videos of themselves as children. The researchers prepared short clips from these videos and showed them to judges, who were also gay and straight men and women. Although the judges were not told the subjects' sexual orientations, they nevertheless rated the pre-gay children as far more gender-nonconformist than the pre-straight children, consistent with the findings of the retrospective studies just discussed. What's more, the observers' judgment of the videos correlated quite well with the subjects' own description of their childhood characteristics, suggesting that such self-recall is fairly accurate. The differences between the pre-gay and pre-straight children began to emerge at about 3 years of age and increased over the following few years. I will return to this study in Chapter 9, when I discuss the topic of "gaydar."

PROSPECTIVE STUDIES

The ideal method to pin down the relationship between child-hood traits and adult sexual orientation would be to recruit a large group of children from the general population, study them in as much detail as possible, and then follow them through to adulthood. Something like this may eventually be possible, given the existence of longitudinal studies such as the National Children's Study, now getting under way, which is intended to closely follow 100,000 American children from birth until 21 years of age.[44] Still, political and social considerations may limit researchers' ability to use this and similar studies to address sensitive topics like gender-nonconformity and sexual orientation.

In the meantime, a few dedicated researchers have carried out longitudinal studies on their own initiative. The strategy of these studies has been to select a group of markedly gender-nonconformist children, along with a comparison group, and to see what becomes of these children as they grow up.

The best-known of these studies is one conducted between the late 1960s and early 1980s by psychiatrist Richard Green while he was at UCLA.[45] Green later became research director of the Gender Identity Clinic at London's Charing Cross Hospital; he is the life partner of Melissa Hines, whose research on gender development was discussed earlier in this chapter.

Green recruited 66 feminine boys, as well as 56 boys who were matched for a number of demographic variables but were unselected for gender traits. (They were not specifically chosen to be "masculine.") The feminine boys were not just slightly unmasculine: Most said that they would have preferred to be girls, and some came across almost like miniature transexuals. They often expressed severe dissatisfaction with their biological sex (*gender dysphoria*). Here is part of an interview with a 5-year-old boy, "Richard," whose parents brought him to Green on account of his persistent cross-dressing and avoidance of male playmates:

> *Green*: Have you ever wished you'd been a girl?
>
> *Richard*: Yes.
>
> *Green*: Why did you wish that?
>
> *Richard*: Girls, they don't have to have a penis.
>
> *Green*: They don't have to have a penis?
>
> *Richard*: They can have babies. And—because they—it doesn't tickle when you tickle them here.
>
> *Green*: It doesn't tickle when you tickle them here? Where your penis is?
>
> *Richard*: Yeah. 'Cause they don't have a penis. I wish I was a girl.
>
> *Green*: You wish you were a girl?
>
> *Richard*: You know what? I might be a girl.

Green interviewed the boys, and their parents, repeatedly during the boys' childhood and adolescence. The results were striking: of the 35 boys in the control group whom Green was able to follow through to adolescence or young adulthood, all were heterosexual; of the 44 feminine boys whom Green was able to follow up, only 11 were heterosexual and 33 were homosexual or bisexual. In other words, the markedly feminine boys were likely to become gay or bisexual adults. Still, there were exceptions, and "Richard" was one of them: Interviewed at age 18, he gave every indication of being heterosexual, both in feelings and actual sexual behavior.

Several other prospective studies, mostly less ambitious than Green's, have reached similar conclusions: Marked femininity in boys is a predictor of adult homosexuality.[46] Perhaps counter to expectations, only a few feminine boys in these studies developed into transexual adults.[47] It should be borne in mind, however, that transexuality is very much less common than homosexuality; thus, even if male-to-female transexuals have a history of marked childhood femininity—and many do—a small sample of feminine boys may not include any future transexuals.

A recent Dutch study helped clarify this issue.[48] The researchers studied 41 young adults (both male and female) who had been diagnosed with gender dysphoria during childhood. The majority were no longer gender dysphoric, meaning that they were now satisfied with their biological sex. Some, however, were still gender dysphoric, and those tended to be the individuals who were most strongly gender dysphoric when they were children. All of the girls and boys who remained gender dysphoric in adulthood were homosexual or bisexual. Of the boys who were no longer gender dysphoric, about half were homosexual or bisexual. In contrast, of the five *girls* who were no longer gender dysphoric, all described themselves as heterosexual. A similar recent study from Ken Zucker's research group at Toronto's Centre for Addiction and Mental Health focused on 25 gender-dysphoric girls.[49] Again, in adulthood, most of these girls became satisfied with their biological sex. In this study, however, about one-third of the subjects were sexually attracted to women (or to both sexes), and these were not just the minority who remained gender-dysphoric.

Looking at all of the prospective studies, it seems that marked gender-nonconformity in childhood, especially when the child expresses a persistent wish to be of the other sex, greatly increases the likelihood that a child will develop sexual attraction to his or her own sex in adulthood. The predictive power of this association is greater for boys than for girls: Perhaps 50%–80% of such boys develop sexual attraction to males, but only about one-third of girls develop sexual attraction to females.

The retrospective and prospective studies have strengths and weaknesses that complement each other. The retrospective studies look at the broad population of gay people, but could suffer from problems caused by inaccurate recall. The prospective studies avoid problems of recall, but focus on what is probably an atypical minority of pre-gay children. Looked at together, the studies make a very strong case that pre-gay children are gender-nonconformist when compared with pre-straight children.

At the same time, the future sexual orientation of any particular girl or boy, no matter what his or her gender characteristics may be, cannot be predicted with certainty. The "average" gay adult has a history of only moderate gender-nonconformity, but the average child who is moderately gender-nonconforming may very well become a heterosexual adult. In fact, for girls at least, the majority go that route. Thus, the point of this survey is not to demonstrate that a child's future sexual orientation is predictable—it may be for a few children, but for most it is not. Rather, the point is to clarify that there is a general and statistically very significant association between childhood gender traits and adult sexual orientation, an association that requires some explanation.

CONTRASTING MODELS

Two general kinds of explanations have been put forward. In one, childhood gender characteristics, whatever their origin, are a causal link in the development of adult sexual orientation—a link that involves social interactions of some kind. To give a concrete example, psychologist Daryl Bem of Cornell University proposed what he called the "exotic becomes erotic" theory of sexual orientation.[50] This theory proposes a five-step causal sequence leading to an adult person's sexual orientation:

1. Biological factors such as prenatal hormones influence a child's personality, especially gendered traits such as aggressiveness.
2. These personality traits induce the child to prefer certain gender-conforming or gender-nonconforming activities, and therefore to socialize with same-sex or opposite-sex peers.
3. Children come to feel similar to the children with whom they usually associate, and different from the children with whom they do not usually associate.
4. The sense of difference causes psychological arousal (antipathy, apprehension) in the presence of children with whom

they do not usually associate. For example, gender-conforming girls are aroused in the presence of boys, while gender-nonconforming girls are aroused in the presence of girls. In the case of gender-nonconforming children, this arousal is heightened by taunting from same-sex peers.

5. This psychological arousal later becomes transformed into sexual attraction. Thus, gender-conforming girls develop sexual attraction to males, and gender-nonconforming girls develop sexual attraction to females, and vice versa for boys.

Because theories such as Bem's propose that biological factors such as genes and sex hormones have direct effects only on non-sexual childhood gender traits, and not on sexual orientation, they imply that a child's psychosexual outcome as gay or straight will depend, not only on these biological factors, but also on the proposed intervening social factors. In Bem's model, for example, a child who was moderately gender-nonconformist due to biological factors, but who nevertheless associated happily with same-sex peers and did not experience taunting, would not become gay, because the "arousal" linking gender-nonconformity to homosexuality would be missing. Thus, Bem's model seems to imply that adult homosexuality could be averted—if that was desired—by identifying gender-nonconformist children and applying measures to reduce their gender-nonconformity, to increase their socialization with same-sex peers, to diminish their anxiety or apprehension, or to reduce taunting. There is no actual evidence that interventions of this kind affect a child's ultimate sexual orientation, however, and I am somewhat skeptical that they would do so.

Another model of the same general kind was put forward earlier by Richard Green.[51] Green suggested that femininity in boys triggers rejection from fathers and male peers, leading to a yearning for close contact with males ("male-affect starvation," in Green's phrase). This yearning may cause the adolescent to seek sexual relationships with males and to derive satisfaction from such relationships. As with Bem's model, Green's model implies that interventions to reduce a boy's femininity or to improve his relationships with his father and male peers would decrease the likelihood of his becoming a gay adult.

In a second kind of explanation, childhood gendered traits are linked to adult sexual orientation, not through a "socialization loop" of the kind proposed by Bem and Green, but because they are both components of a "package" of gendered traits that tend to develop in a more sex-typical or sex-atypical direction under the influence of common biological drivers, such as genes and hormones. This explanation appeals to the concept, outlined earlier on the basis of animal experiments, that levels of androgens during early development organize the brain circuits that mediate a wide variety of gendered traits, including sexual orientation, even though these traits may emerge at quite different times in postnatal life. In this kind of model, there is no particular reason to think that early interventions of the kind just described would change the child's ultimate sexual orientation.

Choosing between these two kinds of explanations requires more information that I've presented so far, and therefore I'll postpone a discussion of which kind of explanation has greater merit until a later chapter. As a general comment, though, it's worth pointing out a widespread misperception. This is the idea that biological factors such as genes and hormones exert their effects only at the beginning of life—giving the individual a hefty kick in a certain direction, as it were—and that socialization and the general vicissitudes of life take over thereafter. In reality, genes and hormones exert a sustained or even growing influence over the life span. Thus, for example, the *heritability* of many psychological traits—the fraction of the variability in these traits that can be attributed to genetic differences between individuals—actually *increases* from childhood into adulthood.[52] Thus, there is no a priori reason to conclude that social processes help decide whether a person becomes gay or straight, simply by virtue of the fact that a many-year gap exists between birth and the awakening of same-sex or opposite-sex desire.

FIVE

CHARACTERISTICS OF GAY AND STRAIGHT ADULTS

For the most part, adults are aware of the direction of their sexual feelings and therefore know what their sexual orientation is. Thus, the central problem of the previous chapter—identifying the pre-gay and pre-straight children—doesn't arise when considering the characteristics of gay and straight adults. It's usually sufficient to recruit samples of adults who are willing to give information about themselves in the confidential setting of an interview, written questionnaire, or Internet-based survey. Thus, a large number of studies have focused on what differences or similarities may exist between people of different sexual orientations. More such studies are added every year.

Many of these studies report on traits that are known to differ, on average, between men and women—gendered or sex-biased traits, in other words. It could perhaps be argued that, by choosing to focus selectively on such traits, investigators are turning a stereotype into a self-fulfilling prophecy. Still, the results are not a wholesale confirmation of the "gender inversion" concept of homosexuality, as we'll see. Some traits appear to be fully gender-transposed in gay people, some are shifted part of the way toward the other sex, some are transposed only in gay men or only in lesbians, some are not shifted at all, and one or two are even shifted in the opposite direction to what stereotypes might lead one to predict. Thus, even if preexisting hypotheses do motivate the choice of research topic, the outcomes don't seem to reflect a consistent bias on the part of the investigators.

Another reason not to be too concerned about the focus on gendered traits is that many, perhaps most mental traits are gendered to a greater or lesser degree. Thus, restricting our attention to gendered traits doesn't exclude as much of the human mind from consideration as we might imagine.

GENDERED TRAITS IN ADULTHOOD

What follows is a brief summary of traits that differ, *on average*, between men and women. Some of these are simply the continuation of gendered traits of childhood, or could be thought of as adult versions of those traits (for example, actual aggression versus play-fighting). Others, especially in the area of sexuality, seem to arise for the first time at puberty.

In the area of cognition, women perform better than men at some memory tasks, including episodic memory (memory of events), verbal memory, and memory of the locations of objects. They are also better at tests of verbal fluency (quickly coming up with words that match a certain category) and some other verbal skills, face recognition, and behavioral tasks requiring fine hand movements. Men perform better than women at a variety of visuospatial tasks such as mental rotation, targeting accuracy, and navigation (especially when navigating by distant landmarks or compass directions rather than by local cues).[1] Men are slightly more likely than women to be left-handed or mixed-handed.[2]

In the area of personality, men rank higher than women on measures of assertiveness, competitiveness, aggressiveness, and independence. (These getting-things-done traits are sometimes referred to collectively as *instrumentality*.) Women rank higher than men on measures of expressiveness, sociability, empathy, openness to feelings, altruism, and neuroticism. (This last item includes the tendency to depression, anxiety, self-consciousness, and low self-esteem.) Men prefer thing-oriented activities and occupations (e.g., carpenter), whereas women prefer people-oriented activities and occupations (e.g. social worker).[3] Women have better-developed aesthetic interests and less-developed technological interests than men.[4] And, as one might expect, when asked to place themselves on a scale of masculinity–femininity men rate themselves more masculine and women rate themselves more feminine.[5] Simon Baron-Cohen, of Cambridge University, has argued that *systemizing*—interest in rule-governed systems outside of the social domain, such as computers—is a basic quality of the male mind.[6]

Marked sex differences exist in the area of sexuality. Men are more interested than women in casual or uncommitted sex, have more accepting attitudes toward such behavior, and make more attempts to engage in it.[7] Men have a greater desire for variety in their sex lives, including a greater interest in having multiple partners.[8] There are sex differences in jealousy: Men are more likely than women to experience *sexual jealousy* (fear that their partner is having sex with another person), whereas women are more likely than men to experience *emotional jealousy* (fear that their partner is becoming emotionally involved with another person).[9] Men are far more likely to have unusual sexual interests (such as fetishisms) and to suffer from *paraphilias* (sexual interests or practices that are sufficiently distressing or harmful to be deemed pathological).[10] They are also more likely to engage in sexual aggression.[11] Men and women differ to some extent in the criteria they use to judge sexual attractiveness: Men focus more than women on the youthfulness of their potential partners, whereas women focus more than men on nonphysical attributes such as personality, wealth, and power.[12] Men are more interested in visual sexual stimuli, including pornography.[13] Men masturbate more than women.[14]

There is, of course, the basic difference in sexual orientation, with men more likely to experience attraction to women (gynephilia—see Chapter I), and women more likely to experience attraction to men (androphilia). This difference carries along with it more specific attractions to physical characteristics of the other sex, such as breasts or a muscular physique. Other differences related to sexual orientation include a greater pre-valence of exclusive homosexuality among men and a greater prevalence of bisexuality among women. There is also a clearer association between genital arousal and self-declared sexual orientation in men than in women. These issues were discussed in Chapter I.

ORIGIN OF GENDERED TRAITS

As with childhood traits, the gendered traits of adults appear to be influenced by biological factors, such as genes and sex hormones. First, many of the sex differences exist widely across different countries and cultures, including illiterate populations as well as among those who are well-educated, and across societies that enforce traditional gender roles as well those that are more egalitarian.[15] In fact, contrary to what one might expect on the basis of a simple socialization model, gender differences in personality seem to become *more* marked as societies cast off traditional expectations about the roles of men and women.[16]

Several of the traits that are gendered in humans are also gendered in nonhuman primates and other mammals. For exam-ple, males and females of other mammalian species, such as rats, differ in their navigational skills and in the cues they use while navigating, and these differences mimic quite closely those described in humans.[17] Even male and female cuttlefish, which are invertebrates related to squid, use different strategies to navigate[18]; these differences could hardly result from socialization, because cuttlefish parents pay no attention to their offspring after hatching.[19]

Genes help establish the diversity in gendered traits that is seen among individuals of the same sex. This conclusion comes mainly from studies of twins—specifically, from the observation that *monozygotic* ("identical") twin pairs, who possess the same genes, are more similar to each other in gendered traits than are same-sex *dizygotic* ("fraternal") twins, who share only about half their genes. Estimates of the heritability of gendered traits range around 40%–50%, which is quite similar to the heritability of a wide range of other psychological traits.[20]

I mentioned in the previous chapter that girls affected by congenital adrenal hyperplasia (CAH)—who were exposed to unusually high levels of androgens before birth—are shifted in the masculine direction in a variety of gendered traits. This shift remains evident through adolescence into adulthood, affecting self-assessed masculinity–femininity, as well as specific *cognitive* skills such as targeting.[21] Still, not all gendered traits are shifted to the same degree: Whereas childhood toy preferences are very strongly affected, pushing CAH girls most of the way toward boys' preferences, the position of adult CAH women on the continuum of self-assessed masculinity–femininity is shifted only a small part of the way toward men's average position on this continuum.

The findings on CAH women don't necessarily tell us whether differences in prenatal hormone levels contribute to the variability in gendered traits among healthy women, or among healthy men. Ideally, this question would be studied by measuring testosterone levels in a sample of healthy fetuses and then examining those individuals' gendered traits when they are adults. There aren't many studies of this kind, because of the long waiting period involved. In one study, however, John Udry and his colleagues at the University of North Carolina took advantage of blood samples that had been drawn from 350 pregnant women and stored for many years.[22]

Before describing Udry's findings, it's necessary to explain a small complication concerning testosterone levels. Testosterone can exist either as free molecules in solution in the blood, or it can be bound to proteins, especially a "carrier protein" called *sex hormone binding globulin* (SHBG). Only the free testosterone is available to exert a hormonal influence on the brain or other tissues. Thus, the higher the SHBG in the mother's blood, the less free testosterone is available to have an effect on the fetus.

Udry's group measured both testosterone and SHGB in the stored blood samples. They also interviewed the women, who by then had reached their late 20s, to obtain a broad measure of the women's gendered behaviors and feelings. There was no relationship between the total testosterone levels in the mothers during pregnancy and their daughters' gender traits. There was, however, a significant relationship between maternal SHGB levels and daughters' gender traits: The lower the SHGB levels (and therefore, the *higher* the fetuses' likely exposure to free testosterone), the more the daughters scored toward the *masculine* end of the gender spectrum. The authors concluded that variations in prenatal testosterone exposure do indeed explain a significant part of the variability in gendered traits among healthy women. Only testosterone exposure during the second (middle) trimester of pregnancy affected the daughters' gender.

There are also less direct ways of probing the relationship between prenatal androgen exposure and adult gender. These involve finding markers—measurable anatomical or physiological characteristics—that are believed to give some indication of an individual's exposure to androgens before birth. The characteristics that are thought to serve as markers include such things as the relative length of different fingers, bodily asymmetries, and certain functional properties of the auditory system. I will discuss these markers in more detail in later chapters. For now, it's just worth pointing out that studies of these markers do offer support for the idea that prenatal androgen levels influence the variability in gendered traits among healthy adults of the same sex, but the findings are sometimes weak or inconsistent between studies.[23]

In line with the idea that sex hormones exert both organizational effects during development and activational effects in adulthood, variations in *adult* sex hormone levels may also contribute to variability in gendered traits. This is most obvious with radical changes such as the profound drop in testosterone levels in adult men whose testicles are removed. Such castrated men experience a major reduction in sex drive and aggressiveness over time. More interesting and subtle are the psychological changes that accompany the rise and fall of sex hormone levels around a woman's menstrual cycle: These include changes both in cognitive skills and in sexual feelings and behaviors. For example, heterosexual women experience a shift in partner preference toward more masculine-looking men near the time of ovulation.[24] (Some popular accounts have represented this as a dramatic swing in sexual preferences—from nurturing sweeties to square-jawed hunks and back—but in reality it's only a very modest shift.)

In addition, differences in hormone levels among individual adults might help generate the diversity of cognitive abilities that exists in the population. For example, according to some studies, women with higher testosterone levels tend to perform better at visuospatial tasks, as if testosterone is important both as an organizer and an activator for visuospatial abilities. Men, on the other hand, may show the opposite relationship: In some studies, *lower* testosterone levels have been associated with better visuospatial performance.[25] This is reminiscent of the paradoxical findings in CAH boys, mentioned in the previous chapter: Those boys, who were exposed to unusually high testosterone levels prenatally, also performed worse at visuospatial tasks than other boys. Thus, it seems that the optimal testosterone levels for visuospatial abilities may lie somewhere in the low masculine range, rather than at the top of the masculine range, as one would intuitively guess. In other words, there might be a nonlinear relationship between testosterone levels and visuospatial ability, both during early development and during adult life.

There is a reason for all the "mays" and "mights" in the previous paragraph, however, because at least one well-designed study failed to detect *any* relationship between adult hormone levels and performance in visuospatial tasks, either in men or in women.[26] (In this study, the women were all tested at the same phase of their menstrual cycles, thus eliminating cycle-related fluctuations.) The association between hormone levels and cognitive function in healthy adults therefore needs further exploration.

The variations in testosterone levels that do occur among healthy adults of the same sex may in part reflect variations in the same hormone during development. In Udry's study, mentioned earlier, the female fetuses that were exposed to high levels of free testosterone developed into adult women who also had relatively high levels of circulating testosterone. So, there may be an organizational effect of prenatal testosterone on adult testosterone levels. Alternatively, prenatal and adult testosterone levels may be correlated because of a common factor influencing both, such as the possession of certain genes. However, environmental factors such as stress, nutrition, and marital status can also affect the adult levels of testosterone and other sex hormones in dramatic ways, and sex hormone levels decline with aging in both sexes. Thus, adult testosterone levels are not set in concrete by any biological mechanism.

SEXUAL ORIENTATION AND COGNITIVE TRAITS: VISUOSPATIAL ABILITIES

I now turn to research on cognitive differences between gay and straight people, starting with visuospatial skills. The visuospatial test that shows the most consistent and large sex difference is the mental rotation test, in which men outperform women. At least six research groups have conducted sizeable studies comparing performance at this task between gay and straight subjects. Five of these studies—one of them an Internet-based test taken by several hundred thousand subjects from around the world (see Figure 5.1)—reported that gay men perform less well than straight men.[27] The sixth study failed to find any difference between gay and straight men.[28] With regard to women, two studies (including the large Internet-based study— see Figure 5.1) found a shift in the opposite direction—that is, lesbians performed better at the task than did straight women.[29] The other four studies found no difference or didn't include lesbians in the study. In other words, both gay men and lesbians are probably shifted toward the other sex in their mental rotation skills, but the shift in lesbians is smaller and doesn't show up reliably in studies with just a few tens of subjects.

Although mental rotation is the visuospatial task that's been investigated most closely, there are also reports of gay/straight differences in related tasks. In a Canadian study, gay men

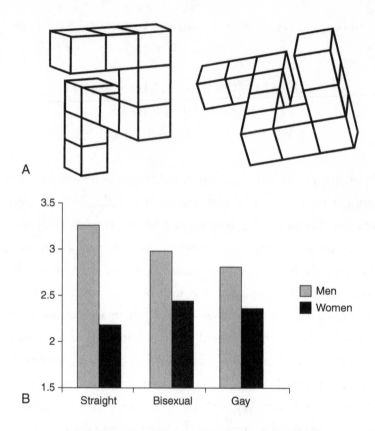

Figure 5.1 (A) In mental-rotation tests, subjects are asked whether figures such as these are the same object viewed from different angles. (B) Mental rotation scores for straight, bisexual, and gay men and women in a large Internet-based study (Peters et al., 2007). Gay men performed worse than straight men, and lesbians performed better than straight women, but gay men still performed better than lesbians. The scores for bisexual men were intermediate between those for straight and gay men; the scores for bisexual women were not significantly different from those for lesbians.

performed worse than straight men at a targeting task (throwing a ball to the center of a target a few feet away), and lesbians performed better than straight women.[30] British psychologist Qazi Rahman and his colleagues examined navigation strategies: They found that the strategy preferred by gay men (use of nearby landmarks) resembled that preferred by straight women, and differed from that preferred by straight men (use of distant landmarks or compass bearings).[31] Finally, two large studies found differences in the ability to judge the orientation of a line—a male-favoring task. Gay men performed worse than straight men on this task, and lesbians performed better than straight women.[32] All in all, then, there is considerable evidence that gay people's visuospatial abilities are shifted, on average, in the direction of the other sex.

VERBAL FLUENCY

As mentioned earlier, women tend to outperform men in verbal fluency and some related verbal skills, although the sex differences are not generally as large or consistent from study to study as they are for mental rotation. In 2003, Qazi Rahman and colleagues measured verbal fluency in 240 individuals—60 straight men, 60 straight women, 60 gay men, and 60 lesbians.[33] The findings are summarized in Figure 5.2: The gay men performed significantly better than the straight men and about as well as the straight women, whereas the lesbians scored significantly worse than the straight women and about as badly as the heterosexual men.

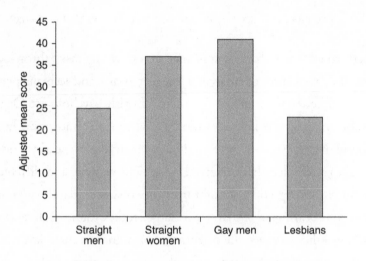

Figure 5.2 Verbal fluency. The bar graph shows the average scores of straight and gay men and women on test questions such as "In one minute, list as many words as you can that begin with the letter 'd.'" Data from Qazi Rahman et al., 2003.

These particular data suggest a complete gender "inversion" in verbal fluency among gay men and women, compared with their heterosexual peers. If we look at all the studies on this topic, however, the picture is more mixed: Some studies have reported a gay/straight difference similar to that just described,[34] some have reported a smaller difference in the same direction,[35] or a difference between gay and straight men but not between lesbian and straight women.[36] Some have not found differences related to verbal fluency as just defined, but have found differences related to another verbal task, verbal association (coming up with as many synonyms for a given word as possible in a given time).[37] One study failed to find any significant differences in verbal tasks,[38] but this could reflect some inadequacy in task design or in the selection of subjects to be tested, because the study also failed to confirm the basic sex difference favoring women, which is reasonably well established. Thus, the weight of the published research suggests that gay men and women's verbal fluency is indeed shifted in the direction of the other sex, but this shift may not be as complete or consistent as suggested by the particular dataset shown in Figure 5.2.

MEMORY TASKS

Few studies have compared gay and straight people's performance on memory tasks, but Qazi Rahman's group has examined object location memory, a trait that generally favors females. (In these tests, the subject is shown a display of many different items; the display is then hidden and the subject is asked to recall as many items as possible, as well as their locations. Sometimes the test is done by showing the subject two displays, one after the other, and asking the subject which items have changed between the displays.) The Rahman group found that gay men outperformed straight men on this kind of task, and in fact did as about well as straight women. They did not find a significant difference between lesbians and straight women, however.[39]

HANDEDNESS

The findings on handedness differ somewhat from the findings just discussed. Comparing men and women in general (without regard to their sexual orientation), men are slightly more likely to be non–right-handed (i.e., left-handed or mixed-handed) than are women.[40] (I'll say that men are slightly "left-shifted" with respect to women.) If this is a basic sex difference resulting from an early developmental process, and if sexual orientation is influenced by the same process, we would predict that gay men will be *right-shifted* with respect to straight men, whereas lesbians will be *left-shifted* with respect to straight women. In fact, however, a meta-analysis of numerous studies concluded that *both* gay men and lesbians are left-shifted with respect to their same-sex counterparts,[41] although some individual studies have failed to detect this shift,[42] or have detected it only in women.[43]*

Richard Lippa has argued, based on the results of a large-scale study, that there is *no* basic sex difference in handedness between heterosexual men and heterosexual women.[44] The reported greater prevalence of non-right-handedness among

* A large Internet-based study (Blanchard & Lippa, 2007) found that people who identified as bisexual had an increased likelihood of identifying as mixed-handed, but this could result simply from the fact that certain people are reluctant to identify themselves at the extremes of any range, no matter what the topic; they quite likely would have identified themselves as bilingual and bicoastal too, if given the chance.

men than among women, Lippa says, is simply due to the fact that random samples of men include more gay men than lesbians, because homosexuality is commoner in men than women, and it is these gay men who shift the average male handedness slightly toward the left end of the handedness spectrum.

Another interesting fact about handedness and sexual orientation is that, in some studies, gay people who are left- or mixed-handed score differently on cognitive tests in comparison with gay people who are consistently right-handed. For example, Cheryl McCormick and Sandra Witelson of McMaster University in Canada reported (in a rather small study) that right-handed gay men scored much worse than right-handed straight men at a certain visuospatial task, whereas the non–right-handed gay men did about the same as the non–right-handed straight men.[45] I'll describe other ways in which handedness may help distinguish between different kinds of gay people in a later chapter.

INTELLIGENCE

One early review of the literature concluded that both lesbians and gay men are more intelligent than their same-sex peers, even when matched for age, educational level, and other factors.[46] It seems very possible, however, that those early studies suffered from "volunteer bias," such that only relatively intelligent gay people were available for study. What's more, commonly used IQ tests, such as the Wechsler Adult Intelligence Scale, include subsets of items that favor one sex or the other (for example, verbal items favoring women), but these subsets are intentionally weighted so as to produce equal IQs in the two sexes. There is no objective reason to believe that these weightings are appropriate for gay–straight comparisons. In recent times, therefore, the issue of differences in general intelligence between gay and straight people has taken a back seat to research on more specific cognitive abilities, as discussed earlier.

PERSONALITY TRAITS: MASCULINITY–FEMININITY

When we ask, "What are gay people like?" it is personality traits rather than cognitive skills that first come to mind. This is the area where stereotypes about feminine gay men and masculine lesbians are most prevalent. What's the reality?

One way to investigate what truth may lie behind the stereotypes is simply to ask gay and straight people how masculine or feminine they consider themselves to be. In 2005, the British Broadcasting Corporation (BBC) ran an Internet-based survey that was taken by nearly half a million individuals worldwide.[47] The survey asked the respondents to classify themselves as "heterosexual (straight)," "bisexual," or "homosexual (gay, lesbian)." It also asked them to assess their own masculinity or femininity on a seven-point scale. As shown in Figure 5.3, the gay and bisexual men assessed themselves (on average) as far

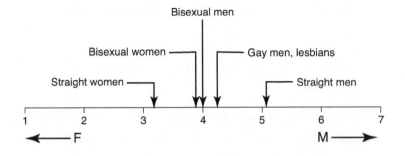

Figure 5.3 Masculinity–femininity and sexual orientation. This shows the average self-assessed masculinity–femininity of subjects in a United Kingdom study, on a 7-point scale. All four non-heterosexual groups cluster near the middle of the scale. Data from Lippa, 2008b.

more feminine than did straight men, and gay and bisexual women assessed themselves as far more masculine than did heterosexual women. All four non-heterosexual groups clustered fairly near the middle of the masculine–feminine spectrum, about half-way between the average positions of the straight men and straight women.

The results shown in the figure are for British respondents, but the results from other regions of the world were almost identical. (Of course, given that the respondents had to have access to a computer, and had to understand English, they must all have been Westernized to some degree.) In other words, homosexuality and bisexuality are associated with a very robust and significant shift in self-perceived masculinity–femininity toward the other sex, but not with a complete "gender inversion." These findings confirm a wealth of smaller studies that have yielded similar results.[48]

OCCUPATIONAL PREFERENCES

Another area that reveals a relationship between sexual orientation and gendered personality traits is that of occupational
preferences. There has long been a stereotype that people who
take up gender-atypical occupations (male nurse, female soldier,
etc.) are likely to be gay. Anecdotal evidence supports the
stereotype. Here's one such anecdote, told by World War II
veteran and lesbian activist Johnnie Phelps:

> One day I got called in to my commanding general's office—
> and it happened to be Eisenhower at the time—and he said,
> "It's come to my attention that there may be some lesbians in
> the WAC battalion. I'm giving you an order to ferret those
> lesbians out, we're going to get rid of them." And I looked
> at him and I looked at his secretary standing next to me, and
> I said "Well, sir, if the General pleases, sir, I'll be happy to
> do this investigation for you, but you have to know that the
> first name on the list will be mine." And he was kind of taken
> aback, and then this woman standing next to me said "Sir,
> if the General pleases, you must be aware that Sgt. Phelps'
> name may be second, but mine will be first." And then I looked
> at him and I said "Sir, you're right, there are lesbians in the
> WAC battalion. And if the General is prepared to replace all
> the file clerks, all the section commanders, all the drivers,
> every woman in the WAC detachment"—there were about

nine-hundred and eighty-something of us—"then I'll be happy to make that list." And he said "Forget the order!"[49]

Phelps's anecdote is just a personal recollection, and even if true, it doesn't necessarily mean that women in today's military are unusually likely to be lesbian, because military service has become a much more "ordinary" occupation for women than it was in the 1940s. The "don't ask, don't tell" policy has made it impossible to survey the sexual orientation of U.S. service personnel in a quantitative fashion. The fact that female personnel are discharged for homosexuality at a far higher rate than male personnel[50] does suggest that there may be more lesbians than gay men in the services, but many other factors affect the number of these discharges besides the actual prevalence of homosexuality.

In 1997, Michael Bailey and Michael Oberschneider focused on one occupation in which gay men are usually assumed to be over-represented—professional dance.[51] They asked a large number of dancers about the prevalence of gay people among their colleagues. The results suggested that nearly 60% of male dancers are gay—an extraordinary degree of enrichment, considering that gay men comprise no more than about 3% of the overall male population (see Chapter 1). The same study concluded that only about 3% of female dancers are lesbian, which is at most a small increase over the percentage in the general female population. Whether so many male dancers are gay because dance is a feminine activity, because it is a form of aesthetic expression (see next section), or for some other reason, is not completely clear.

Military service and professional dance are two extremes in terms of stereotypes about "gay" occupations for women and men, respectively. Whatever the proportion of people in these occupations who are gay, it's obvious that the vast majority of lesbians are not in the military and the vast majority of gay men are not professional dancers. What's more, people's actual occupations are not as informative about personality as are their occupational *preferences*. That's because people don't necessarily work in the field they would most prefer or that would best suit their talents: World War II-era lesbians, for example, would have had a hard time making a living as professional dancers whatever their talent or motivation in that direction.

To address occupational preferences in the general population, the BBC Internet study asked about the respondents' interest in eight occupations that—as shown by preliminary testing—were much more attractive to one sex than to the other.[52] The occupations preferred by men were car mechanic, builder, electrical engineer, and inventor; those preferred by women were costume designer, dance teacher, florist, and social worker. Again, as shown in Figure 5.4, all the gay and bisexual groups had gender-shifted preferences, and these shifts were similar no matter where in the world the respondents lived. With minor exceptions, the masculinity–femininity of the various groups assessed by occupational preferences corresponded quite well to their self-assessed masculinity–femininity.

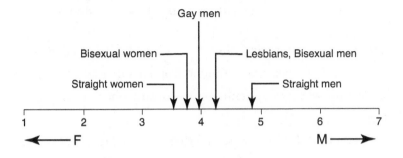

Figure 5.4 Occupational preferences and sexual orientation. This figure
plots the average gendered occupational preferences for subjects in a
United Kingdom study on a 7-point scale, with typically feminine
preferences to the left and masculine preferences to the right.
Data from Lippa, 2008b.

It should be noted that all the "masculine" occupations in
the BBC study were thing-oriented, whereas at least three of the
"feminine" occupations were people-oriented. In fact, Lippa's
analysis pointed to a major gender shift among gay people in the
people–thing dimension, with gay men's interests shifted toward
people and gay women's interests shifted toward things.[53]

OTHER PERSONALITY TRAITS

Gay people tend to be gender-atypical in some other gendered
personality traits in addition to their basic sense of masculinity
or femininity. At least two studies have reported that gay men
score higher than straight men on tests of empathy—a female-
favoring trait[54]—but one study found no difference.[55] Gay and
bisexual men also score higher on tests of aesthetic interest,

another female-favoring trait.[56] Lesbian and bisexual women score much higher than straight women on tests of techno-logical interest and systemizing in Baron-Cohen's sense of the term.[57]

Several studies have reported that gay men are less physically aggressive than heterosexual men, and one of these found that lesbians are *more* physically aggressive than heterosexual women.[58] In a recent study, Paul Vasey and his student Doug VanderLaan investigated sexual coercion: They found that gay or bisexual men were less likely than straight men to have committed acts of physical sexual coercion. They did not find any difference between straight and lesbian or bisexual women in this respect.[59] According to the researchers' statistical analysis, the difference between straight and gay men in sexual coercion reflected the generally greater aggressiveness of straight men; it was not something unique to the context of sexual interactions.

Gay people also tend to be gender-shifted in instrumentality and expressiveness.[60] (These are sets of male-favoring and female-favoring traits respectively, as mentioned earlier.) The basic sex differences in these traits are smaller than for mascu-linity–femininity, and the differences related to sexual orienta-tion are fairly small too—they are definitely "shifts" and not "inversions." In addition, it's notable in the data that lesbians and gay men are much more variable in these traits than are their straight counterparts, suggesting that it might be fruitful to study subpopulations of gays and lesbians who are and are not gender-shifted in these characteristics.

SEXUALITY

Given that sexual orientation is an aspect of sexuality, one might expect that gay people would differ from their same-sex peers most strongly in those facets of personality that are also sexual in nature. Yet, that turns out not to be the case, or not in any very consistent way.

About the only sexual traits that are fully gender-reversed in gay people are those that are almost part of the definition of homosexuality. The fact that gay men are sexually attracted to men carries with it a preference for masculinity—both physical and psychological—in their sex partners. In fact, femininity in looks or manner is strongly rejected by many gay men, according to a study of personal ads and questionnaire data by Michael Bailey's group.[61] Some gay men fantasize about or actually seek sexual relationships with straight men, presumably because straight men are perceived as particularly masculine. Even among the majority who seek gay partners, it's fairly common for gay men who place personals to mention "straight-acting" as a desirable attribute in the sought-after partner or as a selling-point in themselves—however politically incorrect that may seem. (The first gay rights activist, the 19th-century German lawyer Karl-Heinrich Ulrichs, thought it inconceivable that a pair of homosexual men would be sexually compatible, because they would be insufficiently masculine to attract each other.[62]) Conversely, Bailey's group found that lesbians prefer feminine- over masculine-looking women as partners, although they do not reject masculine-*acting* women. Of course, these generalizations mask considerable variability in what individual lesbians and gay men find attractive in their partners, both within the present-day gay community and across the course of history.[63]

One other sexual trait in which *some* gay people may be viewed as gender-reversed has to do with the actual roles they prefer to take during sexual encounters. A gay man who prefers to take the receptive role in anal intercourse—a *bottom* in gay slang—could be seen as feminine by virtue of the fact that he is being penetrated by a penis, just as a woman is penetrated during heterosexual intercourse. Certainly that's how popular cultures construe the act: Not only are bottoms seen as feminine, but men who have sex with men *without* taking the anal receptive role may not be viewed as "gay" or unmasculine at all, either by themselves or others; this is particularly true within non-White cultures.[64]

There is a certain amount of research connecting gay men's preference for receptive anal sex with a broader femininity—for example, it has been reported that bottoms are more likely than *tops* to have been very feminine during their childhood.[65] Still, more research is needed into the motivations of gay men who prefer one or the other role in anal intercourse, as well as the many who are "versatile" or don't engage in anal sex at all.

Similar considerations apply to lesbians. One study reported that butch (masculine-acting) lesbians, who may be expected to take a dominant role in sexual encounters, were more gender-nonconformist during their childhood than femme lesbians.[66]

Again, some caution is called for in interpreting these findings. Even if we take the most masculine-seeming sexual behavior that a lesbian can engage in—donning a strap-on dildo to vaginally penetrate her partner—we can't be sure whether a woman who engages in this practice is doing so out of an innate masculinity or is simply motivated by a concern for her partner's sexual pleasure.

In some other aspects of their sexuality, lesbians are fairly like straight women and gay men are fairly like straight men. Lesbians have the same low interest in uncommitted sex and multiple partners as do straight women, whereas gay men have the same high interest in uncommitted sex as straight men.[67] In terms of their actual behavior, gay men have even more sex partners than straight men do, although the numbers have varied greatly over time, even within a single country such as the United States.[68] The behavioral difference probably reflects the fact that men who seek sex with men are not limited by women's reluctance to engage in uncommitted sexual encounters, rather than resulting from any fundamental difference between gay and straight men's interest in such encounters. Another trait in which gay people resemble their same-sex peers is the emphasis they place on their partners' physical attractiveness: Gay men rate this as important as do straight men, while lesbians rate it as unimportant as do straight women, or perhaps slightly *less* important.[69]

Some other sexual characteristics do differ between gay and straight people, but only for one sex. For example, according to Bailey's group, gay men are as interested in visual sexual stimuli as are straight men, but lesbians are more interested in visual stimuli than are straight women—they are intermediate between straight men and women in this regard. Similarly, gay men are as unconcerned with their partners' status as are straight men, but lesbians are less concerned with their partners' status than are straight women—again, they are intermediate between straight men and women on this measure. And lesbians, but not gay men, tend to use strategies typical of the other sex when attempting to prevent their partners from straying, according to a study by Doug VanderLaan and Paul Vasey.[70]

Conversely, Bailey's study identified two sexual traits that are gender-atypical in gay men and not in lesbians. Lesbians are more affected by emotional jealousy than by sexual jealousy, just like straight women, but gay men closely match the two female groups in this regard: They are much less affected by sexual jealousy than are straight men. And finally, lesbians are as unconcerned with the youthfulness of their partners as are straight women, but gay men are significantly less concerned with this issue than are straight men—they fall about halfway between straight men and women in this regard. This last finding may reflect the fact that the gay male community comprises a mix of men who prefer younger and older partners.[71]

Gay men are at least as likely as straight men to be interested and involved in unusual sexual practices, such as fetishism and sado-masochism (S/M). In fact, they may well be more likely than straight men to engage in S/M practices, especially the more extreme or unusual practices.[72] Again, the willingness of their (male) partners may be a factor here. With regard to women, information is limited, but one survey of several hundred lesbians and bisexual women found that 40% had engaged in at least one S/M or related practice, and 25% had engaged in multiple practices. This seems higher than what would be expected in the general female population.[73] It's possible that the experience of having a minority sexual orientation encourages both gay men and women to explore unconventional sexual practices.

OVERVIEW

The mind of the "average" gay individual is a patchwork of gendered traits—some indistinguishable from those of same-sex peers, some shifted part way toward the other sex, and others typical of the other sex. All in all, though, what's striking is the large number of traits in which gay people's minds are at least part-way shifted in a gender-atypical direction. In other words, the stereotype about "feminine" gay men and "masculine" lesbians is a stereotype because it is an exaggeration and because it generalizes across diverse populations of gay men and of lesbians, but it contains a substantial kernel of truth.

Most people, gay or straight, accept that there is some truth to the stereotype, but they may have a range of explanations for it. One idea heard from time to time is that gay people develop or act out cross-gendered characteristics as a reaction to the realization that they are gay. For example, a gay man might go through a thought process of the following kind: "I'm attracted to men, so I must be a woman, so I should act like a woman." Alternatively, a gay person might be pressured into a cross-gendered personality by the force of social labeling.

It's possible that these factors do operate to some limited degree, but they are woefully inadequate as an explanation for the findings of this chapter and the foregoing one. For one thing, gay people are already quite gender-nonconformist during their childhood—perhaps more so than when they reach adulthood. Yet, childhood is a phase of life when most people are still unaware of their sexual orientation. Given this timetable, it would be much more logical to argue that gay people are gay as a consequence of their gender-nonconformity than the reverse. This in fact is the logic behind Daryl Bem's "exotic becomes erotic" theory, and although I don't believe that that theory is likely to be correct, it at least has things arranged in a believable temporal order.

Another reason for doubting the idea that the awareness of homosexuality (by oneself or others) is what induces gender-nonconformist traits is the nature of the traits themselves. Some of them, especially in the cognitive area, are things about which most people know little and care less. Few people have preconceived ideas about how men and women should perform on arcane tasks such as mental rotation or object location memory, and for the most part it's not obvious how parental pressure or any other forms of socialization would cause gay people to develop attributes or skills in these areas that differentiate them from straight people.

Sometimes, to be sure, socialization does come to mind as a possible causal factor. Gay men's relatively poor targeting skills, for example, might be explained by a failure to participate in childhood sports that hone those skills. When the researchers in that study used statistical procedures to "factor out" the effect of sports experience, however, the gay–straight difference persisted.[74]

Thus, in general, the researchers who have carried out the studies described earlier have interpreted their findings in terms of a biological difference between gay and straight people, most likely related to the levels of testosterone during early brain development, rather than to environmental factors operating during childhood or adult life. The association between sexual orientation and a "package" of gendered traits arises, according to this idea, because several brain systems that mediate such traits develop in the same developmental time period and are all sensitive to circulating testosterone level. The parallels with the research on nonhuman animals, described previously, as well as the observations on CAH girls, support this interpretation.

In the following chapters, I will look more closely at two biological factors, sex hormones and genes, to see whether the evidence supports a role for them in the development of sexual orientation.

SIX

THE ROLE OF SEX HORMONES

The idea that sex hormones influence sexual orientation goes back to the experiments of the Austrian endocrinologist Eugen Steinach (1861–1944). During the first decade of the 20th century, Steinach demonstrated that secretions from the testes and ovaries influence sexual behavior in laboratory animals. He later claimed to have discovered that the testicular secretions of gay men were abnormal, and he even reported that transplantation of testicular tissue from heterosexual men into gay men converted gay men to heterosexuality—an assertion that turned out to be wrong.[1]

Initially, the focus was on the nature and quantities of sex hormones in gay and straight adults; later, attention shifted to the idea that prenatal hormones had a more important influence on sexual orientation. For much of the 20th century, these hypotheses were used as the rationale for attempts to convert gay people to heterosexuality through hormonal means, or for proposed interventions to prevent fetuses from becoming gay adults.[2]

Few, if any, scientists working in this area today think in terms of pathology, cures, or prevention. Still, the idea that hormones hold the key to understanding sexual orientation is, if anything, even more widely held today than it was in the past. In part, this reflects the increasingly obvious weaknesses of competing theories, especially psychodynamic ones, as discussed in Chapter 2. In addition, the emphasis on hormones has come about as a result of new research that points more strongly to their importance than ever before. Here, I review this research.

HORMONE LEVELS IN GAY AND STRAIGHT ADULTS

In 1984, neuroendocrinologist Heino Meyer-Bahlburg of Columbia University reviewed the studies published up to that time that compared serum testosterone levels in gay and straight adults.[3] He concluded that there is no consistent difference between testosterone levels in gay and straight men. With regard to women, the data suggested that most lesbians have testosterone levels in the same range as straight women, but that up to 30% of lesbians may have elevated testosterone levels (although still below the male range).

Very little research has been done in this area since the time of Meyer-Bahlburg's review. There seems to be a consensus that gay and straight men have similar testosterone levels and that further research on that topic is not warranted. With regard to women, there are two studies suggesting that self-identified butch lesbians may have relatively high testosterone levels, or that butch lesbians in partnerships with femme lesbians have higher testosterone levels than their partners.[4] By itself, this doesn't mean that there's some fundamental endocrinological difference between butch and femme lesbians, because testosterone levels at any particular time are influenced by a variety of circumstances such as relationship status, sexual activity, social dominance, stress, phase of the menstrual cycle, time of day, and so on.[5] I will revisit the question of whether there are biologically different types of gay people later, when I've had the chance to describe other kinds of research that bear on the question.

WHY FOCUS ON PRENATAL
SEX HORMONES?

The hypothesis that prenatal hormone levels influence people's sexual orientation comes from three main sets of observations.

First, the experiments conducted using nonhuman animals, described in Chapter 3, indicate that testosterone levels during a "critical period" before and around the time of birth influence an animal's preference for male or female sex partners after puberty. It's reasonable to suspect that a similar developmental mechanism might operate in ourselves as in other animals. The critical period, if it exists in humans, would probably be entirely before birth, given that humans are born at a much later stage of brain maturation than most laboratory animals.

Second, observations in humans suggest that gendered traits other than sexual orientation are indeed influenced by prenatal hormones. For example, the observations on CAH girls (Chapter 4) and CAH women (Chapter 5) support this point of view.

Third, the fact that homosexuality is linked to a variety of other gendered-atypical traits in childhood and adulthood, as discussed in Chapters 4 and 5, suggests that sexual orientation might be part of a gender "package" that has some common developmental roots. Thus, if those other gender traits are influenced by prenatal hormones, then it's reasonable to ask whether sexual orientation is too.

These three sets of observations are the impetus to form a hypothesis about a causal connection between prenatal testosterone and adult sexual orientation, but they do not by themselves prove that any such relationship exists, let alone that the relationship is a causal one. We need to consider whether there is more direct evidence.

HORMONE LEVELS DURING
DEVELOPMENT

There appear to be three main periods during which testosterone levels are markedly elevated in males.[6] The first period begins about 6 weeks after conception, peaks at about 12 weeks, and lasts until about 20 weeks after conception. During the early part of this period, testosterone drives the development of the male genitals and reproductive system; during the latter part, it influences development both of the genitals and of the brain. The second period of raised testosterone begins at or shortly before birth and tails off during the first 6–12 months of postnatal life.[7] The function of this second period—sometimes described as a "mini-puberty"—is not well understood, but it appears to play a role in the maintenance of male genital development.[8] The third period begins at real puberty and is lifelong, although with a gradual decline with aging; during this period, testosterone and its metabolites induce and sustain most of the anatomical and behavioral changes associated with male puberty.

On average, females have lower testosterone levels at all times, but there is overlap between the sexes during some portions of fetal life, as well as during the neonatal "mini-puberty."[9] Although low, the levels of testosterone and other androgens in female fetuses (which are secreted by the adrenal glands) are thought to play a role in the development of the female genitals, because some women who are completely insensitive to androgens (see below) have an underdeveloped clitoris and labia minora.[10]

Females experience a transient rise in estrogen during the neonatal period. Although estrogen levels then fall to very low in girls and remain so until puberty, these low levels are still about eightfold higher than they are in boys, and this childhood sex difference could be relevant to some aspects of development, especially development of the bones (see Chapter 9).[11]

Testosterone levels do rise in girls at puberty (along with the estrogen and progesterone secreted by the ovaries), and they fluctuate with the menstrual cycle, but they remain well below male levels. Testosterone influences sexual feelings and other gendered traits in women. The question of the relative contributions of testosterone and estrogen to sexual feelings in women is not completely settled: Most likely, both hormones play a role.

CONGENITAL ADRENAL HYPERPLASIA

I've already mentioned studies of females affected by CAH as evidence that elevated levels of prenatal testosterone and other androgens are capable of shifting a variety of gendered traits in a masculine direction. What about sexual orientation? No less than 19 studies have investigated the sexual orientation of CAH women, and most (especially those that have compared CAH women with matched control groups, such as their unaffected sisters) have found these women to be very significantly shifted, on average, in the homosexual direction[12] (see Figure 6.1).

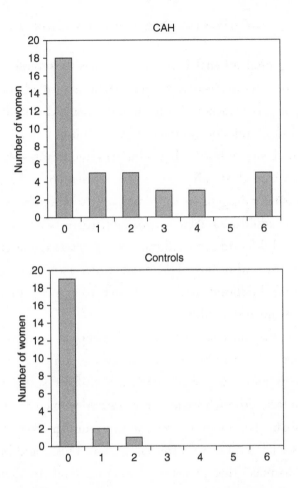

Figure 6.1 Congenital adrenal hyperplasia (CAH) and sexual orientation. The histograms compare the Kinsey ratings of 39 women with the severest ("salt-wasting") form of CAH and a control group consisting of 22 unaffected sisters or female cousins of CAH women. 0 = exclusively heterosexual, 6 = exclusively homosexual. Data from Meyer-Bahlburg et al., 2008.

Congenital adrenal hyperplasia comes in several different forms that vary in severity; the most severe (so-called "salt-wasting") form is associated with the most marked shift in sexual orientation, while the mildest (so-called "nonclassical") form is associated with only a modest—but still significant—shift. This suggests that those affected female fetuses with the greatest exposure to androgens are the most likely to experience same-sex desire in adulthood. Not surprisingly, there is an association between childhood gendered traits and adult sexual orientation: CAH women who showed the most gender-atypical play behavior during childhood are the most likely to report sexual attraction to women in adulthood.[13]

Even the most severely affected group of women—those with the salt-wasting condition—show only a moderate (although statistically very significant) shift of sexual orientation. In fact, although some of the affected women are out-and-out lesbian (Kinsey group 6), a greater number are completely heterosexual, as shown in the Figure 6.1. This could be interpreted to mean that prenatal testosterone levels by themselves do not dictate sexual orientation but merely influence it. It's also possible, however, that the levels or timing of testosterone exposure in many female CAH fetuses do not match the levels or timing of exposure that typically characterize male development. Thus, the observation that there is *any* shift in the sexual orientation of CAH women is probably more meaningful than the fact that the shift is incomplete.

It would be useful to have the converse "experiment of nature," namely a genetic condition that exposed *male* fetuses to

unusually *low* levels of testosterone. The closest to that is a condition called *androgen insensitivity syndrome (AIS)*, in which the gene
coding for the androgen receptor—the molecule that senses the
presence of testosterone and other androgens—is mutated,
giving rise to a receptor that functions poorly or not at all. This
condition causes XY fetuses, who would otherwise have become
normal males, to develop with the outward appearance of
females, because their bodies simply don't respond to the testosterone that is being secreted by their testes. Once born, these
children are reared as girls, and they identify as girls. In adulthood, they are psychosexually similar to other women; that is,
the great majority are sexually attracted to men and are feminine
in other gender traits.[14] This finding is certainly consistent with
the idea that testosterone is the key biological player in the
development of sexual orientation and gender, but it does not
distinguish between biological and socialization factors, given
that these individuals look like females and are raised as such.

FINGER LENGTH STUDIES

Are the findings on CAH and other unusual conditions relevant
to healthy people? To approach this question, researchers have
looked for anatomical or functional "markers" that might give
some indication of the extent to which an individual was exposed
to androgens during her or his fetal life. If these markers do in
fact provide such information, then comparing the markers in
gay and straight people would help establish whether prenatal

androgen levels are related to sexual orientation in the general population.

One potential marker that has triggered a lot of interest is finger length—not the absolute length of the fingers, but the ratios of the lengths of different fingers (see Figure 6.2).[15] The most informative finger appears to be the index finger (second digit). This finger tends to be slightly shorter in males than in females—when measured in relationship to other fingers. The usual way that the measurement is done is simply to divide the length of the index finger by the length of the ring finger (fourth digit), giving what is called the 2D:4D ratio. (However, the results of one study indicate that the 2D:5D ratio may yield a

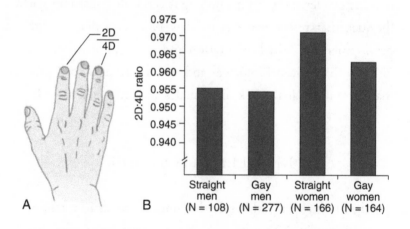

Figure 6.2 Finger-length ratios. (A) The 2D:4D ratio is the length of the index finger divided by the length of the ring finger. The measurements are taken on the front surfaces of the fingers, not the backs as shown here. (B) The average 2D:4D ratios for straight and gay men and women. From data of Williams et al., 2000.

more consistent sex difference than the 2D:4D ratio.[16]) Thus, the 2D:4D ratio is lower in males than females, on average; this sex difference is more marked for the fingers of the right hand than for those of the left hand.[17] The sex difference in 2D:4D ratios exists prenatally, but it probably becomes more marked during the first 2 years of postnatal life.[18]

Several lines of evidence support the notion that the 2D:4D ratio is influenced by prenatal androgens:

- High testosterone levels in a fetus's amniotic fluid are correlated with a low (more male-like) 2D:4D ratio at 2 years of age, independent of the child's sex.[19]
- Women with CAH, who were exposed to unusually high androgen levels before birth, have a lower 2D:4D ratio in the right hand than unaffected women,[20] although possibly not in the left hand.[21]
- Women with polycystic ovary syndrome—another condition thought to be associated with high prenatal testosterone levels—have lower 2D:4D ratios in the right hand than unaffected women.[22]
- XY individuals with AIS (chromosomal males who develop as women because their bodies are insensitive to testosterone—see earlier discussion) have 2D:4D ratios that are *higher* than those of unaffected XY males, and in the same range as typical XX females.[23]
- Women who were members of an opposite-sex twin pair, and who therefore may have been exposed to testosterone from

their brother during fetal life, have lower 2D:4D ratios than do women who were members of same-sex twin pairs.[24]

- Administering testosterone to pregnant rats lowers the 2D:4D ratio of their offspring when measured in adulthood.[25]

So, are there differences between gay and straight people in their finger-length ratios? The answer appears to be yes, although there is not unanimous agreement among different studies. Let's look at the findings for women first. Out of ten studies that have compared 2D:4D ratios between lesbian and straight women, six reported that lesbians have lower (more male-like) ratios.[26] Three studies found no difference.[27] A recent statistical re-analysis of all available studies confirmed that the difference between lesbian and straight women is real.[28]

Another study (from Marc Breedlove's research group, then at the University of California, Berkeley) was perhaps the most interesting: It found that self-identified butch lesbians had a lower 2D:4D ratio than straight women, but that lesbians who identified as femme did not.[29] Another study, published only in abstract form, made the same observation.[30] These reports could be taken to bolster the idea, discussed earlier, that butch lesbians are a biologically different entity from femme lesbians—specifically, that butch lesbians were exposed to unusually high androgen levels prenatally, whereas femme lesbians were not. More studies, however, are needed to verify the butch/femme difference in finger-length ratios.

The data for men are less clear. Out of 11 studies that have compared 2D:4D ratios in gay and straight men, four have reported that gay men have higher (i.e., more female-like) ratios than straight men,[31] four reported that they have *lower* ratios,[32] and three studies found no difference.[33]

This conflict in results is certainly frustrating—it tempts us to throw up our hands and reject the idea that there is any real difference in gay and straight men's finger-length ratios. However, one of the studies that reported that gay men's ratios are higher (shifted in the female direction) was an Internet-based study that had far more subjects than all the other studies combined.[34] This study found the shift only when comparing White gay and straight men, not Black or Chinese men. Because of the size of this study, it does seem likely that a real, but small, shift exists in the average 2D:4D ratios of White gay men in the direction of female-typical values. Still, even more research will be needed to sort out the conflicts among these 11 studies.

The observations on finger-length ratios not only support the idea that prenatal androgens influence sexual orientation; they also strengthen the notion that homosexuality is part of a "package" of gender-atypical traits that share a developmental history. That's because a variety of other gendered cognitive and personality traits have likewise been reported to vary with 2D:4D ratios, and in the expected direction—high ratios being associated with more female-like scores and low ratios with more male-like scores.[35] Still, some of the reported associations are weak or inconsistent,[36] and some researchers have expressed doubts about the usefulness of the 2D:4D ratio as a marker for early androgen exposure.[37]

In my view, finger-length ratios do offer a useful window into people's hormonal history, but the subtlety of the basic sex difference means that detecting differences *within* one sex— between gay and straight men, for example—requires large and carefully designed studies that take ethnicity and other variables into account.[38]

THE INNER EAR

We don't usually think of men and women as differing in their sense of hearing, but in fact numerous subtle differences exist between the sexes in auditory function.[39] Women are more sensitive than men (on average) to very quiet sounds, for example, whereas men are better than women at localizing the source of a sound.

Auditory physiologist Dennis McFadden, of the University of Texas at Austin, has made a close study of the *cochlea*, the auditory sense organ in the inner ear. The cochlea, as it turns out, doesn't just sense sounds, it also *generates* sounds. Although these sounds are extremely weak, they can be detected with the use of a sensitive microphone placed inside the ear canal (see Figure 6.3). The sounds are called *oto-acoustic emissions* (OAEs), and they either occur spontaneously (SOAEs) or they can be evoked in the laboratory by external sounds such as clicks (CEOAEs). Any given SOAE has a certain *frequency* (pitch), and any particular individual generates a certain number of SOAEs, ranging from none to a dozen or so. The number of SOAEs remains

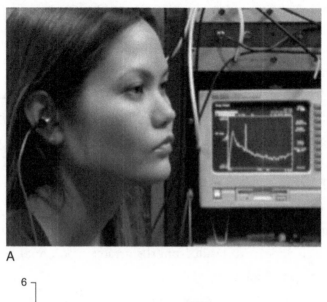

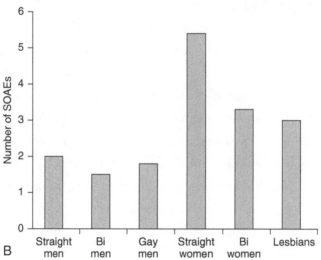

Figure 6.3 (A) Recording of oto-acoustic emissions (OAE).
The oscilloscope trace shows the level of sound recorded from
the subject's right ear across the entire range of audible frequencies.
This subject has one spontaneous OAE (the sharp spike). Photograph
courtesy of Dennis McFadden. (B) Average number of spontaneous
OAEs (SOAEs; right ear), for different sexual orientations. Lesbians
and bisexual women have fewer SOAEs than straight women.
Data from McFadden and Pasanen, 1999.

more or less constant for a given individual from birth until death, unless the ear becomes damaged.

Most of us knew little and cared less about OAEs until it was discovered that they show a sex difference: Women, on average, generate more and louder SOAEs, and louder CEOAEs, than do men.[40] (About half of all men generate no SOAEs at all.) This sex difference also exists in monkeys and even sheep,[41] so it is not likely to be caused by cultural factors such as a difference between boys' and girls' exposure to harmful noise levels. Rather, it appears to result from the greater exposure of males to androgens during prenatal life.

Two lines of evidence support this belief. First, exposing female sheep fetuses to higher-than-usual levels of testosterone causes their CEOAEs in adulthood to be weaker—that is, the testosterone exposure shifts the female pattern to the male pattern.[42] Second, women who were members of opposite-sex twin pairs, and who may therefore have been exposed to higher-than-usual levels of testosterone during fetal life, also have SOAEs and CEOAEs that are more male-like than those of other women.[43] The clincher would be to demonstrate that OAE patterns are also shifted in the male direction in CAH women, but so far that study hasn't been done.

McFadden and his colleague Edward Pasanen have measured both spontaneous and click-evoked OAEs in straight, bisexual, and gay men and women.[44] They found that the OAEs of 60 lesbians and bisexual women were weaker and fewer than those of straight women; in other words, their OAE patterns were shifted in the male direction. The researchers interpreted these findings as evidence that non-heterosexual women have, on average, experienced higher levels of androgens during prenatal life than have their heterosexual peers. McFadden and Pasanen found no difference in OAE patterns among the three male groups (straight, bisexual, and gay). This negative finding does not constitute substantial evidence against the idea that prenatal testosterone levels influence male sexual orientation, however, for reasons that I will discuss later.

One disadvantage of using OAEs as a marker for prenatal hormonal exposure is that measuring them accurately requires considerable expertise, as well as specialized equipment. That's in marked contrast to the use of digit ratios. Anyone with a ruler and 5 minutes' training can carry out a digit ratio study, and as a result there are plenty of published studies on the topic by different research groups—even though digit ratios are less than ideal markers on account of the rather small sex differences that they exhibit. In the case of OAEs, on the other hand, not a single research group outside of Dennis McFadden's lab has compared these phenomena in gay and straight people. Thus, the topic remains somewhat on the fringes of the field, and it deserves to be explored more fully.

CENTRAL AUDITORY SYSTEM

The cochlea represents the first stage in the processing of auditory signals; further processing occurs in the brainstem and in the auditory regions of the cerebral cortex. Although I am putting off my main discussion of the brain until Chapter 8, this is a good place to mention a couple of other studies that have reported functional differences in the central auditory systems of gay and straight people, because these differences, like those already described, have been interpreted in support of a prenatal hormonal influence on the development of sexual orientation.

Dennis McFadden and Craig Champlin have studied central auditory function by means of electrical recordings from the scalp of subjects who are listening to clicks or other sounds.[45] The recordings, called *auditory evoked potentials*, are essentially a kind of electroencephalograph (EEG). Some aspects of these evoked potentials show sex differences, and as with the cochlear responses described earlier, lesbians and bisexual women exhibit patterns of evoked potentials that are intermediate between those typical of heterosexual women and those seen in hetero-sexual men. This finding invites the same interpretation as for the cochlear data, namely, a greater exposure of the brains of bisexual and lesbian women to testosterone before birth.

With regard to men, McFadden and Champlin obtained unexpected results: Some of the patterns of evoked potentials in gay and bisexual men were shifted in a direction *away from* female values. They might be described as "hypermasculinized" rather than "feminized." In terms of the simplest hormonal model, such findings would suggest that gay and bisexual men were exposed to *higher* prenatal testosterone levels than were straight men, contrary to what the majority of data suggest.

Other explanations are possible, however, and I will put off discussion of this finding until later in the chapter.

Another auditory study was carried out by Qazi Rahman and his colleagues.[46] Rahman's group focused on a phenomenon called the "eye-blink auditory startle response," a phenomenon that may be even more esoteric than that of OAEs. Basically, the phenomenon is this: People blink when startled by a sudden loud sound. There is no obvious sex difference in this startle response. However, men's startle response is greatly attenuated if the loud sound is preceded by a much softer sound (a "pre-pulse"—the phenomenon is called "pre-pulse inhibition"). Women's startle response is much less affected by a pre-pulse. When they compared straight and gay men and women, Rahman's group obtained results comparable to McFadden's findings on the cochlea. That is, lesbians showed stronger (more male-like) pre-pulse inhibition than did straight women. There was a trend* for gay men's responses to show weaker (i.e., more female-like) pre-pulse inhibition than straight men's responses.

In summary, then, the three sets of auditory system findings (on OAEs, auditory evoked potentials, and auditory startle responses) are consistent in showing that lesbians (and in McFadden's studies, bisexual women) exhibit response patterns that are shifted in a male-typical direction. The findings in males show little or no

---

* A trend means a difference between groups in the stated direction that fails to reach statistical significance.

difference related to sexual orientation, or may actually be in the opposite direction to what we might have predicted.

ACTION OF SEX HORMONES ON THE DEVELOPING BRAIN

Sex hormones interact with the developing brain in a variety of complex ways. It's worth knowing a little about these interactions because they offer various possibilities for how hormone–brain interactions might differ between fetuses who ultimately become gay adults and those who become straight.

After testosterone enters the fetal brain, some of it is converted into estrogen. As mentioned earlier, the conversion is performed by the enzyme aromatase. Thus, both testosterone itself and the estrogen produced from it are candidates to drive brain development in a male-typical direction. As already discussed in Chapter 3, estrogen appears to be the key player in some animals, but in humans, testosterone may be sufficient, because men who suffer from a genetic mutation that knocks out the aromatase enzyme nevertheless experience male-typical psychosexual development.[47]

The presence of testosterone and estrogen is sensed by *receptor* molecules. Earlier in the chapter, I mentioned the androgen receptor, which senses testosterone and other androgens. (I said that its absence leads to female-like development and, usually, sexual attraction to males.) Estrogen receptors are also present in the brain.

Some of these androgen and estrogen receptors are present on the outer cell membranes of neurons; these are responsible for the rapid actions of sex hormones—within seconds in some cases. Other receptors are present inside neurons; these are responsible for the slower actions of sex hormones—over periods of hours or days. It's these latter receptors that seem to be involved in the long-term effects that we are interested in here, and it's their mode of action that I'll briefly describe.

After a sex hormone molecule binds to a receptor, the hormone–receptor complex interacts with the DNA in the cell's nucleus. Certain genes carry specific DNA sequences that allow the hormone–receptor complex to bind to them and activate the genes, whereas others do not. Thus, androgens activate their own particular suite of genes, and estrogens activate *their* own suite of genes. Further complicating the matter is the existence of a group of proteins called co-activators and co-repressors, which are capable of enhancing or inhibiting hormone action.[48]

Studies of one particular gene offer an interesting insight into how sex hormones exert their effects. This gene codes for a "growth factor" called NELL2. In the developing SDN-POA of the rat's hypothalamus, NELL2 is present in the same neurons that contain estrogen receptors—probably because the NELL2 gene is one of the suite of genes activated by the estrogen receptor.

A group of South Korean researchers, led by J.K. Jeong, wanted to know what would happen if NELL2 were knocked out during development.[49] They therefore injected into the hypothalamus of newborn male rat pups an "antisense DNA"—a stretch of DNA designed to bind to and neutralize the "messenger RNA" that normally carries the genetic instruction to synthesize NELL2. It turned out that, with NELL2 disabled, the male rats' SDN-POA developed to a smaller size than in untreated males—although not as small as in females. This happened because NELL2 normally participates in keeping SDN-POA neurons alive, so without it many cells died. NELL2 is probably just one of several growth factors that are involved in the sexual differentiation of the hypothalamus and other parts of the brain.

Another interesting effect of steroids involves the neurotransmitter γ-aminobutyric acid (GABA). In adults, GABA is the brain's principal inhibitory transmitter, but during early fetal development it has an excitatory action, and this excitation promotes neuronal survival and the formation of synaptic connections.[50] Testosterone delays the switch from excitation to inhibition. Thus, there is a period during development (around the time of birth in rats, probably prenatally in humans) when GABA has exactly opposite effects on testosterone-sensitive hypothalamic neurons in the two sexes: It is still excitatory in males (because males have been exposed to testosterone), but has already switched to an inhibitory function in females.[51] This puts GABA in the position of being able to drive development in different directions in the two sexes, and it seems to actually do so, because reducing GABA levels in newborn rats weakens the development of both male-typical sexual behavior in males and female-typical sexual behavior in females.[52]

The main point of this brief excursion into the world of brain molecules is to point out that a prenatal hormonal theory of sexual orientation actually includes a host of different molecular processes that could potentially be involved. First and foremost, there could be differences between "pre-gay" and "pre-straight" fetuses in terms of the actual levels of circulating testosterone during the critical period for the organization of brain circuits underlying sexual orientation. But alternatively, there could be differences in the activity of the converting enzyme aromatase, or in the function or distribution of the androgen or (less likely) the estrogen receptors—any of which might cause testosterone to have a greater or lesser effect on brain development. The co-activators or co-repressors might differ. Or, there might be differences in the suite of genes that are responsive to androgens and estrogens, such as NELL2. There could also be differences in the GABA mechanisms just described. Thus, a prenatal hormonal theory, broadly defined, could involve other factors in addition to actual differences in hormone levels, and different factors might be operative in different individuals.

Continuing this same line of thought, it is possible to understand how the findings concerning prenatal hormones and sexual orientation may sometimes be inconsistent. Sexual orientation and other sex-differentiated traits (gendered mental traits, finger-length ratios, OAEs, and so forth) may be developmental fellow-travelers, but they don't march in lock-step. This could be for at least three kinds of reasons:

- *Timing effects.* The critical periods for sexual orientation and other traits may be exactly synchronized, or they may partially overlap in time or not overlap at all.
- *Localization effects.* Different regions of the brain and body may respond to hormones in the same way or in different ways.
- *Range effects.* The range of testosterone levels that influence sexual orientation could differ from the range that influences some other traits. To give a specific example, range effects could be the reason why OAEs differ between lesbian/bisexual and straight women, but not between gay and straight men. We would just have to imagine that gay men were exposed to prenatal testosterone levels that were far enough below typical male levels to affect their sexual orientation, but not low enough to give them female-typical OAEs. Lesbian and bisexual women, on the other hand, might have been exposed to testosterone levels high enough to affect both their sexual orientation and their OAEs.

POSSIBLE CAUSES OF VARIABILITY IN PRENATAL ANDROGEN LEVELS

If variations in prenatal androgen levels do influence sexual orientation, how do these variations arise? One possibility is that they are caused by genetic differences between individuals. I've already described one clear-cut example of this genetic effect—CAH.

Women whose sexual orientation has been shifted in the homosexual direction on account of CAH owe their sexual orientation to a specific gene that they have inherited—the gene that caused them to have CAH and thus to be exposed to unusually high androgen levels before birth. Genes may also contribute to variability in androgen levels among healthy individuals; I will discuss the evidence bearing on this in the next chapter.

Prenatal androgen levels may also vary on account of nongenetic factors, including sheer random variability. As discussed in Chapter 3, a good example of this effect from animal research is the uterine proximity effect in rodents—the observation that a female fetus who by chance is located between two males receives an extra dose of testosterone and consequently experiences some behavioral masculinization, including atypical sexual behavior and partner preference. Whether this particular effect influences sexual orientation in humans (in the few women who were members of opposite-sex twin pairs) is not clear. However, there are doubtless many other ways in which random variations in hormone levels can arise during development. I will discuss this issue further in later chapters.

It is also possible that environmental factors could affect prenatal androgen levels sufficiently to influence a fetus's sexual orientation in adulthood. One candidate for such an environmental factor is stress. As I mentioned in Chapter 3, there is evidence that placing a pregnant rat under repeated stress (by immobilization, bright lights, and the like) can alter the sexual behavior and partner preference of male rats born of that pregnancy. This happens because stress hormones secreted by the mother reduce or eliminate the surge in testosterone that usually occurs in male rat fetuses about 4 days before birth.[53] Nevertheless, there have been some reports of failure to observe effects of prenatal stress on rats' sexual behavior.[54]

In the early 1980s, Günter Dörner proposed that prenatal stress was an important cause of homosexuality in men.[55] Dörner and his colleagues reported that the rate of male homosexuality was unusually high among men born in Germany during World War II, when the population was exposed to many kinds of stress. They also found that most gay men (and, to a lesser extent, bisexual men) reported that their mothers had been exposed to stressful events during pregnancy, whereas straight men seldom reported such events. These events included such things as air raids, the death of the father, and the fact that the pregnancy was unwanted. On the basis of Dörner's results, it looked as if prenatal stress was the major cause of male homosexuality.

Subsequent research has not substantiated Dörner's hypothesis. A more careful analysis revealed no effect of World War II on the prevalence of male homosexuality in the German population.[56] Likewise, a recent study found no effect of the Dutch famine of 1944–1945 on the sexual orientation of men (or women) who were fetuses at the time of the famine.[57] (However, the very low rate of exclusive homosexuality reported by men in that study—only 1 out of 374 men overall—raises some doubt about the researchers' ability to correctly assess their subjects' sexual orientation.)

Two U.S. research groups have investigated the incidence and severity of stressful events experienced by women during pregnancies that gave rise to gay men. These groups improved on Dörner's methodology by interviewing the mothers themselves, rather than relying on the men's reports. One study, by Michael Bailey's group, found no tendency for mothers to report more stressful events, or more severely stressful events, during pregnancies that gave rise to gay men than during pregnancies that gave rise to straight men.[58] The other study, by Lee Ellis (of Minot State University) and his colleagues, likewise found no increase in reported stressful events during pregnancies that gave rise to gay men.[59] The study did find an apparently significant increase in severely stressful events during a 3-month period 9–12 months *before* the pregnancies that gave rise to gay men. This unexpected finding could well be a fluke that resulted from subjecting the data to too many statistical tests. It could also result from the fact that gay men are more likely to have older brothers than are straight men (see Chapter 10): Those older brothers could have been a source of increased stress for their mothers. All in all, the idea that stress is a significant cause of homosexuality in men is not supported by data.

Curiously, Bailey's group did find a slight but statistically significant effect in *women:* Mothers of lesbian or bisexual women reported experiencing a somewhat greater number of stressful events during those pregnancies than during pregnancies that gave rise to heterosexual daughters. Because this finding was not predicted by the animal experiments, and was quite weak, it is possible that it was a fluke or was caused by some irrelevant factor, such as mothers' "looking for" events that might have caused their daughters' homosexuality.

Considering all the studies mentioned in the chapter, it does seem to be reasonably well established that prenatal androgen levels have a significant influence on sexual orientation in both men and women. Applying this conclusion to a more general theory of sexual orientation requires consideration of several other factors, starting with genes—the topic of the following chapter.

SEVEN

THE ROLE OF GENES

B oston University psychiatrist Richard Pillard is gay. Not only that; he has a gay brother, a lesbian sister, and a bisexual daughter. And his father—as Pillard found out when he read his father's diaries after his death—was in a sexual relationship with another man early in his adult life.[1] This personal history was Pillard's motivation to investigate whether homosexuality generally runs in families, a line of research he began in the early 1980s.

SIBLING STUDIES

Actually, reports supportive of this idea go back many decades,[2] but Pillard and his colleagues performed more systematic studies.

They recruited gay and straight individuals (*index subjects*) who had siblings, and then ascertained the sexual orientation of the siblings, either from the statements of the index subjects or (whenever possible) from interviews with the siblings themselves.[3]

From these studies, it became apparent that gay men and women have more gay siblings than do straight men or women. In Pillard's early data, about 22% of the brothers of gay men were reported to be gay or bisexual, compared with about 4% of the brothers of straight men. Similarly, about 25% of the sisters of lesbians were reported to be lesbian or bisexual, compared with about 11% of the sisters of straight women.

Subsequent studies by Pillard and others have confirmed the clustering among siblings, although the *degree* of clustering has generally been less than Pillard's early studies suggested.[4] Typically, about 7%—16% of the same-sex siblings of gay people are found to be gay. It may be that the early studies recruited somewhat atypical samples or used broader criteria for deciding whether a sibling was gay.

An important question that hasn't been fully resolved is whether this clustering crosses the sex lines. Are the sisters of gay men more than usually likely to be lesbian, and are the brothers of lesbians more than usually likely to be gay? Pillard's personal history illustrates the clustering of male and female homosexuality in a single family, but that could have been an unusual coincidence, of course. One study, based on data collected in the 1970s, found that opposite-sex siblings of gay index subjects were as likely to be gay as are same-sex siblings,[5] but other studies based on more recent data have failed to detect any increased rate of homosexuality among opposite-sex siblings of gay people,[6] or have reported rates that are increased but less so than for same-sex siblings.[7] Most likely, some cross-sex clustering exists, but not nearly as much as same-sex clustering.

When two brothers are gay, they tend to resemble each other in other traits related to their sexual orientation. Most notably, they are similar in terms of their childhood characteristics. If one brother was a markedly feminine or unmasculine boy, then the same was usually true for his brother; if one brother was conventionally masculine, then the other was usually masculine too.[8] This suggests that family clustering relates not just to homosexuality in general but also to different *kinds* of homosexuality.

IS THE FAMILY CLUSTERING CAUSED BY GENES?

There could be a variety of different reasons why gay people cluster in certain families. If Freud was right, and a close-binding mother or hostile father makes a boy gay, then two or more boys in the same family could easily be subjected to the same influence and thus both end up gay. Alternatively, an older sibling might act as a role model, leading a younger sibling down a shared path toward homosexuality. In fact, pretty much any environmental factor could cause clustering among siblings, so long as it operates before the age at which siblings go their separate ways.

Another possibility, however—and the one that we're concerned with in this chapter—is that the clustering is caused by genes that run in certain families but not in others. In other words, it could be that homosexuality is heritable.

Several methods are available to tease apart the two main causes of family clustering (shared genes vs. shared environment). First, if genes are responsible, then one would expect to find increased rates of homosexuality even among relatives who were not brought up in the same family environment as the gay index subjects—this could include parents, children, aunts, uncles, and cousins, as well as siblings who were separated soon after birth. Conversely, unrelated children who were adopted into a family should not experience any increased propensity to grow up gay, no matter how many other children in the family do so.

A number of studies have reported increased rates of homo- sexuality or bisexuality among nonsibling relatives of gay or bisex- ual people. These include the daughters, nieces, and female cousins of lesbian or bisexual women,[9] and the uncles, male cousins, and possibly the sons of gay men.[10] As with siblings, the increase in homosexuality among other gay relatives applies predominantly to same-sex rather than opposite-sex relatives. These findings sug- gest that genes are at least partly responsible for the clustering of homosexuality in certain families, and that different genes may predispose to homosexuality in men and in women.

A useful adoption study would be to compare the rates of homosexuality among adoptees who have a (genetically unre- lated) gay sibling and among adoptees who lack a gay sibling.

If the rates were the same, this would suggest that the purely social effects of having a gay sibling are not responsible for the clustering of homosexuality in families. Such a study hasn't been done, however. In two studies focused mainly on twins (see discussion in the next section) Michael Bailey, Richard Pillard, and their colleagues included small numbers of adoptive siblings.[11] These limited datasets did not provide strong evidence either for or against a genetic influence on sexual orientation.

TWIN STUDIES

Twins are the workhorses of human behavioral genetics: They offer a fairly straightforward means to distinguish between genetic and nongenetic influences on psychological traits. They can also help distinguish between different kinds of nongenetic influences.

Twin studies compare the trait of interest—homosexuality in this case—in two kinds of twins. Monozygotic (so-called "identical") twins are the products of a single fertilized egg that split into two early in development, so they have nearly all their genes in common. (Not even monozygotic twins have precisely identical genomes, however.[12]) Dizygotic ("fraternal") twins develop from two different eggs fertilized by two different sperm, and they therefore have the same genetic relatedness as regular siblings, which is to say they share about one-half of their genes.

In traditional twin studies, index subjects are recruited who are gay and are members of twin pairs. The researchers then ascertain the sexual orientation of the other member of each pair (the "co-twins")—either by asking the index subjects or, better, by interviewing the co-twins directly. The percentage of the co-twins who are also found to be gay is called the *concordance rate.* To the extent that homosexuality is heritable, the concordance rate will be higher for the monozygotic twin pairs than for same-sex dizygotic pairs. If homosexuality were completely determined by genes, then the concordance rate for monozygotic twins would be 100%, while the concordance rate for dizygotic twins would be 50% or less.

The data from twin studies, along with an estimate of the base rate of homosexuality in the population, can be used to estimate the strength of three different factors on sexual orientation:

- *Genes.* A genetic influence causes the concordance rate for monozygotic twins to exceed that for dizygotic twins, as just mentioned. The fraction of the total variability in a trait in a population that can be ascribed to genes is called the trait's *heritability.*
- *Shared environment.* This includes any nongenetic influences that promote homosexuality in both members of twin pairs; it typically would mean influences that children experience while they still live together, such as similar parental treatment of both twins, or nongenetic factors that affect both twins in the womb. If shared environment is the dominant

factor, concordance rates will be high and roughly equal for monozygotic and dizygotic twin pairs.

- *Unshared environment.* This is a catch-all term for any nongenetic influences that promote homosexuality in one twin but not the other. The word "environment" is a bit misleading in this context: It includes biological sources of variability unique to individuals (such as variations in prenatal hormonal levels that are not controlled by genes), as well as the different life experiences that individuals are exposed to (which could include differential treatment by parents, sexual molestation of one twin but not the other, encountering certain role models or sex partners in adolescence and adulthood, and so on). Any random measurement error also raises the estimate of this factor. If the unshared environment is the dominant factor, the concordance rates will be low and roughly equal for monozygotic and dizygotic twin pairs.

In twin studies published in the early 1990s by Michael Bailey, Richard Pillard, and others, concordance rates for homosexuality in monozygotic twins (both male and female) were around 50%, whereas the concordance rates for dizygotic twins were much lower.[13] Another study from the same period, led by Fred Whitam of Arizona State University, found an even higher concordance rate for monozygotic male twins (65%, compared with 29% for dizygotic twins).[14]

The Bailey-Pillard studies yielded estimates of heritability of roughly 50% in both sexes (although with a considerable range of uncertainty). Unshared environment contributed about as much as genes, whereas shared environment contributed little or nothing. These findings suggested, not only that genes have a strong influence on sexual orientation, but also that parental treatment of children (insofar as it is exerted similarly on both members of a twin pair) plays little or no role.

Because these early studies relied on recruiting gay twins through advertisements, they may have suffered from distortions arising from the recruitment process. For example, if gay individuals who had monozygotic co-twins were especially likely to volunteer if they knew that their co-twin was also gay, then this would artificially inflate the observed concordance rate for monozygotic twins. If dizygotic twins were less susceptible to such a bias, this would give rise to an exaggerated estimate of heritability.

To get away from this kind of problem, more recent studies have recruited pairs of twins from large preexisting lists or registries of twins that were created without reference to the twins' sexual orientation. Studies based on this approach have been conducted in several countries. An Australian study came up with heritabilities of 30% for men and 50%–60% for women.[15] A Swedish study found heritabilities of 34%–39% for men and only 18%–19% for women.[16] A Finnish study (the Alanko study already discussed in Chapter 4) found 45% for men and 50% for women.[17] One U.S. study found 0% for men and 48% for women;[18] another treated men and women together and found a heritability of 28%–65%.[19] The studies found little or no effect of shared environment but a substantial effect of the unshared environment.

The large quantitative differences among the various studies are disconcerting, but they are probably not worth trying to dissect in detail. For one thing, the differences may not be significant, given that these studies tend to have fairly low statistical power. (Although the studies may recruit up to a few thousand twin pairs, most pairs are uninformative because neither member is gay.) Differences may also result from the criteria employed for selecting subjects or for defining homosexuality. The Swedish study relied solely on the numbers of same-sex partners, for example, whereas the Australian study asked about a whole range of issues related to sexual orientation. Finally, it should be borne in mind that measures of heritability can differ between populations, even when there is no actual difference in the prevalence of the relevant genes. That's because the strength of nongenetic effects may vary, leaving genes in greater or lesser control of the trait.

In some of the twin studies, participants were asked about their childhood gender characteristics.[20] It turns out that monozygotic twins who are both gay are also very similar to each other in terms of how gender-nonconformist they were during childhood. From the data in these studies it appears that childhood gender-nonconformity, like homosexuality, is substantially heritable. In fact, a Dutch twin study that focused on childhood gender-nonconformity without regard to adult sexual orientation obtained an estimated heritability for that trait of 70%, which is remarkably high.[21] According to the Finnish registry study, it appears that a shared set of genes is partially responsible both for childhood gender-nonconformity and adult homosexuality.[22]

Monozygotic twins reared separately from birth offer an especially useful paradigm for studying the origin of psychological traits. If such twin pairs share traits on more than a chance basis, those traits are likely to be influenced either by genes or by the shared intrauterine environment, not by the postnatal environment. Unfortunately, it is very difficult to find separately reared monozygotic twin pairs in whom at least one member is gay or bisexual. The research group of Thomas Bouchard Jr. at the University of Minnesota identified six such pairs, two male and four female.[23] With regard to the first male pair, both members were unambiguously gay—in fact, they didn't know of each other's existence until one of them was mistaken for his brother at a gay bar, after which they met each other and became lovers. (This could be considered an extreme example of what is popularly called "genetic sexual attraction"— the strong sexual attraction that can arise between biologically related persons who were raised apart.) The other pair consisted of a man who identified as gay (although he had had relationships with women earlier in his life) and a man who identified as straight (although he had had a homosexual relationship earlier in his life). This pair might be considered concordant for some degree of bisexuality. Another male pair concordant for homosexuality was reported by Fred Whitam and colleagues.[24] Thus, these three cases, although hardly enough to build a statistical case, do support the idea that male homosexuality is strongly influenced by genes or the prenatal environment.

The four female pairs studied by the Bouchard group were all *discordant*: One member of each pair was lesbian or bisexual and the other heterosexual. Thus, the study offered no support at all for the idea that female homosexuality is heritable, although the small numbers prevented any strong conclusion on this score.

Twin studies suffer from various potential shortcomings. The diagnosis of each pair as monozygotic or dizygotic is not always done correctly, especially when it is based on appearance (as was the case in most of the studies just discussed) rather than molecular tests.[25] Recruitment biases can exist, as I've mentioned. And the causes of homosexuality in twins may not always be the same as in singletons.[26] Nevertheless, looking at the twin studies as a whole it seems reasonable to draw the following conclusions: Homosexuality is significantly heritable in both sexes, the unshared environment is also important, but the shared environment plays little or no role.

MOLECULAR GENETICS—
CANDIDATE-GENE STUDIES

The results of the family and twin studies have motivated attempts to find actual genes that might predispose to homosexuality in men or women—so-called "gay genes."* One way this has been done is simply to guess that a specific gene might be involved and then to compare this gene in gay and straight people. This is called the "candidate gene" approach.

In the early 1990s, molecular geneticists Dean Hamer, Jeremy Nathans (of Johns Hopkins University), and their colleagues tried this approach with the gene that codes for the androgen receptor, a key player in the interaction between testosterone and the brain.[27] Obviously, gay men don't completely lack this gene, because if they did they would have androgen insensitivity syndrome and they would have the outward appearance of females (see Chapter 6). However, a range of variations occur in the DNA sequence of this gene that are known or suspected to affect the activity of the androgen receptor in a variety of ways. Hamer and Nathans looked for consistent differences in the gene between gay and straight men, but drew a blank. More recently, a group in Hamer's lab, led by Michael DuPree, focused on the gene that codes for aromatase, the enzyme that converts testosterone to estrogen.[28] Again, they found no evidence that variations in this gene influence men's sexual orientation.

---

* I use the phrase "gay gene" as shorthand for a hypothetical gene that increases the probability that its owner will become homosexual, possibly in conjunction with other genes or nongenetic factors.

GENOME SCANS

Another approach is to search large sections of the genome, or the entire genome, without any preconceived ideas as to which genes might be involved. The initial study of this kind was published by Dean Hamer's group in 1993.[29] Hamer first recruited a sample of gay men and asked about the sexual orientation of their relatives. He found increased rates of male homosexuality among the brothers, uncles, and male cousins of the index cases, in line with what I've mentioned earlier. However, of the two kinds of uncles (maternal and paternal), only maternal uncles had significantly increased rates, and among the four kinds of male first cousins (sons of maternal aunts, sons of maternal uncles, sons of paternal aunts, and sons of paternal uncles) only the sons of maternal aunts had significantly increased rates. In other words, only men connected to the index cases through the female line had an increased likelihood of being gay. This pattern suggests that there might be maternal inheritance of genes predisposing to male homosexuality. Reinforcing this conclusion, Hamer presented several family trees in which multiple gay men were found; in each tree, all the gay men were connected to each other exclusively through females. (An example is shown in Figure 7.1.) Such a pattern of inheritance usually points to genes on the X chromosome, because this is the only chromosome that men inherit exclusively from their mothers. Hamer therefore focused his molecular studies on the X chromosome.

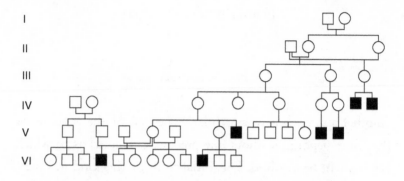

Figure 7.I Family tree including seven gay men (black squares) in three generations. Note that the gay men are connected to each other entirely through women (circles) and not men (squares). From Hamer et al., 1993.

I should say right away that data from subsequent studies have not uniformly confirmed a higher rate of male homosexuality among maternal-line than paternal-line relatives of gay men: Some studies have done so,[30] while others ave not.[31] A recent study led by Gene Schwartz of Northwestern University, for example, found the same elevated rate of homosexuality among all four kinds of first cousins.[32] I will return to this issue later in the chapter.

For the X chromosome study, Hamer and his colleagues recruited 40 pairs of brothers, each pair consisting of two gay men. Recall that women possess two X chromosomes and men just one. Thus, if the brothers in each pair were gay on account of a gene on the X chromosome (an *X-linked* gene), then they should both have inherited the same genetic material from the same maternal X chromosome—the one that carried the putative "gay gene." Because of the phenomenon called *crossing-over*, in which the two maternal X chromosomes break up and rejoin during the development of the ovum, only the region of the X chromosome near to the "gay gene" will be co-inherited by the brothers at an above-chance rate. Hamer therefore examined 22 DNA markers—sites where DNA sequences are known to vary among individuals in the population—that are scattered along the length of the X chromosome. This is called a *linkage study*.

In Hamer's data, the pairs of brothers shared the same markers at an above-chance rate in just one region of the X chromosome, a region named Xq28, which lies near the tip of the long arm of the chromosome. This was interpreted to mean that a gene or genes predisposing to homosexuality lay in that region. Hamer's report seemed to confirm a genetic predisposition to homosexuality—in men at least—and it invited further studies to actually home in on the responsible gene.

Unfortunately, Hamer's report has not been robustly confirmed. Hamer's own group did publish a follow-up study that obtained a similar finding, although with a much lower level of statistical significance than the original study.[33] A Canadian group applied similar techniques but failed to find any evidence for "gay genes" at Xq28.[34] Hamer has argued that the Canadians obtained a negative result because they failed to select subjects who would be likely to show X chromosome linkage.[35]

In 2005, researchers from Hamer's lab, led by Brian Mustanski and Michael DuPree, published another linkage study, this time scanning the entire genome and not just the X chromosome.[36]

This study again made use of families containing pairs of gay brothers; some of these were the same subjects who were used in Hamer's earlier studies and some were newly recruited. The researchers confirmed the linkage to Xq28 in the previously studied families but not in the newly recruited families or in the entire dataset. The likely reason, according to the authors, was that the new families were not preselected to favor maternal inheritance. The study also came up with evidence of linkage to markers on three *autosomes* (chromosomes other than sex chromosomes)—specifically, chromosomes 7, 8, and 10. A similar but independent study by a British-Canadian group came up with evidence for linkage to markers on another autosome, chromosome 14.[37] The statistical power of these findings was low, however, and the findings should be thought of as pointers for future research rather than as actual identifications of regions containing "gay genes."

A new and much larger linkage study has been under way for several years.[38] The study is being led by psychiatrist and behavioral geneticist Alan Sanders of Northwestern University. Sanders' team set itself the goal of recruiting 1,000 pairs of gay brothers. If they even come close to that number they should be able to reliably confirm or disconfirm the findings of the previous studies and perhaps identify other, as yet undiscovered locations of genes that influence male sexual orientation.

As of this writing, the published molecular genetic studies offer no more than suggestive evidence regarding the location of "gay genes." This lack of conclusive results shouldn't be taken to weaken the belief, based on the family and twin studies, that genes do in fact influence sexual orientation. In the field of behavioral genetics, identifying genes with strong effects has been generally difficult. Intelligence is substantially heritable, for example, yet a powerful whole-genome study failed to localize any single gene that accounted for more than 0.4% of the total variation in intelligence in the population.[39]

With regard to sexual orientation, it is certainly possible that there are major genes that simply haven't been localized yet. It's also possible that sexual orientation is weakly influenced by several or many genes. With this kind of polygenic inheritance, however, it would be unlikely that an individual would inherit either all of the genes or none of them. Thus, one would expect sexual orientation to have a more-or-less bell-shaped distribution, with lots of bisexuals and relatively few exclusively homosexual or heterosexual individuals. In fact, that's what we *don't* see, in men at least. Therefore, for polygenic inheritance to work in men there would have to be some other mechanism, either biological or environmental, that converts a bell-shaped underlying distribution into more nearly dichotomous categories of gay and straight. I will return to this issue in the final chapter.

POSSIBLE ROLE OF X INACTIVATION

There exist a variety of molecular mechanisms that can modify the activity of genes or entire chromosomes in a semipermanent way without changing the underlying DNA sequence. These are called *epigenetic processes*. One example is X inactivation. Because men possess one X chromosome and women possess two, a mechanism operates during the development of a female embryo to functionally inactivate (but not eliminate) one of her X chromosomes. The point of this inactivation is to make sure that cells in males and females have the same number of functionally active chromosomes: If this were not the case, cells in females would produce too many copies of proteins coded by X-linked genes.

Women's bodies are usually a roughly equal mix of cells in which one or the other X chromosome (the one inherited from her mother or the one inherited from her father) has been inactivated. According to a study led by Sven Bocklandt of UCLA, some mothers of gay men are unusual in this respect: Most of their cells (or their blood cells at least—the cells that were studied) have inactivated the same X chromosome.[40] To give numbers: Only 4% of control women with no gay sons showed an imbalance to the point that 90% of their blood cells had inactivated the same X chromosome, whereas 13% of women with at least one gay son and 23% of women with at least two gay sons did so.

This reported finding could mean that an X-linked gene that promotes homosexuality in men also affects the rate of cell division in their mothers. By slowing down or speeding up the division of the cells in which the "gay gene" is active, it would cause those cells to become an increasingly small or large fraction of the total cell population over the course of development. Other explanations are possible, however. In general, the finding supports the idea that X-linked genes play a role in the development of male sexual orientation, and potentially open the door to clarifying the underlying mechanism. Bocklandt's report remains to be confirmed, however. Because Bocklandt included subjects from Dean Hamer's 1993 study, who were selected to favor X-linked inheritance, the results might not be replicated in a broader sample.

GENES AND SEXUALITY IN FRUIT FLIES

In a state of nature, the male fruit fly, *Drosophila melanogaster*, is resolutely heterosexual. In the early 1960s, however, Indian geneticist Kulbir Gill, working at Yale University, created a mutant strain of fruit flies in which males courted males and females with equal enthusiasm.[41] When these flies were put together in all-male groups they formed long moving chains resembling conga lines, with each male attempting (unsuccessfully) to mate with the male in front of it. The change from a heterosexual to a bisexual orientation was caused by a single mutation affecting a gene that Gill named "fruity," with the standard three-letter abbreviation *fru*. The full name was a crude joke at the expense of gay people, and it was later changed to the less obnoxious "fruitless."

The *fru* gene was isolated and sequenced in 1996, by a group working at Stanford University,[42] as well as by a Japanese group led by Daisuke Yamamoto.[43] Both male and female flies possess the *fru* gene, but the product of the gene (the messenger RNA) is processed differently in the two sexes.[44] The male *fru* product activates a cascade of lower-order genes in the brains of male flies, thus enabling male-typical sexual behavior and suppressing female-typical behavior. If female flies are engineered to process *fru* in the male fashion, they remain anatomically female but they court other females rather than males, as shown in Figure 7.2.

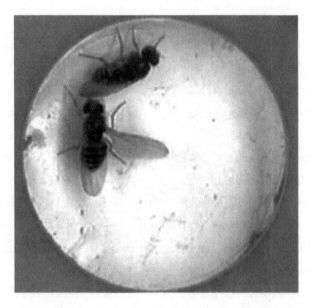

Figure 7.2 Homosexual courtship. The lower of these two fruit flies is a female that has been genetically engineered to process the fru gene in a male fashion. She is courting another female by "singing" to her with the vibrations of her right wing. Photo courtesy of Barry Dickson.

Rather as testosterone does in the developing brain of male mammals, the male *fru* promotes the survival of certain clusters of neurons, so these clusters end up sexually dimorphic—they contain more cells in males than in females.[45] The main difference is that testosterone in mammals is a hormonal signal that enters the brain and masculinizes it, whereas the male-processed *fru* in *Drosophila* operates within brain cells themselves if the chromosomal sex of those cells is male.

Yamamoto's group used molecular-genetic trickery to insert just one of these male-specific neuronal clusters, named P1, into the brains of female flies. Even though the rest of the brain, and the body, of these flies was female, they displayed male-typical sexual behavior, including courtship of females.[46] This was a striking demonstration of the relevance of sexual dimorphism in the brain to sex differences in partner choice.

Many different mutations or other genetic manipulations are now known that can induce homosexual behavior in fruit flies.[47] In addition, two neurotransmitters, *glutamate* and *dopamine*, are known to play a role. Suppressing glutamate neurotransmission in male flies causes them to court other males.[48] Raising dopamine levels in male flies has the same effect.[49]

Finally, *lowering* dopamine levels in male flies, although it does not cause them to court males, does cause other males to court *them*.[50] This is thought to happen because, without sufficient dopamine, males produce less than usual of a chemical that is aversive to males—a kind of "no-males-need-apply" pheromone. A similar effect has been observed in flies that are entirely male except for the pheromone-secreting tissue, which has been genetically engineered to be female. Like the low-dopamine flies, these male flies court females but are courted by males.[51] These observations serve as a reminder that sexual attraction involves two participants, an attractor and an attractee, and characteristics of either can induce or suppress homosexual behavior.

No one considers it likely that the detailed findings in *Drosophila* apply to humans—too much is different between the two species in terms of genetics, development, and brain organization. Still, there may be some useful lessons to be learned. First, there is simply the fact that it is proving possible to understand the basis of sexual partner preference in flies at the level of specific genes, molecules, and brain cells, and the interactions among them. This offers hope that it will eventually be possible to do the same for our own species.

A second lesson from *Drosophila* is that the lower-level neural circuits that mediate courtship of males and females exist in all flies: What differ between flies are the higher-level control centers that activate one circuit and inhibit the other. There is reason to believe that the same might be true in mammals, including humans, as I will discuss in the next chapter.

Finally, it's worth pointing out that, although the sexual differentiation of the mammalian brain is largely controlled by circulating hormones, some influence is also exerted by the intrinsic chromosomal sex of the brain itself, as happens in *Drosophila*. I already touched on this issue in Chapter 3. The evidence for this comes from a variety of studies, including the use of genetic-engineering technologies that allow researchers to manipulate the intrinsic brain sex of mice independently of the sex of the gonads.[52] There is no direct evidence as yet that these hormone-independent processes influence partner preference either in mice or humans, but Sven Bocklandt and Eric Vilain (of UCLA) have raised the possibility that they do so.[53]

GENES, HOMOSEXUALITY, AND EVOLUTION

The idea that genes might predispose certain people to homosexuality is paradoxical: We might expect such genes to reduce their owners' *reproductive success*[†] and thus to be eliminated from the gene pool by natural selection. Doesn't this throw doubt on the very existence of "gay genes"?

Actually, plenty of genes exist that lower reproductive success. I've already mentioned a couple: The gene that causes androgen insensitivity, which renders its owner infertile, and the genes that cause congenital adrenal hyperplasia (CAH), which (untreated) can kill their owners long before they are old enough to have children.

[†] *Reproductive success* is a standard term meaning the total number of an individual's offspring that survive to maturity. I don't mean to imply that there is anything particularly meritorious about having large numbers of children.

A number of factors may help save such a gene from extinction. If it is a *recessive gene* it will only harm its owner's reproduction when the owner has inherited copies of the harmful version of the gene from both parents (the so-called *homozygous state*), and not when the owner has inherited a copy from just one parent (the *heterozygous state*). The homozygous state isn't common, so natural selection acts only slowly to eliminate harmful recessive genes. New mutations may occur fast enough to compensate for the gradual elimination of the gene. In the case of androgen insensitivity syndrome (which is caused by an X-linked recessive gene in which XX female heterozygous carriers of the gene are healthy), about one-third of all cases of the disorder are caused by new mutations.[54]

In some cases, "harmful" genes are actually beneficial when they occur in the heterozygous state. The classic example is the gene that causes *sickle cell anemia*: Persons with two copies of the gene develop the disease, but persons with one copy (the heterozygous state) are actually better off than those who have no copies, because the heterozygous state confers resistance to malaria. Therefore, in malaria-prone regions, the sickle-cell gene persists.

In real life, genes may have multiple effects, and they may interact with each other and with the environment in complex ways that make it hard to predict what their net effects on reproductive success may be. That's particularly true for genes that haven't yet been identified, such as the genes that may predispose to homosexuality. Still, that uncertainty hasn't prevented people from coming up with hypotheses about how "gay genes" are able to stay afloat in the gene pool, and even looking for evidence in support of them.

One idea is this: Maybe being gay doesn't have as severe an impact on reproductive success as we imagine.[55] After all, many famous gay people, such as Oscar Wilde, have been parents. Perhaps traditional societies forced everyone to marry and have all the children they were capable of, regardless of their sexual orientation. In that situation, genes predisposing to homosexuality would not have been weeded out.

This idea doesn't hold water, however—for men, at least. Whatever the situation in traditional societies, gay men in contemporary Western cultures are far less likely to have children than are their straight peers. In one U.S. random-sample survey conducted in 1994, for example, only 27% of men who identified as gay or homosexual said they were fathers, compared with 60% of other men.[56] A more recent Italian study found that gay men have only one-fifth the number of children that straight men have,[57] and a British study (which focused on White men) found an even larger difference.[58] These huge disparities should eliminate any gene for male homosexuality in the blink of an evolutionary eye. The 1994 U.S. study found only a small difference between lesbians and other women (67% vs. 72% said they had children), but even that difference, if consistently maintained, should eliminate genes for female homosexuality quite quickly.

About the only way that the existence of gay genes could be compatible with the lower reproductive success of gay people is if there is a compensatory increase in the numbers of hetero-sexual *relatives* of gay people: individuals who, because of their relatedness to the gay person, have some likelihood of also carrying the "gay genes." The transmittal of these extra copies of the genes into the next generation could balance the loss of copies caused by the lowered reproduction of gay people them-selves, thus maintaining "gay genes" in a state of equilibrium through the generations. This, of course, would require that not every person carrying a "gay gene" is actually gay.

Gay men do indeed seem to have more relatives than straight men. In the British study just mentioned, which was led by psychiatrist Michael King, the combined total numbers of siblings, aunts, uncles, and cousins (i.e., relatives belonging to generations that were likely to be complete at the time of the survey) was 19.8 for the gay men and 16.9 for the straight men; in other words, the gay men had nearly three extra relatives.[59] These extra relatives were fairly evenly spread across all the classes of relatives just mentioned, but the paternal relatives contributed more to the increase than did maternal relatives. Gay men also had more nephews and nieces than did straight men, but this generation was probably incomplete at the time of the survey, so the numbers were more difficult to interpret.

A smaller British study, led by Qazi Rahman, failed to find a significant difference between the family sizes of gay and straight White men, and found the opposite relationship—a greater family size for straight men—among their non-White subjects.[60]

This latter finding might have resulted from a recruitment bias, however.[‡]

An Italian study, like King's British study, found that gay men had more relatives than did straight men, but the extra relatives were not evenly spread across all classes of relatives—an issue I'll return to later.[61]

KIN SELECTION

What causes gay men to have extra relatives? One possibility is that gay men (and possibly lesbians, too) actually help their relatives reproduce. For example, gay people might give their siblings money or assist them with child care, thus enabling them to have extra children. There are known examples of non-human species in which some individuals do not have offspring themselves but dedicate themselves to the reproductive success

---

[‡] Non-White immigrants who are not yet fully acculturated tend to belong to larger-than-average families, and they use more inclusive definitions of relationship terms like "cousin." They also tend to be less accepting of and open about homosexuality. I speculate that the straight non-White subjects were representative of the entire non-White population, whereas the gay non-White subjects came from the more acculturated families, leading to a smaller estimate of family size for the gay men. (This by way of demonstrating that, with sufficient ingenuity, any inconvenient finding can be explained away.)

of their close relatives. The best-known examples are the social insects, such as ants and bees, in which sterile female workers help the queen reproduce.

This "kin selection" model, which was first invoked to explain homosexuality by sociobiologist E.O. Wilson,[62] does not work well to explain the persistence of "gay genes" in humans, however. Admittedly, there is one set of studies that seems to support it: Paul Vasey and his student Doug VanderLaan have reported that homosexual men in Independent Samoa, who are known locally as *fa'afafine*, are significantly more willing to assist their siblings with child-rearing duties than are straight men.[63] This helpfulness is not directed to the children of nonkin, and it is not explained simply by the men's general femininity, so in those respects it fits well with the kin selection model. However, it is very unclear that a *fa'afafine* provides *enough* assistance to his kin to satisfy the model. For a *fa'afafine*'s behavior to satisfy kin selection theory, he must help a sibling have an extra *two* surviving offspring for every *one* offspring that he gives up on himself. That is a very difficult condition to fulfill.

Comparable studies in the United States and the United Kingdom have found no evidence in favor of a kin selection model.[64] What's more, gay people devote considerable resources to their own (reproductively inefficient) sex lives, but this behavior has little value in terms of a kin selection model. And, however benevolent gay people's feelings toward their relatives might be, this benevolence could hardly increase the number of their relatives in the generation *before* their own, yet there are in fact extra relatives in that generation, according to the King study.[65]

THE "FERTILE FEMALE" HYPOTHESIS

A more likely explanation for why gay people belong to larger extended families than straight people is that "gay genes" act directly within some of the relatives of gay people to increase their reproductive success. At least two models exist for how this might work. Both require than "gay genes" have other effects besides conferring a predisposition to homosexuality.

In one model, "gay genes" promote the reproductive success of the opposite-sex relatives of gay people. Because the relevant research has been done on the relatives of gay men, this model is usually called the "fertile females" hypothesis.[66] It could be, most simply, that a male "gay gene" is not really a gene for homosexuality per se, but for sexual attraction to males (androphilia). If so, those female relatives of gay men who inherited the gene might be, as it were, "hyper-heterosexual." That is, they would have the regular tendency to experience sexual attraction to males that most women share, plus an extra dose conferred by the androphilic gene that runs in their families. As a result, they might engage in more sex with men and thus become pregnant more often.

To the extent that this *sexually antagonistic model* is correct, the larger average size of gay men's extended families should result from the greater fecundity (number of children) of their female relatives rather than of their male relatives. Although the King study mentioned earlier did not observe this effect, an Italian research group led by Andrea Camperio-Ciani of the University of Padua has reported a difference of this kind in two studies.[67] In fact, the specific distribution of enhanced fertility found in the Italian study was suggestive of at least one "gay gene" on the X chromosome, consistent with Dean Hamer's 1993 study. Similar data were obtained by Qazi Rahman and colleagues for the relatives of White men in the U.K.[68]

Thus, the "fertile females" hypothesis for the maintenance of genes promoting male homosexuality has some observational support. What's more, detailed mathematic modeling has shown that, with certain assumptions (that two genes influence male sexual orientation, at least one of them located on the X chromosome), the sexually antagonistic model explains why male homosexuality persists at a constant low frequency in the population without either dying out or increasing in frequency.[69]

BENEFICIAL EFFECTS ON SAME-SEX RELATIVES

I've just described a mechanism whereby a gene predisposing to homosexuality in one sex might increase the reproductive success of heterosexual persons of the other sex. There are other possible mechanisms, however, in which a gene promoting homosexuality in one sex might increase the reproductive success of heterosexual persons of the *same* sex, or of both sexes. The most detailed model of this kind was developed by economist Edward Miller of the University of New Orleans.[70] As with the other models, this one was directed primarily at explaining male homosexuality, although it could be applied to both sexes.

Miller started from the assumption (for which I have described evidence earlier in this book) that male homosexuality is not an isolated trait but rather is part of a package of gender-variant traits. Miller proposed that several "feminizing" genes control these traits. If a man inherits a few of these genes, he will have some feminine characteristics, which might include increased empathy and kindness, decreased aggressiveness, and the like. These genes, Miller suggests, increase his attractiveness to women, permitting him more sexual access to women and thus offering him the likelihood of having more offspring. If a man inherits *all* of these genes, however, he will be feminized to the point of homosexuality, and his reproductive success will drop markedly. This leads to an equilibrium state that maintains a certain constant percentage of gay men in the population. Because each feminizing gene is present in many more straight men than gay men, it only has to raise each straight man's reproductive success by a small amount to compensate for the lowered reproductive success of gay men.

There are three predictions that one could make on the basis of this model. First, straight men who exhibit certain feminine traits should experience greater reproductive success than straight men who lack such traits. Second, straight men who have gay relatives should be more likely to exhibit feminine traits than straight men who lack gay relatives. And third, straight men who have gay relatives should experience greater reproductive success than heterosexual men who lack gay relatives.

Miller did not test these predictions, but a group led by Brendan Zietsch of the Queensland Institute of Medical Research (and including Michael Bailey) made an initial attempt to do so, using nearly 5,000 male and female subjects from the Australian twin registry mentioned earlier.[71] The subjects filled out questionnaires that investigated their masculinity or femininity, their sexual orientation, and the number of opposite-sex sex partners they had had over their lifetime. (The researchers used the number of sex partners in preference to fecundity—the total number of offspring—on the theory that modern culture has divorced fecundity from the psychological traits that used to regulate it.)

Zietsch's group found, first, that femininity in men and masculinity in women were associated with an increasing likelihood of being gay. This was fully expected, of course. However, among *straight* men, femininity was associated with a larger number of female sex partners, and among straight women, masculinity was associated with a larger number of male sex partners. Thus, in accordance with Miller's model, gender-atypical traits do seem to promote reproductive success in both straight men and straight women.

Second, by analysis of concordance rates in the monozygotic and dizygotic twin pairs, the researchers were able to show that overlapping genetic factors were partly responsible for the correlation between gender identity and sexual orientation and (in straight men and women) between atypical gender identity and number of sex partners. This is also consistent with Miller's model.

Finally, the researchers found that the heterosexual individuals with gay co-twins had more opposite-sex sex partners than did heterosexual individuals without gay co-twins, although the difference only reached statistical significance for females. This suggests that, among females at least, close same-sex relatives of gay individuals inherit genes that aid their reproductive success by conferring atypical gender characteristics.

These findings need to be replicated and extended. In general, though, it is clear that there are robust models that can account for the persistence of "gay genes" through their beneficial effect on the reproductive success of gay people's relatives.[72] Evolutionary considerations do not rule out the existence of genes that promote homosexuality—in fact, such considerations may be the key to identifying them and understanding their mode of action.

EIGHT

THE BRAIN

All mental traits, including sexual orientation, have some durable representation in the brain. These representations are not merely a matter of neuronal activity patterns; we know this, because their influence reemerges after our thoughts have been diverted into other channels, after we have been asleep or under general anesthesia, and even after our brains have been cooled to a temperature at which all neuronal activity ceases. Therefore, these brain representations are structural in a broad sense, which could include the number, kind, and arrangement of neurons, synapses, or molecules.

Finding these representations could be difficult. Take our preference for one musical composer over another. This too has to have some representation in the brain, but it is likely to be an inconspicuous one. Finding it might be like finding, in a haystack, not a needle but an unmarked stalk of hay. Our hope that the representation of sexual orientation is findable rests on the assumption that there is something unusual about this trait— that it involves very basic and specialized neural hardware rather than general-purpose networks.

Even finding a brain representation for a person's sexual orientation—whether straight or bisexual or gay—doesn't mean that we have understood how it came into being. Figuring that out requires putting together information from many different approaches, some of which I have discussed in previous chapters. I will make only some brief comments on this topic at the end of the chapter, and postpone further consideration of it until later in the book. In this chapter, I will focus on what has been learned from studying the brains of people of different sexual orientations.

A BRIEF TOUR OF THE BRAIN

The brain has a dauntingly complex organization, but for the present purposes I need only give a quick sketch, focusing on a few structures that may be relevant to our enquiry (see Figure 8.1). The brain consists of two general parts: the forebrain, which takes up most of the brain's volume, and the brainstem, which connects the forebrain to the spinal cord. It's the forebrain that interests us here.

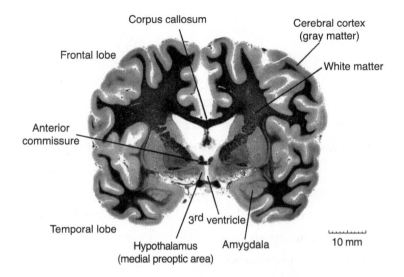

Figure 8.I Transverse section through the human brain, showing some of the structures mentioned in this chapter. The white matter (fiber tracts) has been stained dark. Image by permission of Michigan State University Brain Biodiversity Bank, produced with support from the U.S. National Science Foundation.

The most obvious feature of the forebrain is the cerebral cortex, the wrinkled, layered sheet of *gray matter* (neurons and synapses) that forms most of the outer surface of the left and right cerebral hemispheres. The cerebral cortex is the principal site of cognitive processing. On each side of the brain, the cerebral cortex is divided into four major lobes—the frontal, temporal, parietal, and occipital lobes—and these lobes are further divided into anatomically and functionally specialized regions that are designated with numbers or names. Under the cortex is *white matter* (stained black in the figure), which consists of neuronal fibers connecting cortical regions with each other and with other brain regions. The major band of white matter than inter-connects the left and right hemispheres is called the *corpus callosum*; another, much smaller one is called the *anterior commissure*.

Even deeper under the white matter are large groups of *nuclei*—clusters or masses of neurons that are not organized into layers. I'll mention just three of these groups. The *thalamus* acts as a way-station between lower centers and the cerebral cortex, converting sensory signals into a form that the cerebral cortex can digest. It also participates in cognitive processes by way of its two-way connections with the cortex.

Below the thalamus is the hypothalamus, which I've already mentioned several times in earlier chapters. The hypothalamus can be seen on the underside of the brain. It is situated on either side of the *third ventricle*, a slit-like space filled with cerebrospinal fluid that lies in the brain's midline. In spite of its rather small size, the hypothalamus participates in a wide variety of "life-preserving" functions, such as feeding and drinking, keeping our body temperature in the right range, and reproduction. The hypothalamus also controls the function of the pituitary gland, the master gland of the endocrine system that sits immediately under the hypothalamus. The hypothalamus is divided into many small nuclei with specialized functions, and these are con-nected with many other brain regions, including the cerebral cortex. The hypothalamus is one of the most ancient parts of the brain in evolutionary terms.

Another subcortical structure that needs to be mentioned is the amygdala, which lies to the side of the hypothalamus at the base of each cerebral hemisphere, within the temporal lobe. Each amygdala is a ball-like mass of neurons about 1 cm in diameter, and like the hypothalamus, it consists of several individual nuclei. Although the different nuclei within the amygdala have a variety of connections and functions,[1] one important function of the amygdala is the processing of emotion—most notably, the forming of emotional associations sparked by, for example, seeing happy or fearful faces.[2] Parts of the amygdala are involved in sexual functions, connect richly with hypothalamic nuclei that are concerned with sexual behavior,[3] and differ between the sexes in terms of their synaptic architecture.[4]

THE HYPOTHALAMUS AND SEXUAL ORIENTATION

As I already discussed in Chapter 3, a region at the front of the hypothalamus called the medial preoptic area is involved in the regulation of male-typical sexual behaviors, and within this area lies at least one cell group that is larger, on average, in males than in females. In rats, this cell group is called the sexually dimorphic nucleus of the preoptic area (SDN-POA), and in humans it is called the third interstitial nucleus of the anterior hypothalamus (INAH3) (see Figure 8.2A). It is suspected, but not proven, that the rat's SDN-POA and the human INAH3 are homologous structures, meaning that they evolved from the same structure in the common ancestor of rats and humans.[5]

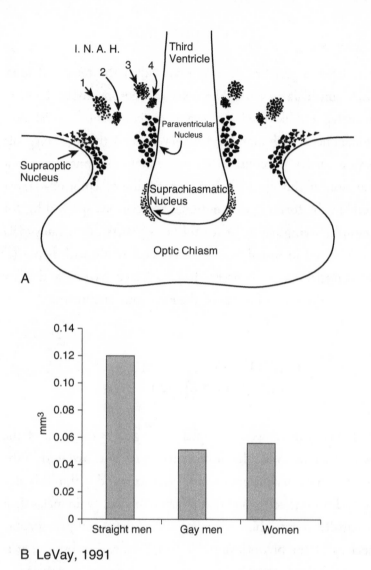

B LeVay, 1991

Figure 8.2(AB) (A) Transverse slice through anterior hypothalamus (same level as Figure 8.1), showing layout of the interstitial nuclei of the anterior hypothalamus (INAH1-4). (B) Volume of INAH3 in straight and gay men, and in women, from study by LeVay, 1991.

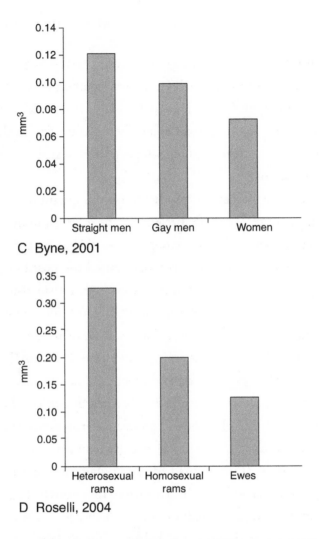

C Byne, 2001

D Roselli, 2004

Figure 8.2(CD) (C) Same as (B), but from study by Byne et al., 2001).
(D) Volume of the equivalent cell group in sheep (oSDN), for
heterosexual and homosexual rams and for ewes, from study by
Roselli et al., 2004.

In the 1991 study already mentioned at the beginning of this book, I reported that INAH3 was significantly smaller, on average, in gay men than in straight men (Figure 8.2B). In fact, there was no significant difference between its size in the gay men and in the women in my sample (whose sexual orientation was unknown).[6]

Because it was an autopsy study, various questions of interpretation arose, especially because all the gay men in my study, but only about half of the straight men, died of complications of AIDS. A number of critics have raised the possibility that I was seeing an effect of that disease rather than something related to the men's sexual orientation. I don't think that was the case, for a variety of reasons. There was no difference between the size of INAH3 in the straight men who died of AIDS and those who died of other diseases; there was no obvious pathology in the specimens I studied; other nearby nuclei (INAH1, INAH2, and INAH4) showed no size differences between subject groups; and the INAH3 of one gay man who died of non-AIDS causes (which I obtained after publication of the 1991 study) was as small as in the gay men in the study. Still, autopsy studies do have their limitations: I will discuss brain imaging studies on living, healthy people later in the chapter.

Only one attempt has been made to replicate my study, by psychiatrist and neuroscientist William Byne of Mount Sinai School of Medicine, New York, and several colleagues.[7] Byne's group confirmed that INAH3 was sexually dimorphic, and that it did not differ in size between persons who died of complications of AIDS and those who died of other causes. With regard to sexual orientation, they found INAH3 to be intermediate in size between the average sizes for (presumably straight) men and women (Figure 8.2C). The size difference between the gay and straight men did not quite reach statistical significance by the test that Byne employed, so he described it as a "trend."*

Byne's group also measured neuronal packing density (the number of neurons per cubic millimeter) in INAH3, and found a "strong trend" for neuronal density to be higher in the gay men than in the straight men. Neuronal density is relatively high when the structures that usually occupy the spaces between neurons, such as synapses, are smaller or fewer, allowing the neurons to pack more closely together; Byne suggested that this might be the case in gay men relative to straight men.

Byne's findings were in no way a refutation of the findings of my study, but neither were they a clear-cut confirmation. Further studies are certainly needed. Other studies have strengthened the general conclusions of my own in indirect ways, however. First, very similar findings to those of my human study have been made in sheep (see later discussion). Second, Dick Swaab's group at the Netherlands Institute for Brain Research

---

* Byne used a two-tailed t-test, which is the appropriate test in cases where there is no advance prediction about the direction of a difference. Given that my study had already reported INAH3 to be smaller in gay men, a one-tailed test might have been appropriate. Such a test would have yielded a significant difference.

reported that INAH3 was smaller in male-to-female transexuals than in non-transexual men.[8] Third, activity patterns in this region of the hypothalamus have been reported to differ between gay and straight men (see later discussion).

One other structure in the hypothalamus has been reported to differ in size between gay and straight men. As I mentioned in the Introduction, Dutch researchers (Dick Swaab's group) reported in 1990 that a cell group called the suprachiasmatic nucleus was larger in gay men than in straight men.[9] The suprachiasmatic nucleus is concerned with the regulation of circadian rhythms, not sex. Swaab's report has not been followed up by other groups. If the finding is real, its significance is uncertain. (In a preliminary study that has not been followed up, Qazi Rahman and Kevin Silber did report on apparent differences between the sleep–wake cycles of gay and straight people.[10])

For the sake of completeness, and to clear up some confusion that has developed in the literature, I should mention that Dick Swaab's group reported in 1985 on a different hypothalamic cell group, now generally known as INAH1, which they claimed was larger in men than in women.[11] They named the cell group "SDN-POA," described it as "analogous" to the rat's SDN-POA, and performed a number of subsequent studies of its structure and development.[12] They also reported failing to find any difference between the size of INAH1/"SDN-POA" in gay and straight men, and used this finding to reject the idea that the hypothalamus of gay men develops in a sex-atypical fashion.[13]

Since that time, however, three other laboratories have failed to confirm the basic sex difference in INAHI.[14] Thus, the reliability of Swaab and Fliers' 1985 observation, the merits of any theoretical conclusions based on it, and the appropriateness of the name "SDN-POA" in reference to INAHI, are open to serious question. Swaab continues to believe that this nucleus is sexually dimorphic, however.[15]

OTHER BRAIN REGIONS

Several brain regions outside of the hypothalamus have been reported to differ in structure between gay and straight people. Both of the fiber tracts interconnecting the two cerebral hemispheres that were mentioned earlier—the anterior commissure and the much larger corpus callosum—have been reported to be larger in gay men than straight men, a difference in the opposite direction from what I reported for INAH3.

The anterior commissure study—based on autopsy material— was carried out by Laura Allen and Roger Gorski of UCLA.[16] They had previously reported that the anterior commissure was larger, on average, in women than in men; thus, their report that the anterior commissure was larger in gay than in straight men seemed to be another example of a brain structure that is shifted in the feminine direction in gay men. When Byne's group attempted to replicate this finding, however, they were unable to find any difference in the size of the anterior commissure—either between gay and straight men or between men and women.[17]

The study on the corpus callosum was carried out much more recently by Sandra Witelson and her colleagues at McMaster University, using magnetic resonance imaging (MRI) in living subjects.[18] The corpus callosum is a single band-like structure, but it is conventionally divided into a series of sectors, from front to back, that interconnect different lobes of the cerebral cortex. Among Witelson's subjects, who were all right-handed, all the sectors of the corpus callosum were larger in gay men, but the difference was only significant for one sector called the *isthmus*, which interconnects parts of the parietal and temporal lobes in the left and right hemispheres.

There has been a long-running controversy on the subject of whether the corpus callosum is sexually dimorphic. If it is, the difference is subtle, and it may affect different parts of the callosum in different ways. Witelson had previously reported, however, that the isthmus is larger in non-right-handed people—i.e., people who are left-handed or mixed-handed—compared with people who are consistently right-handed, and this has been independently confirmed.[19] Thus, Witelson's finding of a difference in the isthmus between gay and straight men (which has not yet been independently replicated) is relevant to the question of a connection between handedness and sexual orientation, a topic I discuss in Chapters 5 and 9.

A group led by Jorge Ponseti of the University of Kiel, Germany, used MRI to examine the distribution of gray matter and white matter throughout the brains of gay and straight men and women.[20] They found no differences between gay and straight men, but they did find several locations where lesbians had significantly less gray matter than did straight women. The most marked difference was in a region of the left cerebral hemisphere called the *perirhinal cortex* (see Figure 8.3). This region typically has more gray matter in women than in men, so Ponseti's finding was another example of a sex-atypical structure in gay people—in lesbians, this time. The perirhinal cortex is involved in olfactory processing, spatial processing, and memory encoding; all of these functions differ between men and women in some respects.

Yet another anatomical study was carried out by Ivanka Savic and Per Lindström of the Karolinska Institute in Stockholm,

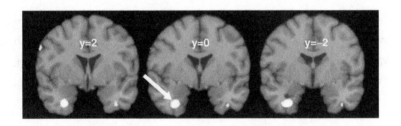

Figure 8.3 Brain structure and sexual orientation in women. These are three transverse slices through the brain, showing the location of a region (indicated by the arrow) where there is less gray matter in lesbians than in straight women, according to a magnetic resonance imaging study by Ponseti et al., 2007. This region, the perirhinal area of the left cerebral cortex, typically has less gray matter in men than in women: Thus it is gender-shifted in lesbians.

Sweden, using both MRI and positron emission tomography (PET).[21] They studied 90 subjects, including both straight and gay men and women. In the MRI portion of the study, Savic and Lindström compared the volumes of the left and right cerebral hemispheres. In the straight men, the right hemisphere was 2% larger than the left—a modest but highly significant difference. In the straight women, the two hemispheres were the same size. In gay men, the two hemispheres were also the same size; in other words, gay men were sex-atypical in this regard. In the lesbians, the right hemisphere was just slightly larger than the left, perhaps indicating a small shift in the male direction in this measurement.

The Swedish researchers used the PET scanner to visualize functional connections within the brains of their subjects.[†] The main findings of interest concerned the left and right amygdalas. There were marked differences between straight men and women. In straight men the right amygdala was more richly connected with other brain regions than was the left amygdala, whereas in straight women the left amygdala was more richly connected. What's more, the main functional connections formed by the

---

[†] The PET scans, performed while the subjects are not engaged in any specific mental activity, produce an estimate of how neuronal activity varies over time at many small regions (voxels) throughout the brain. To the extent that any two regions tend to be active simultaneously, a functional connection is likely between them. The demonstration of a "functional connection" does not specify exactly how the two regions are connected in anatomical terms.

amygdala were to different brain regions in the two sexes. (These findings confirmed earlier reports from the laboratory of Larry Cahill at the University of California, Irvine.[22]) In the gay men and lesbians, however, these characteristics were almost entirely sex-atypical: The findings in gay men resembled those in straight women, and the findings in lesbians resembled those in straight men.

BRAIN ACTIVITY

In Chapter 6, I mentioned two studies that reported on differences in brain activity related to sexual orientation, both of them focused on the auditory system. Several more recent studies have used functional magnetic resonance imaging (fMRI) to reveal activity patterns in the brains of gay and straight people while they were viewing potentially arousing images. These images have included male and female faces,[23] male and female genitals in a state of arousal,[24] and video clips of male–male and female–female couples engaged in sexual behavior.[25]

In general, these studies have revealed widely distributed brain systems that are active during the viewing of erotic images, when those images are appropriate to the viewer's sexual orientation. That is to say, roughly the same brain regions are active when straight men view female images as when gay men view male images, and similarly for lesbian and straight women. This is not particularly surprising.

I mentioned in Chapter I, however, that most women (unlike men) respond with similar genital and subjective arousal to erotic videos showing male–male and female–female couples, regardless of their own stated sexual orientation.[26] It is therefore rather surprising that brain responses in women viewing genitals are fairly specific: According to Jorge Ponseti's group, several brain regions including parts of the thalamus and the frontal lobe of the cerebral cortex were more active in straight women when they viewed male genitals than when they viewed female genitals, and vice versa for lesbians.[27] The reason for this apparent disconnect between the specificity of brain activity and the lack of specificity in genital and subjective arousal is unclear and merits further study.

Although, as just mentioned, activity patterns in the brains of gay and straight people are generally similar (so long as they are viewing images of their preferred sex partners), there does seem to be one difference, which concerns the amygdala. In gay men, according to a Northwestern University group led by Adam Safron, the amygdala is far more active when the subject is viewing male than female erotic videos, consistent with their sexual orientation. In straight men, on the other hand, the amygdala is equally active during viewing of male and female erotic videos, as well as during viewing of nonerotic videos.[28] This unexpected finding needs to be confirmed, and its meaning is unclear. One possibly relevant fact is that the amygdala contains nuclei with a variety of functions, not all of them related to sexual behavior; a signal representing the sum of activities in all these nuclei might fail to detect important differences in straight men's responses to different images. A recent Chinese study reported on some other apparent differences in the brain responses to sexually arousing images in gay and straight men.[29]

PHEROMONE STUDIES

Perhaps the most intriguing functional imaging studies have been carried out by the Karolinska Institute group. In these studies, the Swedish researchers examined brain activity patterns in gay and straight men and women while they were exposed to substances suspected of being human sex pheromones.

Some background is in order here. I already mentioned the relevance of pheromones to the sex life of the fruit fly, *Drosophila*. In that case, the pheromones are present on the cuticle (hard outer surface) of the fly, and are detected by other flies through the sense of taste. Rodents also produce sex pheromones, but these are volatile substances, often derived from steroid sex hormones, that are released from the animals' urine or body secretions into the air; they are detected through the sense of smell (olfaction). A small sensory structure within the rodent's nose called the *vomeronasal organ (VNO)* is specialized for detecting pheromones.

The importance of pheromones to rodent sexuality has been demonstrated in many studies. For example, Catherine Dulac's group at Harvard University studied mutant mice that were unable to sense any urinary pheromones.[30] Male mice with this mutation were unable to tell the difference between males and females; these mice courted and attempted to mount males and females equally, unlike wild-type male mice that have a strong preference to interact sexually with females. Female mice with the mutation showed the entire sequence of male-typical sexual behaviors, including solicitation, mounting, and pelvic thrusting and, like the mutant males, they directed these behaviors indiscriminately toward males and females. Even simply removing the VNO in otherwise normal female mice had the same effect as the mutation.

These findings suggest that sex pheromones play an important role in directing the sex behavior of male and female mice to animals of the opposite sex. They also indicate that the neural circuitry responsible for male-like sexual behavior is present in adult female mice, but that this circuitry is normally suppressed by inputs from the VNO.

There has been a great deal of controversy about whether sex pheromones exist in humans and, if so, what their function may be. On the one hand, the olfactory system is less well developed in humans than in many other mammals; the VNO is vestigial at best and does not contain sensory cells that connect with the brain; and the genes that code for the vomeronasal receptor molecules are nonfunctional in humans.[31]

On the other hand, there is some evidence that substances suspected of being human sex pheromones may be detected by the main olfactory sense organ rather than by the VNO.[32]

And pheromone enthusiasts point to a variety of studies in which sniffing body secretions or substances purified from secretions appears to have some psychological effect, such as improving the person's mood or affecting his or her judgments of attractiveness.[33]

Human sex pheromones are suspected of being sex steroids that have been chemically altered by bacteria that inhabit the skin. Some researchers hold that, to be considered a pheromone, a substance must act through unconscious channels, while others refer even to consciously perceived odors as pheromones. It's very possible that a substance will have a perceptible odor at a high concentration but also work as a pheromone at concentrations too low to be consciously sensed.

In 2005, researchers at the Monell Chemical Senses Center in Philadelphia asked straight men, straight women, gay men, and lesbians to compare the attractiveness of odors derived from the armpits of these same four subject groups.[34] Oddly, neither straight men nor straight women showed any consistent preferences when comparing odors derived from straight men and straight women. However, straight men, straight women, and lesbians all liked the odors from gay men *less* than those from other subject groups, while gay men themselves liked the odors from gay men *better* than those from other subject groups, especially in comparison to odors from straight men or lesbians.

That the odor of gay men is recognizably different from the odor of other people is believable, although the claim hasn't been independently verified and its chemical basis hasn't been studied.

It seems unlikely to me, though, that gay men have an *innate* preference for the odor of gay men over that of straight men, because many gay men are attracted to straight men and, given the opportunity, will have sex with them even in preference to gay partners. Thus this finding, if replicable, is more likely to represent a learned association resulting from gay men's prior history of intimacy with other gay men.

James Kohl, an independent researcher who also markets "human pheromones" to the general public, believes that pheromones may have a primary influence in setting up a person's basic sexual orientation. Other, more consciously perceived aspects of attractiveness, such as facial appearance, are attached to a person's basic orientation through a process of association during early postnatal life, according to Kohl.[35]

This model is attractive in that it solves the "binding problem" of sexual attraction. By that I mean the problem of why all the different features of men or women (visual appearance and feel of face, body, and genitals; voice quality, smell; personality and behavior, etc.) attract people as a more or less coherent package representing one sex, rather than as an arbitrary collage of male and female characteristics. If all these characteristics come to be attractive because they were experienced in association with a male- or female-specific pheromone, then they will naturally go together even in the absence of complex, genetically coded instructions.

Still, even in fruit flies, other sensory inputs besides pheromones—acoustic, tactile, and visual stimuli—play a role in sexual attraction, and sex-specific responses to these stimuli appear to be innate rather than learned by association.[36] We simply don't know where the boundary between prespecified attraction and learned association lie in our own species, nor do we have compelling evidence for the primacy of one sense over another.

Turning now to the Karolinska study, Ivanka Savic and her colleagues used PET technology to visualize brain activity in volunteers who were exposed to two compounds that they referred to at "putative human pheromones." One, a substance called 4,16-androstadien-3-one (AND), is a steroid derivative that is present in armpit secretions of both men and women.[37] (Savic, as well as other authors, refer to AND as a male-specific compound derived from testosterone, but the evidence does not appear to support this assertion.[38]) The other, called estra-1,3,5(10),16-tetraen-3-ol (EST), is an estrogen-like compound present in the urine of pregnant women. When sniffed, AND and EST have a variety of effects on mood. Some of these effects differ between the sexes, but that doesn't seem to be the case with regard to sexual arousal: Both AND and EST are reported to enhance sexual arousal in both men and women.[39]

Some effects of these substances can be elicited even when they are diluted to concentrations that are too low for conscious detection. In the studies discussed here, however, Savic's group used the pure undiluted chemicals, and their subjects did have conscious experience of the odors that were presented to them.

Savic's subjects were heterosexual men and women, along with gay men.[40] In a later study the researchers added lesbians to the mix.[41] Some brain regions were activated in a rather non-specific fashion: These included cortical regions known to be involved in the processing of odors, as well as the amygdala. The most interesting pattern, however, was seen in the hypothalamus—specifically, in a zone at the front of the hypothalamus, which included the medial preoptic area (where INAH3 is located), as well as nuclei behind the medial preoptic area that are also thought to be involved in the regulation of sexual behaviors. (The PET technique lacks the resolution to image individual hypothalamic nuclei, unfortunately.) The front zone was active in straight men when they smelled EST but not AND, whereas straight women showed the exact opposite pattern: The zone was active when they smelled AND but not EST. In gay men, this area responded to AND and not EST, just as in straight women and in sharp contrast to straight men. In lesbians, as in straight men, this zone did not respond to AND. It did respond to EST, but not as strongly as this region did in straight men. Thus, the response pattern in lesbians was strikingly different from that in straight women but not precisely the same as that seen in straight men.

It would make a neat story if AND was a male-specific sex pheromone and EST was a female-specific sex pheromone. Then one could conclude that cell groups in the front part of the hypothalamus are selectively responsive to odors from persons of whichever sex is attractive to the subject, and unresponsive to odors from the other sex. In reality it's not that neat, because AND is present in the armpits of both sexes, and EST, although female-specific, is only present during the latter part of pregnancy, which is hardly an ideal time to solicit sex partners. What's more, as mentioned above, AND and EST have not been shown to promote sexual arousal in a sex-specific fashion. Thus, Savic's findings, although intriguing, leave many unanswered questions that need to be resolved in future studies. Perhaps most immediately, it is important to find out whether similar orientation-specific activity patterns are seen when AND and EST are sniffed at the very low concentrations present in real life. If so, one might go on to study whether the brain responses to these compounds result from a learning process (reflecting a history of sexual contacts with males or females, for example) or whether they exist prior to the onset of sexual activity and possibly contribute to a person's choice of sex partners.

SHEEP

Among domesticated breeds of sheep, 6% to 10% of rams mate with other rams and do not mate with ewes, or do so much less readily. Aside from the preferred sex of their partners, the sexual behavior of these homosexual rams resembles that of heterosexual rams.[42] The existence of substantial numbers of individuals with a durable homosexual orientation (as opposed to a bisexual or heterosexual orientation) seems to be unusual among animal species. Thus, even though sheep are not ideal laboratory animals, several researchers have focused on them with a view to understanding the biological basis of male sexual orientation in this species.

According to studies by Anne Perkins of Carroll College in Montana, Charles Roselli of Oregon Health and Science University, and their colleagues, the brains of homosexual rams differ in several important respects from those of heterosexual rams:

- As I reported for humans, the sexually dimorphic nucleus in the medial preoptic area, known as oSDN in sheep, is about half the size in homosexual rams compared with heterosexual rams (Fig. 8.2D).[43]
- The levels of the aromatase enzyme are lower in the oSDN of homosexual rams than in heterosexual rams.[44]
- The levels of receptors for estrogen in the amygdala are lower in homosexual rams than in heterosexual rams.[45]

The sheep, like the rat, is a species in which conversion of testosterone to estrogen (by aromatase), and the binding of estrogen to its receptors, have been considered important for masculinization of the brain during fetal life, at least with regard to some traits.[46] If so, the differences noted here between heterosexual and homosexual rams suggest that homosexual rams may have experienced lower levels of testosterone, and of estrogen formed from it, during the prenatal sexual differentiation of the brain, and their brains may therefore have been masculinized to a lesser degree than is typically the case. There cannot have been a global lack of masculinization, however, because most of the sexual behaviors of the homosexual rams, except for their choice of partners, are typically male.

Roselli's group examined the effect of treating pregnant ewes with an aromatase-blocking drug.[47] The idea was that the drug would block conversion of testosterone to estrogen in the brains of male fetuses, possibly leading to homosexual partner choice in adulthood. The results were quite mild, however: The treated rams showed slightly less mounting behavior but did not choose male sex partners, and the drug did not prevent male-typical differentiation of the brain. Initially, the authors conjectured that the dosage of the aromatase blocker might not have been sufficient, but more recent experiments with larger and more frequent doses also failed to prevent masculinization of the rams' brain or behavior.[48] Roselli's group has therefore adopted a different interpretation, which is that testosterone by itself plays an important role in the development of sexual orientation in sheep, even without conversion to estrogen. Thus, sheep may be more similar to humans than to rats in this respect.

The existence of an animal model for male sexual orientation that quite closely parallels what is seen in humans offers a variety of possibilities for exploring the underlying mechanisms in ways that would be difficult with human subjects. For example, it should be possible to compare gene activity, transmitter distribution, neural connections, and synaptic architecture in homosexual and heterosexual sheep, and thus to form hypotheses about how the gross differences already reported translate into circuitry that mediates sexual behavior with male or female partners.

OVERVIEW

There is growing evidence for structural and functional differences between the brains of gay and straight people. These involve brain systems that could well be involved in the regulation of sexual attraction to one sex or the other, such as the hypothalamus and amygdala, as well as systems that are unlikely to have any close involvement with sexuality.

With regard to the former, the findings are supportive of the idea already put forward several times in this book, that prenatal sex hormones control the sexual differentiation of brain centers involved in sexual behaviors, and that this process goes forward differently in individuals who become gay as compared to those who become straight. The brains of "pre-gay" male fetuses may undergo less masculinization and/or more feminization in comparison to those of "pre-straight" male fetuses, and vice versa for "pre-lesbian" female fetuses.

The parallels with the results of animal experiments, described in earlier chapters, are a large part of the reason for leaning toward this conclusion. Still, some caution is in order. One possible interpretation of Byne's findings on INAH3 is that sexual orientation affects only the packing density of neurons in the nucleus, not their total number.[49] If true, this might take the focus away from the early developmental period when—if animal studies are relevant—testosterone promotes the survival of neurons in INAH3. Instead, the key difference might arise during some poorly defined later period when the neurons are elaborating their synaptic connections.

As I did not measure cell packing density in my own subjects, I cannot strongly confirm or refute such an interpretation. Still, I am skeptical that changes in packing density alone could explain my results, for, if so, the density would have to be very much increased in the subjects with small INAH3s, and that is something I would have noticed. In fact, several of my gay subjects had virtually *no* detectable INAH3, which is incompatible with possessing a full complement of neurons. Thus, I tend to believe that, in at least some of the gay subjects, the small size of INAH3 is accounted for by programmed cell death during early development, the same process that is thought to account for the small size of the nucleus in females.

The findings of differences between gay and straight people in brain regions that are not obviously concerned with sexuality, such as parts of the cerebral cortex, could be connected with the existence of cognitive differences between these same groups, as discussed in Chapters 4 and 5. Because, as with the cognitive differences, the brain differences generally represent shifts toward the other sex, they could be taken as further evidence for sex-atypical brain development in gay people.

What is lacking at this point is a clear correlation between form and function. That, for example, could involve demonstrating that lower mental-rotation skills in gay men are associated with sex-atypical development of the brain structures or connections that underlie this skill. Such correlations have been difficult to establish even with respect to male–female differences, however, because the brain basis of individual cognitive skills, such as mental rotation, has not been pinned down. Some structure–function correlations can be made in connection with the lateralization of cognitive functions, and I will discuss this issue in the next chapter.

INHIBITION AND
SEXUAL ORIENTATION

Some observations suggest that male heterosexuality might involve, not just the existence of sexual attraction to the opposite sex, but also the active suppression of sexual attraction to the same sex. Most of the evidence comes from animal studies. Damage to the medial preoptic area in male rats or ferrets causes a change in their preference from female sex partners to male partners, suggesting that SDN-POA might normally both activate attraction to females and suppress attraction to males.[50] Conversely, as mentioned earlier, removing the VNO in female mice causes them to court both males and females, as if the input from the VNO usually exerts a suppressive effect on courtship toward females.[51]

There is some evidence in humans too—at least in men—for the active suppression of brain circuitry serving same-sex attraction in heterosexual individuals. Homosexual attraction and behavior can appear in previously heterosexual men afflicted by the Klüver-Bucy syndrome, which is caused by damage to structures in the temporal lobe including the amygdala, a major source of input to the medial preoptic area.[52] Homosexual attraction can also appear in heterosexual men who undergo surgical or chemical castration for prostate cancer,[53] or who take female hormones as a prelude to sex reassignment surgery.[54] It is certainly only a minority of men in these categories who experience novel homosexual attraction, but the fact that this change occurs at all suggests that the brain circuitry serving attraction to males does exist in at least some heterosexual men, albeit in a functionally suppressed form.

At least in the rat's SDN-POA, the predominant neurotransmitter used by the neurons in this nucleus appears to be γ-aminobutyric acid (GABA), which generally has an inhibitory action on other neurons.[55] Thus, it is conceivable that the suppression of attraction to males involves an inhibition exerted directly by the neurons of SDN-POA (or INAH3) on cell groups elsewhere in the brain that promote attraction to males; this suppression may be released when the medial preoptic area is damaged or deprived of its neural or hormonal inputs. Of course, this idea is highly speculative and could be entirely wrong—I mention it simply to point out that there are possible biological mechanisms for setting up sexual attraction to one sex that depend primarily on *preventing* attraction to the other sex.

NINE

The Body

A re there are any differences between the bodies of gay and straight people, and if so how do they come about? In Chapter 6, I already discussed evidence for one such difference—in finger-length ratios. I now look at a broader range of studies. Some focus on gross anatomical features, such as height and weight, and others look at more subtle characteristics, such as bodily symmetry or asymmetry. This latter topic will require us to briefly revisit the brain.

For some reason, many inconsistencies exist among the studies in this field. Still, it is worth reviewing them, because they may shed additional light on the question of what developmental mechanisms are at work in the lives of gay and straight people.

BODY SIZE AND SHAPE

Ray Blanchard (of Toronto's Centre for Addiction and Mental Health) and his colleague Tony Bogaert (now at Brock University in Ontario) have conducted several studies of the relationship between body size and sexual orientation, using very diverse samples.[1] In general, they have found that gay men are slightly shorter and lighter than straight men, on average, whereas lesbians are slightly taller and heavier.

With regard to men, the findings have been fairly robust from study to study, but the findings for women have been less so. In fact, Bogaert's most recent study, based on data from a large national random-sample survey conducted in Britain, found *no* difference in average height or weight between straight and lesbian or bisexual women.[2] Even so, in this study significantly more *variability* was present in height and weight among lesbian and bisexual women than among straight women. Bogaert speculated that there might be subgroups of non-heterosexual women—such as "butch" and "femme" lesbians—whose height and weight differed from the female average, but in opposite directions.

Many factors can influence a person's height and weight. One factor is age at puberty: The later puberty begins, the more time is available for childhood growth, so the person is likely to end up that much taller. Boys enter puberty later than girls, and this is the main reason why men are taller, on average, than women.

Several studies have asked gay and straight people about their age at puberty. The consensus is that straight and lesbian women enter puberty at the same time.[3] One large random-sample survey found that gay men enter puberty a few months earlier than straight men,[4] but another, much more detailed study failed to find any difference.[5] All in all, there is little evidence for differences in the onset of puberty between gay and straight people.

Prenatal influences, which might include genetic and hormonal factors, also influence a person's adult size. This is known because there is a correlation between birth weight and adult weight.[6] A study conducted in Denmark, where detailed birth records are available for the entire population, found that gay men—identified by the fact that they entered a same-sex marriage—were significantly shorter and lighter at birth than the general male population.[7] Only a small minority of gay Danish men enter same-sex marriage, so a replication study on a broader sample would be desirable. Still, this study points to prenatal biological factors as contributing to the differences in height and weight between gay and straight men.

With regard to females, the Danish study did not find an overall correlation between birth length or weight and the likelihood that a woman would enter a same-sex marriage. Nevertheless, heavy, short babies (a combination that is predictive of being overweight or obese in adulthood) did have an increased likelihood of entering a same-sex marriage. This finding again suggested a prenatal biological influence on female sexual orientation, although perhaps only for a subset of females.

Devendra Singh, of the University of Texas at Austin, has made a many-year study of the *waist-to-hip ratio* of men and women; this is the ratio of the circumference of the waist to the circumference of the hips. Women have relatively wide hips and therefore typically have a lower waist–hip ratio than men. According to Singh and his colleagues, lesbians who identify as "butch" have a higher (more male-like) waist–hip ratio than do straight women, whereas lesbians who identify as "femme" have the same ratio as straight women.[8] Because the waist–hip ratio rises if people become overweight, this difference does not necessarily represent a constitutional difference between butch and femme lesbians: It could simply be that butch lesbians have less interest in dieting or maintaining a "feminine" profile. Nevertheless, Singh's group reported on several other indicators, such as higher testosterone levels, in butch lesbians (see Chapter 6), and they interpreted this constellation of sex-atypical traits as indicative of sex-atypical prenatal development.

TRUNK AND LIMB LENGTH

Men have longer limbs, longer trunks, and wider shoulders than women, but these sex differences are not all in proportion. In men, the limbs are longer, in relationship to the dimensions of the trunk, than they are in women. Put another way, leg length forms a greater proportion of total height, and arm length forms a greater proportion of total arm span (the distance between the fingertips of the two hands when the arms are extended to the side), in men than in women.

Both limb and trunk length are strongly influenced by sex hormone levels during development; this influence involves a direct action of testosterone and estrogen on the skeleton, as well as an indirect action whereby sex hormones influence the secretion of growth hormone from the pituitary gland. The extra growth of the male limb bones occurs primarily before puberty, whereas the extra growth of the male trunk occurs mainly after the onset of puberty.[9] Estrogen is responsible for the closure of the growth zones in the limb bones at puberty, in both males and females, and thus limits the final length of the limbs.

James Martin and Duc Huu Nguyen of the Western University of Health Sciences in Pomona, California, performed a detailed and fairly large anthropometric study of gay and straight men and women; they measured about 100 subjects in each group.[10] They found no differences in the dimensions of the trunk between the straight and gay men, or between the straight and lesbian women. In other words, the sex dimorphism in trunk dimensions was just as marked for gay people as for straight people. They did, however, find very marked differences in limb length: The limbs of the gay men were significantly shorter, in proportion to their trunk dimensions, than those of the straight men, whereas the limbs of the lesbians were significantly longer than those of the straight women; in other words, both gay men and lesbians were shifted toward the opposite sex in these measures. The differences were more marked for the

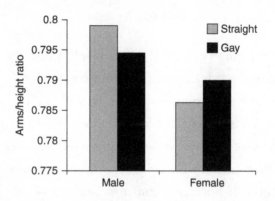

Figure 9.1 Body proportions. This bar graph shows the ratio of the length of the arms (left and right arms combined) to height. Men generally have a higher ratio than women, but both gay men and lesbians have ratios that are shifted about one-third of the way to the values for the opposite sex. Data from Martin and Nguyen, 2004.

arms than the legs (Figure 9.1). There were also differences in the length and shape of the hands, again with the values for gay individuals shifted toward those typical for the opposite sex.

Martin and Nguyen interpret their findings to mean that gay men had less exposure to sex steroids during development than did straight men, and that lesbians had greater exposure than did straight women. This conclusion is supported by animal studies. For example, administration of testosterone to newborn female rats (which shifts their sexual partner preference toward females) also increases the length of their limb bones compared with untreated females.[11]

The differential limb growth between gay and straight individuals probably occurs during childhood, because that is when the basic sex difference arises. The timing of the postulated differences in hormone exposure is less clear. It could be during childhood, or it could be during fetal life. In the latter case, it would exert a kind of priming effect, probably by influencing the sensitivity of the bones to sex hormones.

PENIS SIZE

When Alfred Kinsey and his colleagues conducted their famous sex surveys in the mid-20th century, they gathered data about the size of their male subjects' penises. The men were given instructions on how to measure the length and circumference of their own penis at home. They were supposed to mail the answers back to the researchers, but less than half of them actually did so.

Kinsey himself did not use these data to investigate whether there was any relationship between male sexual orientation and penis size, or at least did not publish any findings on the topic. More recently, however, Tony Bogaert, along with Scott Hershberger of California State University, Long Beach, mined Kinsey's files for information on this question.[12] Among the straight men, according to their analysis, the average reported length of the erect penis (measured along the top surface from abdomen to tip) was 5.99 inches (15.21 cm). Among gay men it was 6.32 inches (16.05 cm), or one-third of an inch (0.84 cm) longer. Comparable differences were found in erect circumference and in flaccid length and circumferences: In all cases, gay men reported slightly larger measurements than straight men.

The main strength of the study was the large number of subjects: Complete data were available for more than 3,000 straight men and more than 800 gay men. This ensured that all the size differences were highly significant in statistical terms. There were also potential weaknesses, however:

- Because the men reported their own measurements, there was plenty of room for inaccurate reporting: Perhaps gay men were more prone to exaggeration than straight men. Anyone who has read gay sex ads will acknowledge the legitimacy of this concern.* And in a study that asked gay men to measure their partners' penises on two separate occasions, the reproducibility of the measurements from one test to the other was poor, illustrating the problem with entrusting the measurement to "amateurs."[13]
- Even if all the measurements were accurate, gay men may have been more likely to mail in their data, or to take the measurements in the first place, if they had a larger-than-average penis. The researchers did not consider this possibility, but it is a significant one in view of the low response rate.

---

* In a recent issue of *Frontiers in LA*, a gay newsmagazine, the mean penis length of 20 advertisers was an implausible 8.37 inches (21.3 cm).

- Gay men may have been more sexually aroused, and thus had a more extreme erection, when they took the measurements. After all, gay men are more aroused by the sight of an erect penis than are straight men.[14]

Somewhat alleviating these concerns is the fact that a smaller 1961 study by sexologist Kurt Freund, in which the researchers themselves measured their subjects' penises, is said to have come up with a similar size difference in favor of gay men.[15] (I haven't read the study, which was published in an obscure Czech-language journal; it is cited by Bogaert and Hershberger.)

If the finding of a larger penis size in gay men is correct, what does it mean? Since prenatal and postnatal testosterone both promote development of the penis, the most obvious interpretation would be that testosterone levels were *higher* in gay men than in straight men at some point of pre- or postnatal development. This is, of course, the opposite of the usual hypothesis, which proposes that testosterone levels were *lower* during the gay men's early development.

Bogaert and Hershberger suggest a couple of possible explanations for their paradoxical finding. One is that the usual prenatal peak in testosterone levels occurs earlier than usual in fetuses that become gay men, thus raising it during the most crucial early period for genital development but lowering it during the later period for brain development. The other suggestion is that testosterone levels are in fact lower in pre-gay than in pre-straight fetuses, but that these low levels cause the developing penis to increase its sensitivity to the hormone, so that when testosterone levels rise at birth or at puberty they cause the penis to grow more than usual.

It's very unclear which of these ideas is correct. Although Bogaert and Hershberger's study does suggest a biological difference between gay and straight men, most likely involving testosterone levels during development, it needs to be replicated in a modern sample with objective measurement techniques before it can be given full credence.

SYMMETRY AND DEVELOPMENTAL INSTABILITY

Humans, like all vertebrates, are bilaterally symmetrical, but not perfectly so. The deviations from perfect left–right symmetry are of two kinds. The first occurs when the deviation from symmetry is in the same direction in most individuals. The best-known example is the position of the heart on the left side of the chest; many other internal organs are similarly asymmetric in location or shape. I'll call this *consistent-sided (CS) asymmetry.* (It is often simply called "directional asymmetry.")

Although most obvious in the viscera, there also tend to be small CS asymmetries in the rest of the body, and these may be more marked in one sex than the other. For example, I mentioned in Chapter 8 a report that the right cerebral hemisphere is 2% larger than the left in heterosexual men, but that the two hemispheres are the same size in heterosexual women.[16]

The existence of CS asymmetries in the body means that the developing embryo must somehow distinguish between its left side and its right side, in order to direct different developmental programs on the two sides. The discovery of how the embryo accomplishes this fundamental task makes for a fascinating scientific detective story, which sadly is not relevant enough to retell here.[17] With regard to CS asymmetries that differ between the sexes, however, differential exposure to sex hormones is thought (but not proven) to be the responsible factor.[18]

The other kind of asymmetry involves deviations from perfect symmetry whose direction is unpredictable from individual to individual: Either the left or the right side may be more developed. I will call this *random-sided (RS) asymmetry*. (In the scientific literature it is usually called "fluctuating asymmetry," a phrase whose meaning may not be self-evident.) Any bilateral feature of the body will show some degree of RS asymmetry, if it is measured precisely enough. That's because development always encounters a certain amount of "noise" or "jitter" that ensures slightly different outcomes on the two sides of the body.

Some individuals show more RS asymmetry than others. This may happen because their genes were less able to correct for the "jitter" than were the genes of most people, or because the jitter they encountered was more intense than usual, amounting to a disruption or destabilization of development. Specifically, the embryo, fetus, or child might have encountered an infection, fever, trauma, nutritional deficit, toxin exposure, or other environmental stressor that proved difficult to compensate for, resulting in asymmetry. *Developmental instability* is the catch-all phrase used to refer to the range of factors that can lead to high RS asymmetry, as well as to other effects.[19]

People (and animals) unconsciously check out the visible symmetry or asymmetry of others when forming judgments of their attractiveness—the more symmetrical they are, the more attractive they are thought to be.[20] According to evolutionary psychologists, this is a basic mechanism for assessing the quality of a potential mate.[21] The rationale for this is that individuals with high degrees of RS asymmetry are liable to suffer from more physical and mental health problems than are more symmetrical individuals.[22] Thus, in a sense, low RS asymmetry is "good" and high asymmetry is "bad." Still, the levels of RS asymmetry that are commonly encountered are probably not very significant in any functional sense, at least in our present-day culture.

Several research groups have looked into whether gay and straight people differ in terms of how much RS asymmetry their bodies exhibit. The thought behind the research is this: If gay people have greater RS asymmetry, that could be taken as an indication that they experienced some problem within the general category of developmental instability. This problem, whatever it was, might have derailed the developmental program that usually leads to heterosexuality, leaving them predisposed to becoming gay.

Based on a variety of limb and digit measurements, one research group (Patricia Hall and Catherine Schaeff of American University) has reported that both gay men and lesbians show significantly more RS asymmetry than their same-sex peers.[23] Hall and Schaeff interpreted their findings to suggest that developmental instability does play an important role in the development of homosexuality. Several other studies, however, failed to detect any difference in RS asymmetry between gay and straight people.[24]

A problem with the measurement of RS asymmetry is this: Many of the anatomical features that are used for the measurement of RS asymmetry also display some degree of CS asymmetry (i.e., a consistent bias favoring the left or right side), and the direction and magnitude of the CS asymmetry can vary between the sexes and between gay and straight people. (I mentioned the example of the left and right cerebral hemispheres.) If this CS asymmetry is not carefully assessed and removed from the data for each group of subjects, the measure of RS asymmetry is likely to be incorrect. When James Martin, David Puts, and Marc Breedlove reanalyzed datasets from their own previously published studies, taking this issue into account, they found that gay men and lesbians actually show *less* RS asymmetry than straight men or women.[25] If this finding is correct, one could argue that gay people actually experience less developmental instability than do straight people, not more. Still, given that there are unresolved conflicts between the existing studies, we can be sure that the last word hasn't been spoken on the issue of RS asymmetry and sexual orientation.

In Chapter 5, I mentioned studies indicating that both gay men and lesbians are slightly more likely to be non–right-handed (left-handed or mixed-handed) compared with straight men and women. Because the connections between the brain and the body are crossed, this suggests that the usual dominance of the left cerebral hemisphere is not quite as marked in gay people as it is in straight people. Some researchers have taken this finding as a possible indicator of developmental instability in gay people: Some genetic or environmental problem, according to this idea, might have disrupted the usual pathway to right-handedness, and this same problem might have disrupted the usual pathway to heterosexuality.[26] There is no real reason to favor developmental instability over other causal mechanisms, such as prenatal sex hormones, however.

Handedness is just one window on the lateralization of brain function, and several other such windows have been used to see if the brains of gay and straight people are organized in different ways. Tasks involving simultaneous presentation of two different syllables to the left and right ears (*dichotic listening tasks*) have been used to assess hemispheric specialization for language.[27] Other studies have examined how symmetrically the two sides of the brain process visual, auditory, spatial, and verbal information.[28]

In some of these studies, the data for gay people resemble those for straight people of the other sex, consistent with the idea that they experienced atypical levels of sex hormones during early development. For example, Qazi Rahman and his colleagues reported that lesbians are shifted in a masculine direction in some aspects of language lateralization.[29] And the Swedish study of the connections of the left and right amygdala, which I described in Chapter 8, pointed to sex-atypical functional organization of this part of the brain in both gay men and lesbians.[30]

The findings of different studies have not always been consistent, however, and even the existence of a basic sex difference in brain lateralization for language remains controversial after decades of study.[31] It does seem likely that there are gay/straight differences in the functional lateralization of the brain, but the lessons to be learned from them will depend on a better understanding of how they relate to underlying sex differences.

HAIR WHORL DIRECTION

Most people's scalp hair features a whorl-like arrangement visible on the top of the head. Viewed from above the head, the majority of hair whorls are clockwise in direction, but a minority of people—about 1 in 10—have a counterclockwise whorl. In 2003, a National Cancer Institute geneticist, Amar Klar, claimed that gay men have a greatly elevated rate of counterclockwise whorls. Based on surreptitious observations of men on a gay beach, he reported that 30% of gay men have such a whorl—far higher than the rate among men he observed on a non-gay beach—and he tied this in to a hypothesis linking left-handedness, counterclockwise hair whorls, and male homosexuality to a single gene that supposedly controls all these traits.[32]

Given the enormous difference between the data for gay and straight men—the difference was significant at $p < 0.0001$, meaning that it had less than a 1 in 10,000 likelihood of having arisen by chance—Klar's study attracted considerable attention from the media and from psychologists. Yet, two subsequent studies, carried out with much greater scientific rigor, failed to observe any significant difference in hair whorl directions between gay and straight men.[33] Several studies found no correlation between hair whorl direction and handedness either. It seems that Klar's data may have been distorted by subjective bias; that is, by the fact that he knew which groups his subjects belonged to when he was assessing the direction of their hair whorls. Statistical tests don't identify problems of this kind.

GAYDAR

"Gaydar" is a colloquial expression for the ability to spot people who are gay without the benefit of any explicit information about their sexual orientation. To the extent that gaydar works, there must be something about the discernible characteristics of gay men that distinguishes them from straight men, and something about lesbians that distinguishes them from straight women.

As many studies have shown, gaydar does work, although it is not infallible.[34] And if gaydar works, there must be a corresponding "straight-dar," but this skill isn't usually of much interest because almost everyone is straight. From a scientific point of view, though, the interest is not so much in identifying either gay or straight people as in figuring out the recognizable differences between them. This could throw light on the factors that influence the development of sexual orientation. For present purposes, then, I am mainly interested in what gaydar can tell us about the person observed, rather than what it can tell us about the observer, although the latter is an interesting issue in itself.[35]

I mentioned in Chapter 4 the study by Gerulf Rieger and his colleagues, who showed observers short excerpts from home movies of gay and straight people made when they were children.[36] The observers, who were not told the subjects' sexual orientation, rated the pre-gay boys as much more feminine than the pre-straight boys, and they rated the pre-lesbian girls as more masculine than the pre-straight girls. Because the videos had not been made with research in mind, their content was poorly controlled. Nevertheless, it appears that the judges depended both on the type of activities that the children were engaged in as well as on ill-defined aspects of the children's demeanor—their "vibes," to use a technical term. Whatever the exact cues, the pre-gay children were unconsciously "outing" themselves by virtue of gender-atypical behavioral traits.

In the case of adults, a variety of cues, alone or in combination, can be used to assess a person's sexual orientation. This was shown very clearly in a recent study by Rieger and his colleagues.[37] The Northwestern University group video-recorded interviews with gay and straight men and women (20–25 in each of the four groups). From each interview, the researchers extracted a single 5- to 10-second clip, consisting of the first sentence the interviewee spoke in response to a question about his or her interests. The video was modified so as to emphasize the interviewee's body outline and deemphasize facial appearance and other details. Raters (a mix of gay and straight men and women) were presented with the video without the sound, the sound without the video, a written transcript of the spoken sentence, a still photograph of the standing interviewee, or the video combined with the sound. For each of these except the written transcript, the raters discerned the interviewees' sexual orientation at far above chance levels, and they did best with the combined video plus sound. This suggests that appearance (as seen in the still photo), body motion, and voice all carry independent information about a person's sexual orientation, and that this information can be picked up on with just a few seconds' observation. If the Monell study mentioned in Chapter 8 is correct, there are also discernible differences between the body odor of gay and straight people—particularly between gay and straight men—so this would offer yet another sensory channel through which gaydar could operate.[38]

What exactly is communicated by these various cues that is informative about sexual orientation? To a considerable extent, it is gendered traits. Men who seem feminine and women who seem masculine are judged to be gay. Let's look at examples of research that illustrate this point. Psychologist Kerri Johnson (who is now at UCLA) and her colleagues have conducted studies of walking style (gait).[39] The researchers found, first, that raters judged people's *sex* primarily from body shape. "Hourglass-shaped" figures—those with a low waist–hip ratio—were judged to be female, whereas "tubular" figures—those with roughly similar shoulder, waist, and hip dimensions—were judged to be male. Raters judged the *masculinity–femininity* of walking figures primarily from the relative motion of the shoulders and hips: The more marked the figures' shoulder motion ("swagger"), the more masculine the figures were judged to be; the more marked their hip motion ("sway"), the more feminine they were judged to be. Computer-generated walking figures that had a male shape and moved with a swagger were judged to be straight men, whereas those that had a male shape but moved with a sway were judged to be gay men. Conversely, figures that had a female shape and moved with a sway were judged to be straight women, whereas those that had a female shape but moved with a swagger were judged to be lesbians.

When presented with video clips of real gay and straight men and women walking on a treadmill—clips that had been simplified so as to contain information about body shape and motion and little else—raters identified the figures' sexual orientation at well-above-chance levels, although certainly not with complete accuracy. Thus, it appears that the average person walks with enough of a sex-typical or sex-atypical gait to offer a usable clue to his or her sexual orientation.

In addition, the researchers found that body shape was used in judgments of women's (but not men's) sexual orientation. A high waist–hip ratio raised the likelihood that a woman would be judged to be lesbian. This could relate to Devendra Singh's report, mentioned earlier, that "butch" lesbians do in fact have higher waist–hip ratios than femme lesbians or straight women.

Rieger's study also pointed to the conclusion that gendered traits are used to judge sexual orientation. In that study, raters were asked how masculine or feminine the persons in the video-tapes seemed. There was a strong correlation between judgments of sexual orientation and judgments of masculinity–femininity, even though the judgments were made by separate groups of raters. The more feminine a male subject was judged to be, the more he was likely to be judged as gay, and vice versa for the women. In fact, the male subjects who were most consistently judged to be gay also judged *themselves* to be the most feminine, and vice versa for the women. This correlation certainly suggests that masculinity–femininity is the general characteristic used to decide on a person's sexual orientation.

It's not the case that every feature of gay people's behavior is sex-atypical, however. Just as with the psychological traits discussed in Chapter 5, gay people seem to be a patchwork of sex-atypical and sex-atypical elements, and gaydar seems to pick up on that. Take voice quality as an example. Something about the voice offers a cue to sexual orientation, because judgments based on voice quality are accurate at well above chance levels.[40] Still, raters do make many errors, mostly in the direction of misidentifying gay people as straight.[41] In other words, many gay people have "straight-sounding" voices, but not many straight people have "gay-sounding" voices.

A group led by linguist Ron Smyth of the University of Toronto performed a detailed phonetic analysis of a set of 25 male voices chosen to represent a spectrum from the most straight-sounding to the most gay-sounding.[42] They first looked at the *fundamental frequency* of the voice. This is the characteristic that most obviously differentiates men's and women's voices: Men's voices are lower-pitched, thanks to the lengthening and thickening of boys' vocal cords at puberty. The researchers found that gay-sounding men's voices were no different in fundamental frequency from straight-sounding voices.

Many other characteristics distinguish male and female voices, however, even before the difference in fundamental frequency emerges at puberty, and even if the frequency difference in adult voices is artificially eliminated. One difference is that women typically make the various vowel sounds more distinct from each other than men do. (In technical terms, they exhibit greater "vowel peripherality" or "vowel-space dispersion.") Smyth's group found that gay-sounding male voices were relatively female-like in this characteristic, and a similar finding was made by a group at Northwestern University led by Janet Pierrehumbert, who compared the voices of randomly selected gay and straight people.[43]

Women tend to lengthen vowel sounds more than men do. Here again, Smyth's group found that gay-sounding male voices featured longer vowel sounds, although the differences were observed for some vowels and not others. Further examples of sex-atypical phonetic characteristics involved phenomena called voice onset time (the length of time at the start of a syllable before the vocal cords start vibrating: Women and gay-sounding men have longer onset times), sibilant frequency (the distribution of frequencies in s- or z-like sounds: Women and gay-sounding men use a higher frequency distribution), and clear/dark "l" (the difference between the "l" in "leave" and "old": Women and gay-sounding men more commonly employ a "clear l").

Pierrehumbert's group found much less evidence for sex-atypicality in gay people's voices than did Smyth and his colleagues. This was probably because Pierrehumbert compared unselected gay and straight people and did not test how recognizably gay or straight their voices sounded; thus, many of their gay subjects probably lacked gay-sounding voices.

Although we can conclude that gaydar works to a considerable extent by detecting sex-atypical behavioral traits, that leaves unresolved the question of how these traits develop. Obviously, unconscious imitation of the other sex, or of other gay people, could play a role in causing these behaviors to become sex-atypical. Imitation of the other sex could occur either during childhood or adulthood, while imitation of other gay people would more likely happen after a person joins a gay community.

Smyth's group suggested that gay men's speech develops by imitation because, first, speech in general is acquired by imitation, and second, "gay" phonetic characteristics are those that are not constrained by anatomy or physiology. (They don't involve differences in fundamental frequency, for example, which is tied to the dimensions of the vocal cords.)

Without denying the likelihood that imitation does play some role in gay people's adoption of sex-atypical behaviors, this may not be the whole story. With regard to the voice, the brain is a more important determinant of many phonetic characteristics than is the vocal tract. Although both men and women are physiologically capable of adjusting the duration of their vowel sounds, for example, the fact is that longer vowel sounds have been observed in German-, Swedish-, and English-speaking women than in male speakers of the same languages,[44] as if the gender difference in this trait is driven by something that transcends the acquisition of a specific language.

Genes could play an important role in the development of the unconscious behaviors such as those that are detected by gaydar. Even trivial behavioral characteristics, such as how children hold their hands, are remarkably similar between monozygotic twins and remarkably different between dizygotic twins. Is that because monozygotic twins imitate each other and dizygotic twins don't? No, because when twins are separated very early in life and brought together in adulthood, the monozygotic pairs show the same uncanny similarity in hand posture, while the dizygotic twins are as different from each other as ever.[45] Yet, if genes play such an important role in the development of these unconscious behaviors, it means that these behaviors emerge from specific developmental programs in the brain—programs that could easily differ between men and women and between gay and straight people.

Studies of flirting behavior make a similar point. The seemingly trivial unconscious behaviors that people exhibit when they are flirting—head turns, touching of hair, and so on—differ between men and women, and these differences have been observed consistently across dozens of cultures, both Western and non-Western.[46] This indicates the importance of biological programs in the development of unconscious gendered behaviors, and raises the real possibility that the atypicality of these behaviors in some gay people arises, not through imitation, but because the underlying biological programs are themselves sex-atypical.

Although I have focused on what gaydar tells us about the people observed, rather than what it tells us about the observers, there is one point about the observers that is worth making. We might intuitively suppose that gay people would have more accurate gaydars than straight people. After all, gay people have strong motivation and frequent opportunity to hone this skill. For straight people, on the other hand, the skill is largely irrelevant to their lives. Yet most studies—such as Rieger's—have found only minor differences in the accuracy of gay and straight people's gaydar, and some—such as Smyth's—have found none at all. And people, gay or straight, demonstrate their good gaydar skills with exposure to just a brief and highly reduced specimen of speech or movement.

If gaydar were based on the recognition of characteristics that are unique to gay people, this uniformly high performance level would defy explanation. But it isn't. Rather, gaydar appears to involve the detection of ordinary gendered traits, by and large—traits that distinguish men and women and that are important to anyone's life as a social being. What turns "gendar" into gaydar, for the most part, is simply the mismatch between some of these discernible gendered traits and a person's physical sex.

OVERVIEW

In this chapter, I've reviewed studies that focus on the bodies of gay and straight people. I described studies that looked for differences in stature and body proportions, penis size, and hair whorl direction, and other studies that looked for differences in bodily symmetry. Finally, I surveyed studies on the basis of gaydar—what clues to their sexual orientation gay (and straight) people give off in the course of ordinary, unconscious behaviors. The results of many of these studies suggest that gay people are gender-atypical in subtle aspects of their anatomy and behavior.

Because of the lack of consistency between studies, some caution is obviously called for interpreting these reports. There are contradictory studies on whether gay people exhibit more random-direction asymmetry than straight people, for example. The initial report on hair whorl direction was followed by two failures to confirm it. The single study on penis length actually found gay men to be "hypermasculine" rather than gender-atypical in this trait. And even studies that reported robust shifts in a gender-atypical direction did so only for some of the measured traits, not all.

Even so, the studies described in this chapter do bolster the conclusions from previous studies, providing more indications that early development follows somewhat different pathways in gay and straight people, probably because of differences in levels of sex hormones or in the response of the brain or body to those hormones. The reported anatomical differences in height, limb/trunk proportions, finger-length ratios (described in Chapter 6), and size of the cerebral hemispheres (Chapter 8), as well as the behavioral differences in voice quality and gait that are detected by gaydar, all tend to support this model. In contrast, the studies offer little support for an alternative biological theory—the idea that weak genes or prenatal environmental stressors ("developmental instability") are the cause of homosexuality.

I will postpone a more detailed review of these issues until the final chapter of the book. Before that, however, I need to describe a set of studies that point to a fairly novel factor that seems to influence sexual orientation, in men at least: birth order.

TEN

THE OLDER-BROTHER EFFECT

According to Ray Blanchard and his colleagues, gay men have more older brothers, on average, than do straight men.[1] This apparent influence of older brothers on the sexual orientation of later-born boys is biological rather than social in nature, the Canadian researchers believe. They hypothesize that the influence of one boy on another is not a direct one but is mediated by their mother—more specifically, by their mother's immune system.

The idea that being a later-born member of a family predisposes men to homosexuality was put forward by psychiatrists at London's Maudsley Hospital—Eliot Slater and (separately)

Edward Hare* and Pat Moran—in the 1960s and 1970s.[2] But the real heavy lifting in this area has been done by Canadians Ray Blanchard, Kenneth Zucker, Tony Bogaert, and various colleagues. Since the early 1990s, they have published at least 25 papers on the topic, many of them being replications of the basic finding in a wide variety of subject groups.

One way to represent a person's birth order position is by use of an index devised by Slater, which is the number of the person's older siblings divided by the person's total siblings. Thus, a first-born child has a *Slater's Index* of 0 and a last-born child has an index of 1. My own index, as the second of five children, is 1 divided by 4, which equals 0.25. The Toronto group has found in study after study that the average Slater's Index is slightly higher for samples of gay men than it is for straight men. The data for seven such studies are shown in Figure 10.1.

If gay men have a higher (later-born) Slater's Index than straight men, this could be for any of four reasons: They could have more older brothers, more older sisters, fewer younger brothers, or fewer younger sisters. As shown in Figure 10.2, an analysis of Blanchard's data showed that all four of these possibilities were true: Gay men had significantly more older brothers and sisters than did straight men, as well as significantly fewer younger brothers and sisters.

---

* Edward Hare was stepfather to myself and my four brothers. From oldest to youngest our sexual orientations are gay, gay, straight, straight, and straight—a sequence that's at odds with his theory.

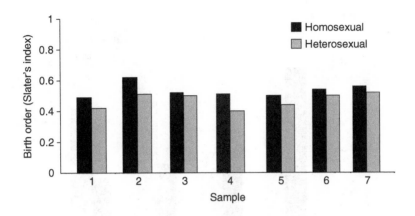

Figure 10.1 Birth order and sexual orientation. The bar graphs show the average Slater's Index for gay and straight men for seven samples studied by Blanchard and colleagues. An index of 0 would represent a first-born child; an index of I would represent a last-born child. Single children are excluded because they cannot be represented by this index. In all samples, gay men are later-born (on average) than straight men. From Blanchard, 2001.

This doesn't mean that all four of these factors played a causal role in the men's homosexuality. If, for example, it is only older brothers that play a causal role, gay men will of course have more older brothers than straight men, but they will also tend to have more older sisters. The older sisters will "come along for the ride," because it takes time to produce older brothers, and girls may also be born during that time. Similarly, they will tend to have fewer younger brothers and sisters, simply because having older brothers increases the likelihood that they will be late-born in their families.

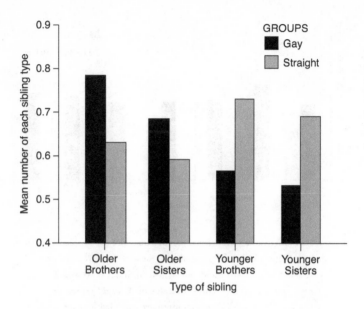

Figure 10.2 The numbers of the four kinds of siblings of homosexual and heterosexual men. These data represent the unweighted averages of 14 samples, taken from studies by Blanchard's group, that collectively included about 3,000 gay men and 7,000 straight men. ("Unweighted" means that each sample was treated equally regardless of the number of men in each sample, which varied greatly.) From Blanchard, 2004.

The Toronto group used a statistical technique called logistic regression to sort out which of the four factors was playing a causal role and which were "coming along for the ride." The results indicated that only the number of older brothers influenced the men's sexual orientation. The differences in the numbers of older sisters, younger brothers, and younger sisters were all secondary consequences of the increased number of older brothers. Thus, Blanchard calls this influence the "fraternal birth order effect," and it is often simply called the *older-brother effect*.

HOW WELL-ESTABLISHED IS THE
OLDER-BROTHER EFFECT?

Blanchard, Bogaert, and their colleagues have reported observing the older-brother effect in (by my count) 12 studies, some of which dealt with more than one group of subjects. Four of the studies were based on data collected long ago by Alfred Kinsey, psychoanalyst Irving Bieber, sexologist Alan Bell, and psychologist Marvin Siegelman.[3] Six of the studies were based on groups of North American volunteers recruited by the investigators.[4] One was based on a multinational sample recruited through the Internet.[5] One study was based on two national random-sample surveys—potentially the most accurate kind of study.[6] In another national random-sample survey, which involved British subjects, Bogaert failed to observe an older-brother effect.[7] He attributed this failure to insufficiently precise information about the subjects' birth order and siblings.

In addition to these studies on gay men, the Canadian researchers have reported an older-brother effect for other, potentially related groups. These included gay male adolescents and feminine (probably pre-gay) boys,[8] androphilic ("homosexual") male-to-female transexuals,[9] and male sex offenders whose victims were adult, pubescent, or prepubescent males.[10] In each case, these males had more older brothers than comparable gynephilic males—for example, male sex offenders whose victims were female.

The results of studies by other researchers have not been in complete accord with the findings of the Toronto group. In a Northwestern University study led by Gene Schwartz, which recruited about 1,700 gay and straight male subjects, a significant older-brother effect was found. In addition to having an excess of older brothers, however, the gay men also had an excess of older and younger sisters.[11] According to a logistic regression analysis, the younger sisters, and possibly the older sisters as well, had an influence that was independent of the number of older brothers. A British study led by Michael King obtained similar results to the Northwestern study, except that it was the older sisters rather than the younger sisters who influenced the men's sexual orientation independently of the older brothers.[12]

Two Italian studies, led by Andrea Camperio Ciani of the University of Padua, did get results similar to the Canadian studies: Gay men were later-born, and this was due entirely to an excess of older brothers.[13] In London, Qazi Rahman performed two studies that assessed the older-brother effect in fairly small samples. In one study, he saw a robust effect,[14] while in the other, the effect was equivocal: The gay men did not have a greater average number of older brothers, but they were more likely to have at least one older brother.[15] Rahman did not present data on sisters. Doug VanderLaan and Paul Vasey reported that Samoan *fa'afafine* (homosexual men, many of whom are markedly feminine—see Chapter 7) have excess older brothers compared with other male Samoans, but they have excess older sisters too, and the older sisters had an influence that was independent of the older-brother effect.[16] On the basis of their most recent analysis, VanderLaan and Vasey conclude that two factors are associated with an increased likelihood of homosexuality among Samoan men: an older-brother effect of the kind proposed by Blanchard, as well as a general effect of large family size.[17]

Particularly surprising are the negative results from two very large, apparently well-designed studies. Danish researchers started with all the 2 million Danes who were born in a certain three-decade time span.[18] They compared the family data of 3,500 persons who entered into homosexual marriages with those of nearly half a million persons who entered into heterosexual marriages—gay and straight people respectively, one may presume. The gay men did not have an excess of older brothers, but they did have an excess of older sisters. Of course, men who entered same-sex marriages may not have been typical of all gay Danish men. Interestingly, the *women* who entered into same-sex marriages had significantly fewer older sisters than women who entered heterosexual marriages, suggesting that older sisters *decrease* the likelihood that their younger sisters will be lesbian.

The other study, by economist Andrew Francis of Emory University, used data from the National Longitudinal Study of Adolescent Health,[19] which has followed about 10,000 American teenagers through to their early 20s. Francis found that men with a single older brother were no more likely to be gay than men with no older brothers. Men with multiple older brothers were slightly more likely to be gay, but the effect didn't reach statistical significance, perhaps on account of the small numbers of men in the study with multiple older brothers.

Richard Green studied a large group of male-to-female transexuals.[20] He confirmed Blanchard's finding that androphilic transexuals have more older brothers than gynephilic transexuals, but he maintained that his data undercut the theoretical explanation that Blanchard has put forward to explain the older-brother effect, as we'll see later.

My take on the entire collection of studies is that gay men do have significantly more older brothers, on average, than straight men. If this were not the case, some systematic error would have to have biased the Canadians' many studies and the positive findings of several other researchers. No one has been able to pinpoint such an error. That some studies have failed to detect an older-brother effect may result from methodological issues, atypical samples, or pure chance. (Blanchard has spelled out what he considers the weaknesses of some of the negative studies.[21])

It is not quite so clear that older sisters and younger siblings have no effect on men's sexual orientation. Most of the research suggests that they don't, but a few studies do seem to show a positive influence of older sisters that is independent of the older-brother effect, and not every one of Blanchard and Bogaert's studies, considered singly, rules out such an influence. If having older sisters does increase the chances that boys become gay, it is likely to be a weaker effect than the effect of older brothers. Still, to the extent that an older-sister effect exists, it suggests that being late-born in a family, or simply being born into a large family, may be as important as having older brothers in predisposing boys to homosexuality.

HOW STRONG IS THE OLDER-BROTHER EFFECT?

The Toronto researchers have put a great deal of effort into quantifying the older-brother effect. They have assessed the strength of the effect in two complementary ways. First they have asked: By how much does having an older brother increase the likelihood that a man will be gay? Second, they have calculated the percentage of all gay men who owe their sexual orientation to the older-brother effect—a measure that provides an estimate of the importance of the older-brother effect in relation to all the other potential factors that may predispose men to homosexuality.

According to Blanchard and Bogaert, the effect of older brothers on the sexual orientation of their younger brothers is linear. Compared with having no older brothers, each older brother increases the likelihood that a man will be gay by the same fixed percentage, which they have estimated at 33%.[22] The results of some large-scale studies, however, suggest that the effect may be nonlinear. One such study, by Gene Schwartz and colleagues, found that the first and second older brothers have only small effects, but that the effect grows rapidly stronger with three or more older brothers.[23] Francis's study, which found no effect of one older brother but a trend toward an effect with multiple older brothers, also raises the possibility of a nonlinear effect.[24]

Let's stay with Blanchard's linear model and the 33% estimate, however. This is a sizable influence of an older brother. It is much larger, for example, than the effect of older brothers on gendered traits in childhood, as discussed in Chapter 4.

Looked at another way, however, it's quite a modest effect. According to estimates from Blanchard's group, the rate of homosexuality among men with no older brothers is 2%.[25] Thus, having one older brother will raise the likelihood of being gay to less than 3%, and having two brothers will raise it to less than 4%. It will take more than ten older brothers to give a man a better-than-even chance of being gay by the older-brother effect, but families with 11 or more boys almost never crop up. It's still very possible that some men with just one or two older brothers are gay on account of the older-brother effect, but some other factor would have to be acting in concert with that effect: either another cause of homosexuality, or just a hefty dose of good luck.

Blanchard and Bogaert (along with James Cantor and Andrew Peterson) borrowed statistical techniques from medical epidemiology to estimate the percentage of all gay men who owe their sexual orientation to the older-brother effect.[26] The figure they came up with was 15%, or about one in seven gay men. In a more recent study, using different samples and methods,

Blanchard and Bogaert increased this figure to 29%, meaning that between one-quarter and one-third of all gay men owe their sexual orientation to their older brothers.[27]

Taken literally, this claim can hardly be correct, at least for contemporary samples of young gay men, because well under 29% of such men have any older brothers.[28] The claim also seems to imply that for every gay man there is one cause for his homosexuality, and only one. There is no reason to accept this idea, however, rather than the alternative idea that fraternal birth order and other factors such as genes can add together or inter-act in a man's psychosexual development. Thus, I interpret Blanchard and Bogaert's statement that 29% of gay men owe their homosexuality to their older brothers simply as a figure of speech intended to convey some idea of the magnitude of the older-brother effect in relation to all factors that influence men's sexual orientation.

There's another problematic aspect of these figures, which has to do with historical trends in family size. Since the early 19th century, the average number of children born to American women has dropped from seven (for White women) or eight (for Black women) to barely more than two today.[29] This drop is part of a global phenomenon known as the *demographic transition*. Thus, most American men used to have older brothers, and many had several.[†] Today, on the other hand, few young men

---

[†] Many of these older brothers died early in life, but this fact is irrelevant to Blanchard's theory of the older-brother effect, as we'll see.

have even one. If, even in today's brother-poor society, the older-brother effect is responsible for producing 29% of the gay men in the United States, then the overall rate of male homosexuality should have been much higher two centuries ago than it is now. The same should be true for contemporary societies that have not yet undergone the demographic transition to small family size.

Bogaert has discussed this issue.[30] He believes that the rate of male homosexuality in the U.S. has indeed declined—he points to a 10% estimate made by UCLA psychiatrist Judd Marmor in 1980,[31] and compares it with the 2%–3% figure coming from a national random-sample survey published in 1994.[32] Yet this apparent decline in less than two decades is far too precipitous either to be credible in itself or to mesh with the slow decline in family size over the last two centuries. We don't know the rate of male homosexuality early in the 19th century, but it seems unlikely that it was much higher than it is today. Fred Whitam's studies, mentioned in Chapter 1, suggest that the rate of (urban) homosexuality is similar in the Philippines and Guatamala to what it is in the United States, even though family size is smaller in the United States.[33]

Thus, the older-brother effect, if it is as strong as Blanchard and his colleagues maintain, implies that the rate of homosexuality, and particularly the numbers of men who are gay on account of their older brothers, should change significantly across time or between cultures. So far, such changes haven't been well documented. It might be worth investigating this issue by comparing different ethnic groups in the United States. Hispanic-Americans, for example, have more siblings than other groups,[34] and Hispanic-American men (but not women) are slightly more likely than men of other ethnicities to experience same-sex attraction and to identify as gay.[35] It would be interesting to study whether these differences are linked through the older-brother effect.

THE OLDER-BROTHER EFFECT
AND HANDEDNESS

In three studies, Blanchard's group have reported a rather surprising finding: The older-brother effect only applies to right-handed gay men; gay men who are mixed- or left-handed do not have any excess of older brothers.[36] In a very large Internet-based study, Blanchard and Lippa reached a similar conclusion, although their data provided only moderately strong evidence in favor of it, in spite of the large numbers.[37]

The reason this finding is surprising is that, as described in Chapter 5, gay men in general are slightly left-shifted in handedness compared with straight men. Thus, both being non–right-handed and having older brothers are factors that, considered individually, increase the likelihood that a man will be gay. Putting these two factors together in the same man might be expected to increase the likelihood of his being gay even further. But in fact they have no such effect. Instead, the two factors seem to cancel each other out: Non–right-handed men with older brothers are no more likely to be gay than are men who lack either of these predisposing factors. I'll consider why this might be at the end of the chapter.

WHAT CAUSES THE OLDER-BROTHER EFFECT?

Why should having an older brother increase a boy's likelihood of growing up gay? The explanations that most readily come to mind are social ones. These require that there is something about the experience of growing up with an older brother that helps drive a boy down a path toward homosexuality. For example, parents might (consciously or unconsciously) guide their oldest son toward heterosexuality but give later-born sons free rein to be different. Younger sons might become gay as part of a general tendency toward rebelliousness or openness to experience.[38] Younger sons might even become gay because of the opportunity for sexual interactions with an older brother. (Not that the evidence actually supports any of these ideas.)

The findings of a 2006 study by Tony Bogaert appear to have ruled out all social explanations of this kind.[39] Bogaert recruited about 950 gay and straight men (index subjects), many of whom had been brought up in nonstandard families (i.e., they had adopted brothers or step-brothers, or they were adopted themselves). It turned out that only older brothers who had the

same biological mother as the index subjects increased the likelihood that the index subjects would be gay. Adoptive brothers,
step-brothers, and half-brothers who had only the father in
common had no such effect. What's more, the influence of biological older brothers existed even if those brothers never actually lived with the index subjects (because the index subjects
were adopted out of the birth family, for example).

Given the crucial importance of this study to the interpretation of the older-brother effect, it needs to be replicated by other
investigators. As it stands, however, it points strongly away from
social explanations and toward biological ones operating before
birth—specifically, to an influence exerted on male fetuses by
mothers who previously had at least one male child.

Blanchard, Bogaert, and their colleagues have proposed that
it is the mother's immune system that "remembers" the earlier
pregnancy and exerts an influence on subsequent male fetuses.[40]
In their maternal-immunity model, women who are pregnant
with males may be exposed to certain *antigens* (molecules capable
of stimulating an immune response) that are possessed by male
but not by female fetuses. The exposure may happen during the
pregnancy or because of leakage of fetal cells into the mother's
circulation at the time of birth.

The mother may develop *antibodies* against those male-specific
antigens. If so, when her immune system encounters those
antigens again—during a later pregnancy with another male
fetus—her antibodies bind to the antigens and block their
function. If the usual action of those antigens is to guide brain

development in a male-typical direction, the fetus might therefore end up less stereotypically masculine than other boys,
and this might include a tendency toward homosexuality. With
each successive pregnancy with a male fetus, the likelihood
and strength of such an immunological reaction will increase,
heightening the likelihood that the fetus will develop into a
gay man.

The male-specific antigens that are thought to be involved
are *histocompatibility antigens* (antigens that provoke immune reactions when tissue is grafted from one person to another). More
specifically, they are "minor histocompatibility antigens" that
are coded by genes on the Y chromosome, a chromosome that
is possessed only by males. Thus, they are often referred to
simply as *H-Y antigens*. They include a number of different molecules with quite diverse functions. Molecules coded by genes
on other chromosomes could also be involved, so long as those
genes are expressed (active) only in males.

In evaluating this model, it's important to remember that
every fetus, no matter whether it is male or female, is immunologically foreign to its mother. That's because half its genes
come from its father, who is usually unrelated to the mother.
There exists a specific mechanism that causes the mother's
immune system to "tolerate" her fetus rather than reject it, and
this mechanism should, in principle, prevent any response to the
H-Y antigens possessed by a male fetus.

Nevertheless, immunological reactions to fetal antigens can
occur. The best-known example is Rh disease. Rh (or rhesus
factor) is a cell-surface antigen possessed by some individuals.

Rh disease may occur if the mother is Rh-negative and she becomes sensitized to an Rh-positive fetus: The sensitization is usually caused by fetal bleeding into the maternal circulation during the birth process. During a subsequent pregnancy with a second Rh-positive fetus, her anti-Rh antibodies attack the fetus's red blood cells, causing a potentially fatal anemia. Blanchard suggests that something analogous happens to cause the older-brother effect.

The maternal-immunity hypothesis neatly explains why (in most of the Toronto researchers' data, at least) only males exert the effect, and why only males are sensitive to it. It also explains why the older-brother effect becomes stronger with increasing numbers of older brothers, and why older brothers exert an effect even if they don't actually live with their younger brothers.

Another relevant finding has to do with birth weight. Several studies have reported that children with older brothers have a lower birth weight than children with older sisters. According to Blanchard's group, it is only later-born boys, not girls, who are subject to this effect.[41] What's more, they reported that gay men with older brothers had an even lower birth weight than did straight men with older brothers. Blanchard and colleagues interpret these findings in the following way. Usually, the anti-male antibodies generated during the first pregnancy are fairly weak: They reduce the birth weight of later-born boys somewhat, but don't affect their sexuality. Occasionally the anti-male antibodies are stronger, in which case they reduce the weight of later-born boys more, and also predispose them to homosexuality.

Somewhat undermining this interpretation are the findings of a recent and far larger Danish study, which found that older brothers reduce the birth weight of later-born girls as well as boys, although not to the same extent.[42] The Danish researchers do believe in the anti-H-Y mechanism, however: They suppose that the effect on girls results from a kind of innocent-bystander effect that is technically called "determinant spreading."

The Danes made another intriguing observation: If a woman's two sons were fathered by different men, the second son did not show the expected reduction in birth weight. This, the researchers surmise, was because the second son's paternal antigens were different from the first son's, and therefore were not recognized by the mother's antibodies. With a large enough sample, it might be possible to assess whether switching fathers also prevents homosexuality in a woman's later-born sons.

Another study of newborns, published in 1979, may be relevant to the older-brother effect. Eleanor Maccoby (of Stanford University) and colleagues reported that later-born boys have lower testosterone levels at birth than do first-born sons.[43] The effect was particularly marked for sons born soon after their older siblings. This difference is in the expected direction to increase the likelihood of homosexuality in these later-born boys. The researchers did not report that *male* older siblings had any greater influence on the later-born boys' testosterone levels than *female* older siblings, however, which would have been a key finding supportive of the maternal-immunity hypothesis.

Richard Green pointed out a different potential problem with the maternal-immunity hypothesis.[44] In his study of transexuals, he confirmed the older-brother effect, as mentioned earlier: Androphilic male-to-female transexuals had more older brothers than did gynephilic transexuals. But the androphilic transexuals with older brothers were not necessarily the last-born males in their families. What about those males who were born even later? Green identified 22 such men, and found that 21 of them were heterosexual and one was bisexual. None was homosexual. If the maternal-immunity theory was right, Green reasoned, at least some of these males should have become gay men or androphilic transexuals, but they didn't.

Actually, Green's observation is not fatal to the maternal-immunity hypothesis, but it does constrain the hypothesis somewhat. We can think about it this way: We know that most boys with older brothers don't become gay. This could either be because most mothers don't generate anti-male antibodies, or because most boys are unaffected by those antibodies. If the former case were true, Green's observation would be a real problem, because the few mothers who generate the antibodies should exercise the same influence on the sexual orientation of all their later-born sons, and they evidently don't. If, on the other hand, all mothers generate antibodies to male fetuses but most fetuses are unaffected by them, there would be no particular reason to expect large numbers of those late-born sons to follow their gay brothers toward homosexuality, so Green's observation would be not be a show-stopper. Thus, if Green's observation is found to be generally true, it suggests that some intrinsic characteristic of the fetus itself is the crucial factor affecting whether maternal anti-male antibodies will predispose it to homosexuality or not. This characteristic could be a certain gene, for example.

In summary, the maternal-immunity hypothesis offers a credible biological explanation for the older-brother effect, but it lacks direct supportive evidence. It is known that women who have been pregnant with boys have an immunological memory of exposure to H-Y antigens, and that this memory lasts for many years.[45] But do the mothers of later-born gay men differ immunologically from women whose sons are all straight? And do antibodies or cells in the blood of these women actually have the capacity to push a male fetus down the path toward homosexuality? Studies relating to these questions have not been reported.

Let me give an example of the kind of direct experiment that can be done. In 2009, researchers at Johns Hopkins Medical School published a study on the cause of autism.[46] They had formed the hypothesis that autism results from maternal antibodies that interfere with fetal brain development. They therefore purified antibodies from mothers of autistic children and from mothers of nonautistic children, and administered the antibodies to pregnant mice. Later, they tested the behavior of the adult mice that were born of those pregnancies. The mice that had been exposed to the antibodies from the mothers of autistic children showed autistic-like behavior, and their brains showed signs of having been subject to immunological attack, whereas the mice that had been exposed to antibodies from the mothers of healthy children showed no unusual behavior or brain pathology. Thus, the experimental findings supported the researchers' original hypothesis.

I know little about autism and have no idea whether this study represents an authentic breakthrough in our understanding of the condition. My point is simply that no comparable studies have been done to investigate the basis of Blanchard's older-brother effect as a cause of homosexuality. Without such studies, the maternal-immunity hypothesis remains an intriguing but speculative hypothesis.

IS THE OLDER-BROTHER EFFECT ADAPTIVE?

In Chapter 7, I discussed Edward Miller's ideas about how genes predisposing to male homosexuality might be maintained in the population in spite of the negative effect of being gay on a man's reproductive success.[47] Briefly, Miller suggested that there are a number of *feminizing genes* circulating in the population. Each of these genes, acting independently, has no effect on a man's sexual orientation but enhances his attractiveness to women and thus increases his reproductive success. When all the genes happen to be present in the same man, however, they cause him to be gay. The positive reproductive effect of these feminizing genes in heterosexual men outweighs their negative effect in gay men.

In the same paper, Miller proposed an analogous explanation for the older-brother effect. Miller noted that competition
among offspring for resources lowers their reproductive success
and thus reduces the benefit to a female of having multiple offspring in the first place. Diversification among offspring reduces
competition for resources, however, and thus enhances the
mother's reproductive success. (In fact, this may be part of the
reason why sexual reproduction is preferred over asexual reproduction by so many species. Sexual reproduction produces
genetically diverse offspring, whereas asexual reproduction produces genetically identical clones.) Miller suggested that the
maternal-immunity phenomenon has evolved because it slightly
feminizes most of a woman's later-born sons, thus altering their
personalities in ways that make them less likely to compete with
their older brothers. That the process occasionally produces gay
sons is, in this model, simply an accidental by-product—a sort
of "too much of a good thing" phenomenon. The adaptive
value of the mechanism is expressed in the greater total number
of grandchildren a woman may have as a result of it.

Miller's explanation is, of course, speculative, and it does not
have a great deal of supportive evidence. In fact, there is some
evidence to the contrary. Qazi Rahman wanted to know whether
there was a detectable feminizing influence of older brothers on
gendered traits other than sexual orientation—something that
would be predicted both by Miller's explanation and by Blanchard
and Bogaert's basic model for how the older-brother effect works.
In a sample of gay and straight men, he confirmed both the

older-brother effect (more of the gay men had older brothers) and a broad femininity of the gay men (they scored lower on the male-favoring mental rotation test, and they were shifted in the feminine direction on a test of masculinity–femininity). But there was absolutely no tendency for men with older brothers— whether gay or straight—to score in a more feminine direction on these tests than men without older brothers.[48] Bogaert has made a similar observation, although limited to childhood femininity and not cognitive skills such as mental rotation.[49]

This is a puzzling result, and it needs to be confirmed. But taken at face value it suggests that, if the maternal-immunity mechanism is the explanation for the older-brother effect, it does not work by broadly feminizing the brain development of later-born sons. It could work by some other effect that acts more specifically on sexual orientation. If so, there would seem to be alternative developmental pathways leading toward male homosexuality: one leading to a combination of homosexuality and a broader gender-nonconformity, and the other (operative in gay men who have older brothers) that predisposes to homosexuality but not to other gender-nonconformist traits.

Earlier, I mentioned the finding that both being non–right-handed and having older brothers are associated with an increased likelihood of homosexuality, but not if both factors are present in the same person. This also suggests that more than one developmental mechanism may lead to homosexuality in men, and furthermore that they may do so in a mutually antagonistic fashion. Blanchard and his colleagues have proposed a specific model for how this might work.[50] A certain level of testosterone in male fetuses is associated with a heterosexual outcome, they propose, and levels both above and below that level predispose to homosexuality. Non–right-handedness, they suggest, is associated with higher-than-average testosterone levels, whereas having older brothers is associated with lower-than-average levels. Thus, both factors, operating singly, predispose to homosexuality, but when present together, fetal testosterone levels end up in the average range that leads to heterosexuality.

I don't think that this particular mechanism is correct, for two reasons. First, there is little reason to believe that non–right-handedness is associated with high fetal testosterone levels. (If it was, straight men should be left-shifted with respect to straight women, but as discussed in Chapter 5, they don't seem to be. The "sex difference" in handedness is due entirely to the left-shifted handedness of gay men, according to Richard Lippa's data.[51]) Second, if gay men with older brothers had lower-than-usual testosterone levels, they should be shifted toward femininity in other traits, but they are not, according to Rahman's study just described. Still, Blanchard's data do seem to call for more than one developmental pathway leading toward homosexuality. I will take up this issue again in the next chapter.

ELEVEN

Conclusions

Sexual orientation is an aspect of gender that emerges from the prenatal sexual differentiation of the brain. Whether a person ends up gay or straight depends in large part on how this process of biological differentiation goes forward, with the lead actors being genes, sex hormones, and the brain systems that are influenced by them.

The biological perspective on sexual orientation stands in marked contrast to traditional beliefs, which have remained largely silent on the origin of heterosexuality while ascribing homosexuality to family dynamics, learning, early sexual experiences, or free choice. As I discussed in Chapter 2, there is no actual evidence to support any of those ideas, although we cannot completely rule out that they play some role. In my view, differences of opinion on this score often result from differences in what we mean by sexual orientation. Biological factors give us a sexual orientation in the sense of a disposition or capacity to experience sexual attraction to one sex or the other, or to both. Other factors influence what we do with those feelings.

Two theories that invoke environmental factors in the development of sexual orientation merit special consideration because they intersect with biology in interesting ways. Günter Dörner's prenatal stress theory (Chapter 6) emerged from research in rats: Prenatal stress has been reported to alter the timing of the prenatal testosterone surge in male rat fetuses, leading to "demasculinization" of the brain and to atypical sexual behavior in adulthood. These animal studies offer a theoretical background for investigating the effect of prenatal stress in humans. Yet, carefully controlled studies have not been able to document any such effect in men. Apparently, human mothers and human fetuses are resistant to this kind of stress effect.

The other interesting idea is Daryl Bem's proposal that genes predispose to childhood gender-nonconformity, and that interactions with peers are what propel the gender-nonconformist child toward homosexuality in adulthood. There is no evidence, however, that modifying peer interactions affects the likelihood that a gender-nonconformist child will grow up gay. Again, then, Bem's "exotic becomes erotic" theory lacks empirical support.

SEXUAL ORIENTATION IS LINKED TO OTHER GENDERED TRAITS

If one idea does have empirical support, it is that homosexuality is part of a package of gender-atypical traits. Some characteristics of the bodies and minds of gay men are shifted in a female direction compared with straight men, and some characteristics of the bodies and minds of lesbians and bisexual women are shifted in a male direction compared with straight women.

It's important to stress that these shifts are (for the most part) only shifts and not complete gender reversals, and they don't affect *every* gendered trait. Gay men don't have women's bodies, otherwise they would *be* women. Nor do they have women's minds, otherwise they would be transexuals. Similarly, lesbians don't have the bodies or minds of men. What is impressive is not so much the size of these gender shifts but their number and variety. Here is a quick synopsis of some of the reported findings that I have described earlier in this book:

- *The body.* The ratio of limb length to trunk length—a sexually differentiated trait—is shifted in a sex-atypical direction in both gay men and lesbians. Digit-length ratios are gender-shifted in lesbian and bisexual women, and possibly in gay men too. Some lesbians are sex-atypical in their waist-to-hip ratios. Both gay men and lesbians are gender-shifted in aspects of body function that are recognized by "gaydar," including gait and voice quality.

- *The brain.* Gay men are gender-shifted in the size of INAH3, the sexually dimorphic cell group in a region of the hypothalamus concerned with male-typical sexual behavior. They are also gender-shifted in terms of the relative sizes of the left and right cerebral hemispheres. Both gay men and lesbians are gender-shifted in their brain responses to compounds thought to be sex pheromones and in the functional connectivity of their amygdalas. Lesbians and bisexual women are gender-shifted in their auditory physiology, both at the level of the cochlea and in their central auditory pathways.
- *Childhood characteristics.* Pre-gay children are gender-nonconformist in a variety of traits including physical aggressiveness, engagement in rough-and-tumble play and sports, preference for the company of same- or opposite-sex peers, interests, and the unconscious behaviors that allow raters to judge them as gender-nonconformist from home videos.
- *Cognitive traits.* Gay men and lesbians are gender-shifted in a variety of male-favoring visuospatial traits such as mental rotation, targeting, and navigation, as well as female-favoring tasks such as verbal fluency (both sexes) and object location memory (gay men only).
- *Personality.* Gay men consider themselves less masculine, and lesbians consider themselves less feminine than do straight men and women. Both gay men and lesbians have gender-shifted occupational preferences. Gender shifts have also been reported in physical aggressiveness, instrumentality, empathy, expressiveness, and aesthetic/technological interests.

Gay people remain gender-*typical* in a variety of traits, especially those related to sexuality, such as their interest in casual sex. With regard to gay men, a very few shifts have been reported that seem to be in the opposite direction of those just described, with gay men shifted in a "hypermasculine" direction. These traits are penis size (gay men's penises reported to be larger than straight men's, based on a single study), auditory evoked potentials (again, a single study), and handedness. Considering a large penis to be a hypermasculine trait may be somewhat misleading, however: That idea depends on the assumption that a woman's clitoris is developmentally equivalent to a small penis, which is not really true. (Most of the tissue that develops into the shaft of the male penis forms the labia minora, not the clitoris, in women.) And believing that gay men's left-shifted handedness is a "hypermasculine" trait depends on the assumption that men in general are left-shifted with respect to women but, as mentioned in Chapter 5, the excess left-handedness in men may be contributed by gay men themselves. Thus, the evidence for hypermasculine traits in gay men (or hyperfeminine traits in lesbians) is very thin.

A COMMON ORIGIN
FOR GENDER-SHIFTED TRAITS?

To understand why gay people are gender-shifted in so many and such diverse traits besides their sexual orientation, it makes sense to look to the processes that are responsible for differences between men and women in general. Chief among these is the hormonally mediated sexual differentiation of the body and brain.

In humans, testosterone is the major hormone responsible for sexual differentiation during early development. Before focusing on this hormone, however, it's worth recalling that other factors play contributory roles, as discussed in Chapter 3. The testicular *antimüllerian hormone* (AMH) prevents development of the female reproductive tract in males, and (in mice) is responsible for at least one sex difference in behavior—the greater degree of exploratory behavior shown by males. Another factor is the internal chromosomal sex of brain cells (XX or XY): This contributes to the sex difference in aggressive behavior (in mice, again). It is quite possible that future research will uncover more ways in which these and other "minor" factors influence the sexual differentiation of the brain, perhaps including brain systems responsible for sexual feeling and behaviors.

The central role of testosterone, however, has been amply demonstrated in nonhuman animals by experiments in which this hormone has been administered or its action blocked, in fetuses or newborn animals. When present at high levels (during early and mid-pregnancy in humans), it drives development in a male direction; when present at low levels during that same time span, it permits development to proceed in a female direction. Although testosterone can be converted into estrogen within the human brain by the aromatase enzyme, suggesting some role for estrogen in male brain development that remains to be identified, observations on males who are insensitive to estrogen or who lack the aromatase enzyme have not pin-pointed any effects of estrogen on male-typical psychosexual development or gender identity.

To judge from the animal experiments described in Chapter 3, testosterone exerts organizing effects on brain systems that contribute to a wide variety of gendered traits, including sexual behaviors and sexual partner preference. The same seems to be true in humans, according to observations on persons with congenital adrenal hyperplasia (CAH) and other conditions that affect fetal androgen levels or sensitivity to androgens (Chapter 6).

Thus, the most parsimonious biological explanation for the development of sexual orientation is this: If testosterone levels during a critical prenatal period are high, the brain is organized in such a way that the person is predisposed to become typically masculine in a variety of gendered traits, including sexual attraction to females. If testosterone levels are low during that same period, the brain is organized in such a way that the person is predisposed to become typically feminine in gendered traits, including sexual attraction to males. Bisexuality might result from intermediate levels of testosterone, although there is little direct evidence bearing on this.

A closely related alternative hypothesis is that there is no difference between pre-gay and pre-straight fetuses in the actual circulating levels of testosterone, but that their brains respond to testosterone in different ways, due to differences in the receptors or other molecules that are involved in translating the hormonal signal into actual neuronal architecture. Thus, the same level of testosterone might drive brain development strongly in a male direction in a "pre-straight" male fetus but less so in a "pre-gay" male fetus, and vice-versa for female fetuses.

We do not have definitive information that would allow us to choose between these two models. Because they are so closely related, I lump them together into a "prenatal hormonal" model for the development of sexual orientation. However, some of the gendered traits associated with sexual orientation (such as limb-to-trunk ratios) involve the body rather than the brain. Thus, if we wish to identify a single "decision point" in the development of sexual orientation, we should look to elements that are common to the development of the body and the brain, not to a specifically brain-related element. Actual testosterone levels, or the receptor mechanisms that respond to them, seem better candidates in that regard than, say, differences in brain-specific growth factors, neurotransmitter mechanisms, or the like.

Probably most sex researchers believe at this point that a prenatal hormonal mechanism of this kind is operative. Otherwise, it is too difficult to explain the association of sexual orientation with all the other gendered traits that I've listed. However, there remains considerable uncertainty about the strength of the effect—whether, in other words, these prenatal hormonal factors decide whether a person will experience sexual attraction to males or females, or whether they rather provide a predisposition that can be modified by other factors, such as parenting and life experiences. Because the evidence for these other factors seems so weak, I am inclined to place most of the developmental control in the hands of prenatal hormones. However, I do acknowledge that certain observations—such as the fact that CAH women are only partially shifted in the direction of homosexuality—could be interpreted to mean that other factors play important roles.

THE ROLE OF GENES

The prenatal hormone theory is not an ultimate explanation of how people become straight or gay, because it leaves unexplained how hormone levels might come to differ between two fetuses of the same sex. There are many ways in which this could happen, but one likely possibility is that genes help set these levels.

The family and twin studies discussed in Chapter 7 provide evidence that genetic differences between individuals account for a substantial fraction of the differences in sexual orientation that are observed in the population. Estimates of the heritability of homosexuality have been quite variable but range around 30%–50% for both sexes, which is similar to heritability estimates for many other psychological traits.[1]

The twin studies, especially the Finnish study discussed in Chapter 7, suggest that a common set of genes predisposes both to gender-nonconformist characteristics in childhood and to homosexuality in adulthood.[2] If so, it is likely that these genes work through the hormonal pathway, because childhood gendered characteristics seem to be strongly influenced by prenatal hormones (Chapters 4 and 6).

Working on this assumption, Dean Hamer and others looked for differences in the genes that code for two key hormone-related molecules, the androgen receptor and aromatase, but drew a blank (see Chapter 7). However, a very large number of genes are involved one way or another in the interaction between sex hormones and their target tissues. These include genes for enzymes in the synthesis and metabolism of the hormones; genes for carrier proteins, several kinds of receptors, co-activators, and co-repressors; and the many genes whose activity is regulated by sex hormones. And, given the evidence for the involvement of the neurotransmitter γ-aminobutyric acid (GABA) in the sexual differentiation of the hypothalamus,[3] this introduces another collection of genes—those involved in GABA transmission—as possible contributors to the heritability of sexual orientation. Thus, there is every reason to test for the involvement of other candidate genes, especially if the genome-wide scans continue to yield equivocal results.

In general, few major genes have been identified in the field of behavioral genetics; most heritable psychological traits seem to be influenced by multiple genes, each of modest effect. This could well be true for sexual orientation too. If so, different individuals might carry different complements of "gay genes" and thus exhibit different "kinds" of homosexuality. For example, one gay person might carry genes that influence limb-trunk length in addition to sexual orientation, another person might only have psychological gender-shifted traits and not bodily ones, and yet another person might be gay but lack other gender-shifted traits altogether.

DOES THE OLDER-BROTHER EFFECT WORK THROUGH PRENATAL HORMONES?

In the previous chapter, I discussed the work of Blanchard, Bogaert, and their colleagues, who showed that having older brothers increases the chances that a man will be gay. Those authors have presented evidence that the older-brother effect is biological rather than social in nature. They propose that it involves immunization of the mother against male-specific antigens during an initial pregnancy with a male fetus, and an effect of this immunization on the development of a later male fetus.

The question is, does this immunological process work by lowering testosterone levels in the later male fetuses? Blanchard and his colleagues suggest that it does.[4] I would be happy to believe that, except for the observation by Rahman that older brothers have no effect on childhood gender characteristics or mental rotation.[5] This issue merits further research, but at this point it seems that the older-brother effect does not cause the broad gender shift that would be expected if it lowered fetal testosterone levels. It may therefore work through some other mechanism involving a more specific effect on the brain circuitry that is responsible for sexual orientation.

IS THERE A RANDOM BIOLOGICAL INFLUENCE?

In Chapter 3, I mentioned the idea that random biological processes can influence psychosexual development. The example I cited was the "uterine proximity effect" in rodents: Female fetuses that happen to be located next to males pick up testosterone from those males and are partially masculinized in their sexual behavior as a result. Actually, many developmental processes are "probabilistic" or "stochastic" in nature, meaning that the results are not rigidly specified but are subject to random variability or "noise."

Perhaps the strongest clue that probabilistic processes influence sexual orientation comes from monozygotic twins. If one such twin is gay, there are roughly even odds that the co-twin will be gay or straight. How can this be the case if the twins possess the same genome, developed in the same uterus at the same time, and experienced very similar rearing conditions? If one believes that early sexual experiences determine sexual orientation, these experiences might differ between the twins. One twin might have been sexually molested and the other not, for example. However, the evidence speaks against an influence of molestation or sexual experiences in general on sexual orientation, as discussed in Chapter 2.

Lynn Hall (of New York University School of Medicine) and Craig Love (of Brown University) performed a study that may throw light on this issue.[6] They examined the finger-length ratios (2D:4D) of seven pairs of monozygotic female twins in which each pair was discordant for sexual orientation: one woman in each pair was lesbian, the other was straight. They found that, in each pair, the 2D:4D ratio of the lesbian twin was lower (i.e., male-shifted) in comparison with the straight twin. In another study, Hall identified another consistent anatomical difference between discordant female twin pairs—a lower total number of ridges in their fingerprints.[7] In both studies, pairs of *concordant* twins (both lesbian) showed no differences of this kind.

Given the small numbers of subjects, these studies need to be replicated. Nevertheless, they suggest that, when female monozygotic twins are discordant for sexual orientation, the lesbian twin has experienced higher levels of testosterone prenatally than her heterosexual sister. In other words, the same biological factor (prenatal testosterone levels) appears to guide the development of sexual orientation in discordant twins as it does in gay and straight people generally, but in the case of these twins there is no ultimate cause, such as genetic differences. Rather, it is as if a biological coin has been tossed. Quite likely, such coin-tossing occurs during the development of singletons too. To the extent that this may be the case, we should not expect to identify a specific cause behind every individual's sexual orientation, beyond a general attribution to the prenatal hormonal mechanisms that I've been discussing.

HOW DOES SEXUAL ORIENTATION
BECOME CATEGORICAL?

Most gendered traits are dimensional. An individual's verbal
fluency score, for example, can lie anywhere along a broad spectrum, although women tend to outscore men. Sexual orientation, on the other hand, is categorical, in men at least: There is
a bimodal (two-peaked) distribution of sexual orientations,
with a large cluster of men who are entirely or mostly straight,
a smaller cluster of men who are entirely or mostly gay, and few
men who experience roughly equal attraction to the two sexes.
Although the distribution of women's sexual orientations is not
obviously bimodal, nevertheless there are many women who say
that they are exclusively attracted to one sex or the other.

One could imagine that the categorical nature of male sexual
orientation results from an entirely deterministic process of
development. For example, there might be a gay gene and a
straight gene, and possession of one or the other drives an individual to a sexual orientation at one or other end of the Kinsey
scale. That would be a delightfully simple model, but it doesn't
seem very likely to be correct, at least for the population as a
whole. For one thing, the intermediate factors, such as prenatal
testosterone levels, probably vary continuously. There's no evidence for two sets of male fetuses with completely distinct,
non-overlapping testosterone levels. Also, if male sexual orientation were rigidly determined in this way, we would expect

much tighter correlations with other gendered traits than are actually observed.

It is more likely that some developmental process takes a broad spread of individual trajectories and forces them into just two channels, one leading to heterosexuality and one leading to homosexuality. For example, male fetuses whose prenatal testosterone levels are above some threshold value are steered down the "straight" channel, and those whose testosterone levels are below that threshold are steered down the "gay" channel. Thus, two fetuses whose testosterone levels are quite similar (but on different sides of the threshold) may end up with radically different sexual orientations.

This model implies that something must be keeping the channels separate—a developmental wall or ridge, if you like. What could that correspond to in biological terms? One possibility is that it involves mutual inhibition between neural centers or circuits responsible for sexual attraction to males and to females. Mutual (reciprocal) inhibition produces an unstable, winner-take-all situation and thus leads to a black-or-white outcome, even when the input signals are every shade of gray. If a mutual inhibitory mechanism is at work, it seems to be less strongly active in females than in males. Some observations in rats suggest that there might indeed be a sex difference of this kind, because inhibitory processes in several sex-related regions of the hypothalamus are stronger in male rats than in females.[8]

Mutual inhibition might operate only during development, so as to set up a single dominant channel in any particular individual, while the other channel simply withers away and ceases to exist. This could be part of the reason why organizational effects of hormones are limited to a certain period of development.

Alternatively, the mutual inhibition might continue to operate—perhaps in an attenuated fashion—throughout life. This latter idea is more compatible with the observation that, under certain circumstances, sexual partner preference can change. In Chapter 8, I mentioned two examples of this from animal studies: In adult female mice, destruction of the vomeronasal organ uncovers an entire suite of male-typical sexual behaviors, including mounting of females, that the animals did not previously show,[9] and in adult male ferrets and rats, destruction of the medial preoptic area (including SND-POA) changes their partner preference from female to male.[10]

Although sexual orientation usually remains stable in humans, I have mentioned that homosexual feelings can sometimes emerge spontaneously in previously heterosexual women, as well as in previously heterosexual men who undergo hormone treatments or castration, or who experience brain damage. Thus, there are suggestions that brain circuitry capable of mediating sexual attraction to the nonpreferred sex does exist in adult animals and humans, but is functionally disabled by inhibition from brain centers concerned with attraction to the preferred sex.

If such a mutual inhibitory loop does operate, its neuronal basis remains to be identified. Even so, it is tempting to speculate that INAH3 (and SDN-POA in rats) is one element of the loop, namely the source of inhibition exerted by the male-typical channel on the female-typical channel. That's because SDN-POA is rich in cells that are sensitive to testosterone and that use the inhibitory transmitter GABA.[11] The observation that damage to this region in male rats and ferrets changes the animals' partner preference, as mentioned earlier, is also consistent with the idea. Still, there are other brain regions that are also candidates to play this role: one is the medial portion of the amygdala, which (in rodents) helps create a preference for opposite-sex partners[12] and also contains many neurons that use GABA as a transmitter.[13]

Where the other elements of this hypothetical control system are located is unknown, but several other regions of the hypothalamus are actively involved in the regulation of male and female sexuality; these include regions in the medial preoptic area near INAH3, as well as a region further back in the hypothalamus known as the ventromedial nucleus.

DIVERSITY AMONG GAY PEOPLE

Throughout much of this book, I have been content to break down the population into two classes, "gay" and "straight," with an occasional nod to "bisexual." That's because, for the most part, subjects have been recruited into research studies on the basis of simple questions that lead to this kind of grouping. Yet, there is also evidence for considerable diversity *within* the categories of "gay male" and "lesbian." Here are some of the main lines of evidence:

- Gay people have, to a varying extent, used terminology like "butch/femme" and "top/bottom" to designate types of lesbians and gay men who differ in gendered traits or in their preferred sexual behaviors.

- In many of the quantitative studies reviewed in this book, the scores of gay men and lesbians are not merely gender-shifted with respect to their straight counterparts, but are also more spread out, as if gay men and lesbians do not form monolithic blocs to the same extent that straight men or straight women do.

- Pre-gay boys who are markedly feminine are more likely to be "bottoms" in adulthood than are more conventionally gendered boys. Pre-gay girls who are markedly masculine are more likely to be "butch" in adulthood.

- When two brothers are gay, they are likely to share a similar childhood history of femininity or more conventional masculinity, as if they both belong to the same "type" of gay men. If the brothers are both gay because they have inherited the same "gay genes," then there should be different kinds of gay genes that lead to different kinds of gay people.

- Butch and femme lesbians have been reported to differ in terms of two anatomical measures—2D:4D ratios and waist–hip ratios—and perhaps in terms of testosterone levels in adulthood.

Although these findings hint at the existence of at least two biological pathways that can lead to homosexuality—one accompanied by a broader gender-nonconformity and one less so—it's important to stress that the data in this area are very limited. It has not been demonstrated that there is a specific class of gay people who are conventionally gendered on all the various tests and measurements that I've discussed in this book, and another class who are gender-shifted on all of them. It could equally be that *all* gay people have *some* gender-atypical traits, but few have the entire package. In fact, some of the data, such as Rahman's findings on verbal fluency plotted in Figure 5.2, indicate a gender-shift so complete that it must affect the great majority of gay people. Gender-nonconformity, whether measured in cognitive or personality dimensions, is not the province of some atypical minority of lesbians and gay men.

There is one study that points to a special kind of diversity among *straight* people. This is the taxometric analysis by Steven Gangestad and colleagues (Chapter 1), which concluded that a significant minority of straight people share a predisposing factor with gay people of the same sex. Given the way that the analysis was set up, it seems likely that this predisposing factor is one that predicts gender-nonconformity in childhood and/or in adulthood. Perhaps this relates to Edward Miller's hypothesis, discussed in Chapter 7, that male homosexuality results from inheriting a set of several "feminizing" genes. If that hypothesis is correct, the straight men who share a predisposing factor with gay men might be those who have inherited some of those feminizing genes, but not enough of them to make them gay.

CHANGES IN THE PREVALENCE AND NATURE OF HOMOSEXUALITY

People often assume that, if the prevalence or nature of a trait like homosexuality varies across cultures, or across history in the same culture, then that trait must be a cultural phenomenon. Biological factors are assumed to be a fixed attribute of human populations that could not contribute to such diversity in space or time. In reality, however, biological factors may be closely involved.

I have already discussed one such example in Chapter 10, with respect to the older-brother effect. The demographic transition has led to a dramatic reduction in family size over the last two centuries, such that men with older brothers—the majority of all men in the early 19th century—are an endangered species today. Thus, the number of gay men who owe their homosexuality to the older-brother effect should have declined markedly, at least in those countries that have undergone the demographic transition.

There is another possible effect of the demographic transition on homosexuality. I discussed in Chapter 7 the "fertile female" hypothesis, which states that genes predisposing to male homosexuality increase the fecundity (number of children) of gay men's female relatives, and this increase in female fecundity is what keeps gay genes in the population. Yet, before the demographic transition, women were pregnant so often that they didn't have a great deal of spare reproductive capacity, and this would have limited the positive effect of "gay genes" on their fecundity. Now the situation is quite different—most women could have half a dozen more children than they actually give birth to, and those extra children would almost certainly survive, so there is a great deal of room for genes to increase their reproductive success. Thus, to the extent that the fertile female hypothesis is correct, genes for male homosexuality should have become more prevalent in the population over the last two centuries. And, if it should be the case that the older-brother effect and the "fertile female" genes predispose to different *kinds* of male homosexuality (accompanied by different levels of gender-nonconformity, for example), then the overall "quality" of male homosexuality might have changed perceptibly over the past two centuries—all thanks to an interaction between a cultural process, the demographic transition, with human biology.

Social and biological changes over an even longer term may have influenced the prevalence of homosexuality. Economic historians such as Oded Galor (of Brown University) and Gregory Clark (of the University of California, Davis) have argued that human nature changed over the course of the long "Malthusian era" between the agrarian revolution (which took place about 10,000 years ago) and the Industrial Revolution (which started in the 18th century). During this time, social factors promoted the reproductive success of people who were less violence-prone and more disposed to care for their children.[14] The spread of "feminizing" genes could well be the mechanism that accomplished this change. If Edward Miller's theory of gay genes, discussed in Chapter 7, is correct, the increasing prevalence of these genes would in turn have increased the prevalence of male homosexuality.

SEXUAL ORIENTATION AND GENDER: THE SOCIAL FALLOUT

I have discussed the social implications of a biological perspective on sexual orientation in an earlier book,[15] and I will not attempt another review of this topic here. There is one facet of the science that deserves comment from a social perspective, however. This is the idea that sexual orientation is linked with a broader collection of gendered traits. Does this concept stigmatize gay people, by reinforcing stereotypes of "mannish" lesbians and "queeny" gay men?

Children who are gender-nonconformist do tend to suffer for it, not merely during childhood itself,[16] but also years later. According to Katarina Alanko and her colleagues, when such children reach adulthood they are at increased risk of psychiatric problems, such as anxiety and depression, and this is true for both boys and girls and regardless of whether they end up gay or straight.[17] Gender-nonconformity in adulthood can also lead to stigmatization and resulting psychological distress, but gay men suffer more distress than do lesbians, according to a study by Michael Bailey's group[18]—perhaps because any masculine traits that lesbian or bisexual women may exhibit are more socially acceptable or advantageous than feminine traits in gay men.

Whether gender-nonconformist children experience psychological problems is strongly affected by how they are treated. When parents have cold or controlling attitudes toward these children, the chances of psychological distress in adulthood are greatly increased, but if a warm parent–child relationship is established, the likelihood of such distress in adulthood is reduced.[19] No doubt the same is true for relationships with siblings, peers, teachers, and society in general.

Some critics, such as social psychologist Peter Hegarty of the University of Surrey in England, have taken the position that research into the relationship between gender-nonconformity (especially during childhood) and homosexuality tends to "medicalize" gay people, as well as gender-nonconformist children, and thus perhaps increases their risk of suffering psychological problems.[20] The fact that "gender identity disorder of childhood" is a diagnosable medical condition may worsen the situation by labeling these children as having a disorder.

Still, there may be practical advantages to keeping the diagnosis. This is how Richard Pillard put it to me some years ago: "If these same kids grew up in a culture that had a place for them, they would not be in conflict or distress, and no diagnosis would be relevant. That said, these children are still suffering and can benefit from sensitive treatment. And having a diagnosis allows the psychiatrist to get paid."

Kenneth Zucker, who treats many gender-dysphoric children, takes a more interventionist position. He believes that if such children are caught early enough, they can and should be steered toward an acceptance of their birth sex, no matter how strong their desire to change it. This point of view is controversial.[21]

There have always been gay men who resent any attempt to identify a connection between male homosexuality and gender-nonconformist traits. Benedict Friedländer, co-founder of a German gay-rights organization in the early years of the 20th century, asserted that Magnus Hirschfeld's biological approach reduced homosexuality to a mental disorder. He wrote:

> As long as the love for a male being is presented as a specific and exclusively feminine characteristic . . . there remains an unavoidable image of a partial hermaphrodite, that is, a kind of psychic malformation. Here too one cannot claim respect, but only at most beg for pity and at best tolerance.[22]

Here's a more recent example. In 2009, Sergio Garcia, an 18-year-old gay male high-school senior at Fairfax High School in Los Angeles, ran successfully for prom queen against several female candidates.[23] His action elicited this comment from gay playwright Vincent James Arcuri:

> [B]ecause Garcia is gay, that places him in the feminine role? Are we expected to accept and align "gay" with "girl"? . . . [C]rowning this young man as the prom "queen" only conveys the wrong

message, one that accepts and perpetuates an archaic stereotype of homosexuality and reinforces an inaccurate portrayal of gay men as feminine, girlie caricatures.[24]

Gay men may adopt this point of view because they themselves are not particularly feminine and thus see no truth behind the stereotype, or because they are all *too* feminine, having struggled all their life to present a more masculine image to the world. Arcuri, for example, underwent speech therapy to modify his voice, which he says transitioned at puberty from that of a "girl" to that of a "raging homosexual."[25] Femiphobia—the dislike or fear of femininity in a man—is a potent force in our society, and when internalized by gay men it may be more destructive even than homophobia.[26]

In my opinion, the finding that gay and straight people tend to differ in a wide variety of sex-differentiated traits offers a valuable insight into the origins of sexual orientation, and thus helps us understand this important facet of human diversity. No approach that ignores this reality is going to advance our understanding.

What's more, the kaleidoscopic blend of gender-variant and gender-typical traits that characterizes gay people is exactly what enables us to make our own unique contributions to society. It's the reason that we should be valued, celebrated, and welcomed into society rather than merely being tolerated. The aim should be to foster acceptance of gay people as we are, in all our rich diversity, and not to seek acceptance by shoe-horning ourselves into conformity with the straight majority.

GLOSSARY

2D:4D ratio The length of the index finger divided by the length of the ring finger.

activational effect The functional activation during postnatal life of a brain system whose basic organization has been established earlier in development.

age-stratified relationship A sexual relationship characterized by a substantial age difference between the partners.

amygdala A group of nuclei in the temporal lobe of the brain, involved in the processing of emotion, sexuality, and social functions.

androgen insensitivity syndrome (AIS) A congenital condition in which the androgen receptor is nonfunctional, causing affected XY fetuses to develop with the outward appearance of females.

androgens Sex hormones, such as testosterone, that tend to drive development in a male direction.

androphilic Sexually attracted to men.

anterior commissure A small band of fibers that interconnects the temporal lobes of the left and right cerebral hemispheres. It crosses the midline in the region of the anterior hypothalamus.

antibody A molecular components of the immune system that recognizes and binds to a specific antigen.

antigen A substance that is capable of triggering an immune response.

antimüllerian hormone (AMH) A hormone secreted by the developing testes that suppresses development of the female reproductive tract.

aromatase An enzyme that converts testosterone to estrogen.

auditory evoked potentials Electrical signals that may be recorded from the scalp, and that reflect the activity of auditory brain systems in response to a sound.

autosome A chromosome other than a sex chromosome.

AVPV A nucleus in the preoptic area of the hypothalamus that is larger in females than in males; it helps regulate the reproductive cycle, at least in rodents.

bisexual Sexually attracted to persons of either sex.

bottom In gay slang, a man who prefers to take the receptive role in anal sex.

butch Masculine or dominant, usually in reference to a lesbian.

coactivator An intracellular molecule that enhances the action of a hormone.

cochlea The auditory sense organ in the inner ear.

cognitive Of information-processing aspects of the mind, such as perception; as distinct from emotions or personality.

concordance rate The probability that both members of a twin pair will exhibit some trait, given that one member does.

congenital adrenal hyperplasia (CAH) A genetic condition in which excess androgens are secreted by the adrenal gland during prenatal development.

consistent-sided (CS) asymmetry An anatomical asymmetry that is in the same direction from person to person. Also called *directional asymmetry*.

conversion therapy Psychological treatment intended to change a person's sexual orientation.

co-repressor An intracellular molecule that inhibits the action of a hormone.

corpus callosum The largest band of white matter that interconnects the left and right cerebral hemispheres.

critical period A period during which the development of a certain brain system is particularly sensitive to the influence of hormones or other factors.

crossing over The exchange of genetic material between chromosomes during development of a sperm or ovum.

demographic transition The marked decrease in the number of offspring born to the average woman that has accompanied industrialization and other social changes in many countries.

developmental instability Any of a range of factors that can impair development in such a way as to increase the amount of random-direction asymmetry.

dichotic listening A test of brain lateralization for speech that involves the simultaneous presentation of different syllables or words to the two ears.

dimensional Forming a continuous distribution; opposite of categorical.

discordant Of twins, not sharing a trait such as homosexuality.

dizygotic Of twins, arising from two different fertilized ova.

dopamine A neurotransmitter with a variety of functions within the brain; it is particularly associated with motivation and reward.

egalitarian relationship A homosexual relationship between two persons who are similar in age and gender characteristics.

emotional jealousy Fear that one's partner is emotionally involved with a third party.

ethology The study of animal behavior.

eye-blink auditory startle response A reflex blinking of the eyes in response to an unexpected sound.

fa'afafine A homosexual man in Samoa, who may or may not be transgendered.

feminizing genes Hypothetical genes that promote the development of feminine characteristics in males.

femme Feminine, usually in reference to a lesbian.

flehmen response In some mammals, a curling of the upper lip that facilitates detection of pheromomes by the vomeronasal organ.

frequency In audition, the number of sinusoidal pressure oscillations per second, corresponding roughly to perceived pitch.

fruitless (fru) A gene in fruit flies that regulates the development of brain regions responsible for sexual behavior.

fundamental frequency The lowest periodic component in a complex sound, such as a voice; it is the main contributor to the perceived pitch of the voice.

γ-amino-butyric acid (GABA) A neurotransmitter that has an inhibitory action in adults but may be excitatory during development.

gay Homosexual.

gaydar The ability to identify a person as gay on the basis of his or her appearance or unconscious behaviors.

gender The collection of psychological traits that differ, to a greater or lesser extent, between the sexes.

gender dysphoria Severe dissatisfaction with one's biological sex.

gendered Differing between the sexes, usually in reference to mental or behavioral traits.

gender-stratified relationship A homosexual relationship characterized by a marked difference in gender characteristics between the partners.

gene A stretch of DNA that is expressed as a functional unit; a unit of inheritance.

genome An individual's entire genetic endowment.

glutamate A common excitatory neurotransmitter in the brain.

gray matter Brain tissue containing neurons and synapses, as contrasted with white matter.

growth factor A molecule that signals certain target cells to increase their rate of growth.

gynephilic Sexually attracted to women.

heritability The fraction of the variability in a trait within a population that is attributable to genetic differences between individuals.

heterosexual Sexually attracted to persons of the other sex.

heterozygous state The state in which an individual has inherited different versions of a particular gene from his or her two parents.

histocompatibility antigens Antigens that trigger rejection of tissue grafted from one individual to another.

homosexual Sexually attracted to persons of one's own sex; gay.

homozygous state The state in which the same version of a gene has been inherited from both parents and therefore is present on two homologous chromosomes.

hormone A substance that is secreted by a gland into the bloodstream and that influences the activity or development of tissues elsewhere in the body.

hwame In Mohave culture, a girl who rejects the female role.

H-Y antigens Histocompatibility antigens coded by genes on the Y chromosome, and therefore possessed only by males.

hypothalamus A small region at the base of the brain on either side of the third ventricle; it contains cell groups concerned with sexuality and other basic functions.

INAH3 (3rd interstitial nucleus of the anterior hypothalamus) A cell group in the hypothalamus that differs in size between men and women and between gay and straight men.

index subject A person initially recruited into a study, as opposed to a person drawn into the study later because of a relationship to an index subject.

instrumentality A collection of traits, including assertiveness, competitiveness, aggressiveness, and independence, that tend to be more developed in men than in women.

isthmus A sector of the corpus callosum that interconnects parts of the parietal and temporal lobes in the left and right cerebral hemispheres.

Kinsey scale A seven-point scale of sexual orientation ranging from 0 (exclusively heterosexual) to 6 (exclusively homosexual), devised by Alfred Kinsey.

lesbian Homosexual, gay (of women only); a homosexual woman.

linkage study A method of locating genes of interest on the basis of their proximity to other genetic markers whose location is already known.

lordosis reflex A sexual behavior typically shown by female rodents in response to being mounted; the animal raises its rump to allow for penetration.

mental rotation The ability to tell whether two 2-dimensional drawings represent the same 3-dimensional object viewed from different angles.

monozygotic Of twins, arising from a single fertilized ovum (and thus genetically identical or near-identical).

NELL2 A growth factor involved in the development of the hypothalamus.

nucleus In neuroanatomy, a consistently recognizable cluster of neurons in the brain.

oedipal homosexuality In psychoanalytic theory, homosexuality resulting from a failure to emerge from the oedipal phase of psychosexual development.

oedipal phase In psychoanalytic theory, a period during infancy when a boy is sexually fixated on his mother.

older-brother effect The increased probability of homosexuality in men who have one or more older brothers.

organizational effect An effect of a hormone on the developing brain that influences behavior in later life.

oSDN The sexually dimorphic nucleus in the medial preoptic area of the hypothalamus of sheep.

oto-acoustic emission (OAE) A weak sound produced by the cochlea; it may be spontaneous (SOAE) or it may be evoked by clicks (CEOAE).

paraphilia An unusual sexual interest or behavior that is sufficiently distressing or harmful to be considered a mental disorder.

perirhinal cortex An area of cerebral cortex within the temporal lobe that is involved in the encoding of memory, spatial information, and olfaction.

pre-gay children Children who become gay adults.

pre-oedipal homosexuality In psychoanalytic theory, homosexuality that results from a failure to enter the oedipal phase.

pre-pulse inhibition Reduction in the strength of the eye-blink auditory startle response when the startling sound is preceded by a fainter sound.

programmed cell death The "planned" death of a cell or class of cells as the end-product of an organized sequence of gene expression.

random-sided (RS) asymmetry An anatomical asymmetry whose direction is unpredictable from person to person. Also called *fluctuating asymmetry*.

receptor A molecule or molecular assembly that responds to the presence of a hormone or neurotransmitter.

recessive gene A version of a gene that has little or no apparent effect when present as a single copy.

reproductive success The total number of an individual's offspring that survive to maturity.

sex hormone A hormone that helps regulate sexual function or development. Several important sex hormones are steroids.

sex hormone binding globulin (SHBG) A protein in the blood that acts as a carrier for steroid sex hormones.

sex pheromone A substance produced or released by one individual that affects the sexual feelings or behavior of another individual of the same species.

sex-biased Differing at least to a small degree between the sexes.

sexual jealousy Fear that one's partner is physically involved with a third party.

sexually antagonistic model A model explaining the persistence of a gene, in which a negative effect on the reproductive success of one sex is counterbalanced by a positive effect on the reproductive success of the other sex.

sexually dimorphic Differing in structure between males and females.

sexually dimorphic nucleus of the preoptic area (SDN-POA) A cluster of neurons in the medial preoptic area of the hypothalamus that is typically larger in males than in females.

shared environment Any nongenetic influences that promote a trait in both members of a twin pair.

sickle cell anemia A form of anemia caused by the inheritance of two copies of an abnormal gene for hemoglobin.

Slater's Index A numerical representation of a person's order within a sibship: the number of a person's older siblings divided by the total number of his or her siblings.

SRY A gene on the Y chromosome that confers maleness.

standard social science model The idea, prevalent through much of the 20th century, that the human mind starts out as a blank slate that is written upon by learning and culture.

steroid A class of fatty molecules derived from cholesterol, including the sex hormones testosterone, estrogen, and progesterone.

straight Heterosexual.

suprachiasmatic nucleus A cell group in the hypothalamus that regulates circadian rhythms.

systemizing In the terminology of Simon Baron-Cohen, a male-typical trait involving interest in rule-governed systems.

taxometric analysis A statistical method to look for hidden categories underlying a dataset.

testosterone A sex hormone secreted by the testis and the adrenal gland; it is the principal androgen.

thalamus A large group of forebrain nuclei that receives sensory inputs from the periphery and is reciprocally connected with the cerebral cortex.

third ventricle A fluid-filled space that occupies the midline of the brain, separating the left and right hypothalamus.

top In gay slang, a man who prefers to take the insertive role in anal sex.

transexual A transgendered person who wishes to transition to the other sex, or who has already done so.

transgendered Having the subjective identity or the social role of a person of the other sex.

trend In statistics, a difference between samples that fails to satisfy a minimum criterion for significance, perhaps because the samples were too small.

two-spirit person In Native American culture, a person who is transgendered or who exhibits a mix of male and female characteristics.

unshared environment Any nongenetic influence that promotes a trait in one member of a twin pair but not the other.

vomeronasal organ A sensory structure within the nasal cavity of some animals; it is involved in the detection of pheromones.

waist–hip ratio The circumference of the body at the waist divided by the circumference of the body at the hips.

white matter Brain tissue containing fibers but no neurons or synapses.

winkte A Lakota Indian, biologically male, who adopts a female or mixed-gender role.

X chromosome A sex chromosome: females possess two, males possess one.

X inactivation In females, the inactivation of one X chromosome during early development, leaving the individual with just one functional X chromosome in each cell.

X-linked Of a gene, located on the X chromosome, or caused by such a gene.

Y chromosome The smaller of the two sex chromosomes; males possess one, females possess none.

NOTES

Introduction

1. LeVay, 1996.

Chapter 1

1. Oosterhuis, 1991.
2. Dickson et al., 2003.
3. Diamond, 2003, 2008.
4. Marcus, 1992.
5. Neglia, 2009.
6. Haldeman, 1994.
7. American Psychiatric Association, 2007.
8. Spitzer, 2003.
9. Isay, 2006.

10. Laumann et al., 1994; Wellings et al., 1994; Smith et al., 2003; Statistics Canada, 2004.

11. Laumann et al., 1994.

12. Lewontin, 1995.

13. Chivers et al., 2004; Rieger et al., 2005; Rosenthal et al., 2011.

14. Weinrich, 1987b.

15. Laan et al., 1996; Suschinsky et al., 2009; Chivers et al., 2011.

16. Lippa & Patterson, 2010

17. Diamond, 2008.

18. Bailey, 2009.

19. Gangestad et al., 2000.

20. Whitam, 1983.

21. Wellings et al., 1994.

22. Norton, 1999.

23. Dover, 1978.

24. Reynolds, 2002.

25. Williams, 1986; Nanda, 1990; Vasey & Bartlett, 2007.

26. Lame Deer & Erdoes, 1972.

27. Williams, 1986p. 233.

28. Murray, 2000.

29. Kennedy & Davis, 1983; Faderman, 1991.

Chapter 2

1. Freud, 1905/1975.

2. Bell et al., 1981.

3. Isay, 1989.

4. Green, 1987 p. 275.

5. Taylor, 1992

6. Socarides, 1978 p. 83.

7. Nicolosi & Nicolosi, 2002 p. 27.

8. Freud, 1920/1955.

9. Eysenck, 1985.

10. Koerner & LeVay, 2000.

11. Churchill, 1967.

12. Cameron & Cameron, 1995.

13. McGuire et al., 1965.

14. Tomeo et al., 2001.

15. Wilson and Widom, 2010

16. Herdt, 1981.

17. Wellings et al., 1994 pp. 204–209.

18. Associated Press, 2005.

19. Rafanello, 2004 pp. 123–4.

20. Dominguez et al., 2002.

21. Brannock & Chapman, 1990.

22. Tooby & Cosmides, 1992

23. Eckes & Trautner, 2000.

24. Money et al., 1957; Money & Ehrhardt, 1971.

25. Diamond & Sigmundson, 1997

26. Colapinto, 2000.

27. Bradley et al., 1998.

28. Reiner & Gearhart, 2004.

29. Anderssen et al., 2002.

30. Mehren, 2004.

31. Schmalz, 1993.

32. Lever, 1994; 1995.

Chapter 3

1. Gazzaniga, 2008.

2. Gorski et al., 1978; Gorski, 1985.

3. Commins & Yahr, 1984; Tobet et al., 1986; Byne, 1998; Roselli et al., 2004a; Vasey & Pfaus, 2005.

4. Allen et al., 1989; LeVay, 1991; Byne et al., 2001.

5. Goldstein et al., 2001; Cahill, 2005.

6. Hines et al., 1992; Cooke et al., 1999; Mori et al., 2008.

7. McEwen, 2008.

8. Luine & Dohanich, 2007.

9. Wilhelm et al., 2007.

10. Asby et al., 2009.

11. Rodeck et al., 1985.

12. Gorski, 1985; Goto et al., 2005; Sakuma, 2009.

13. Davis et al., 1996b; Forger, 2009.

14. Rhees et al., 1990a, b; Davis et al., 1995.

15. Dugger et al., 2008.

16. Habert & Picon, 1984.

17. Davis et al., 1996a; Yang et al., 2004.

18. Buss et al., 2006.

19. Arai et al., 1996.

20. Forger et al., 2004; Forger, 2009.

21. McEwen, 1998.

22. Cooke & Woolley, 2005a.

23. Arnold & Breedlove, 1985; McCarthy & Konkle, 2005.

24. Romeo, 2003; Koshibu et al., 2004; Ahmed et al., 2008.

25. Cooke et al., 1999.

26. Morris et al., 2008a; Morris et al., 2008b.

27. Phoenix et al., 1959.

28. Goy et al., 1988.

29. de Jonge et al., 1988.

30. Vega Matuszczyk et al., 1988.

31. Adkins-Regan, 2002.

32. Signoret, 1970; Ford, 1983.

33. Mansukhani et al., 1996; Adkins-Regan, 2005.

34. Becker et al., 2002.

35. Bodo & Rissman, 2007; Zuloaga et al., 2008

36. Bakker et al., 1993; Zuloaga et al., 2008.

37. Grumbach & Auchus, 1999.

38. Wang et al., 2009.

39. Arnold et al., 2004; Gatewood et al., 2006; Arnold, 2009b.

40. Compaan et al., 1994.

41. Lephart et al., 2001.

42. Kudwa & Rissman, 2003.

43. vom Saal & Bronson, 1980; Pei et al., 2006.

44. Clemens et al., 1978; Pei et al., 2006.

45. Kerchner & Ward, 1992.

46. Ward, 1972; Anderson et al., 1985; Kerchner & Ward, 1992; Meek et al., 2006.

47. Goldfoot et al., 1984.

48. Cooke et al., 2000.

49. Esquifino et al., 2004.

50. Moore & Morelli, 1979; Moore, 1984, 1992; Moore et al., 1992.

51. LeVay, 1996.

52. Dörner, 1969; Dörner et al., 1991.

53. MacCulloch & Waddington, 1981; Ellis & Ames, 1987.

54. Dörner, 1969.

55. Dörner, 1989/2001.

56. Bagemihl, 1999.

57. Sommer & Vasey, 2006.

58. Kotrschal et al., 2006.

59. Hunt & Warner Hunt, 1977; Hunt et al., 1980; Hunt et al., 1984.

60. Fry, 1993.

61. de Waal, 1995; Fruth & Hohmann, 2006.

62. Vasey, 2006.

63. Vasey & Jiskoot, 2009.

64. Perkins & Fitzgerald, 1992b.

65. Geist, 1971.

66. Roselli et al., 2004a.

Chapter 4

1. Simmons, 1965; Levitt & Klassen, 1974; Taylor, 1983; Kite & Deaux, 1987; Madon, 1997.

2. Eaton & Enns, 1986; Maccoby, 1998.

3. Berenbaum & Snyder, 1995; Serbin et al., 2001.

4. Berman et al., 1977.

5. Kimura, 1999.

6. Beer & Fleming, 1989; Kerns & Berenbaum, 1991; Kimura, 1999.

7. Halpern, 2000.

8. Goodenough, 1957.

9. Maccoby, 1998.

10. Sachs et al., 1973.

11. Fagot et al., 1992.

12. Rust et al., 2000.

13. Braggio et al., 1978; Ward & Stehm, 1991; Wallen, 1996.

14. Alexander & Hines, 2002; Hassett et al., 2008.

15. Lovejoy & Wallen, 1988.

16. Connellan et al., 2001.

17. Moore & Johnson, 2008; Quinn & Liben, 2008.

18. Alexander et al., 2009.

19. Wallen, 1996.

20. Roberts et al., 2009.

21. Money & Ehrhardt, 1971; Berenbaum & Snyder, 1995; Berenbaum et al., 2000; Hines et al., 2003b; Hines et al., 2004; Meyer-Bahlburg et al., 2004; Meyer-Bahlburg et al., 2006; Pasterski et al., 2007.

22 van Anders et al., 2006

23. Cohen-Bendahan et al., 2005a

24. Henderson & Berenbaum, 1997.

25. Hines et al., 2002.

26. Auyeung et al., 2009.

27. Chapman et al., 2006.

28. Hines et al., 2003b.

29. Grimshaw et al., 1995.

30. White, 1994 p. 30.

31. Pallone & Steinberg, 1990 pp. 11–12.

32. Isay, 1999

33. Alanko et al., 2009

34. Blanchard et al., 1983.

35. Grellert et al., 1982.

36. Bailey & Zucker, 1995.

37. Lippa, 2003a; Loehlin & McFadden, 2003; Cardoso, 2009; Lippa, 2008a; Plöderl & Fartacek, 2008; Alanko et al., 2010.

38. Cardoso, 2009.

39. Alanko et al., 2010

40. Williams, 1986; Nanda, 1990; Vasey & Bartlett, 2007.

41. Williams, 1986.

42. Baker, 1985.

43. Rieger et al., 2008.

44. The National Children's Study, 2009.

45. Green, 1987.

46. Bakwin, 1968; Money & Russo, 1979; Zuger, 1984.

47. Davenport, 1986.

48. Wallien & Cohen-Kettenis, 2008.

49. Drummond et al., 2008

50. Bem, 1996; Bem, 2000.

51. Green, 1987.

52. Bergen et al., 2007.

Chapter 5

1. Kimura, 1999; Geary et al., 2000; Halpern, 2000; Halari et al., 2005; Lippa, 2005a.

2. Papadatou-Pastou et al., 2008; Sommer et al., 2008.

3. Lippa, 1998; Su et al., 2009.

4. Nettle, 2007.

5. Costa et al., 2001; Lippa, 2005a; Fink et al., 2007.

6. Baron-Cohen, 2003.

7. Buss & Schmitt, 1993; Oliver & Hyde, 1993; Bailey et al., 1994.

8. Schmitt, 2003; Fenigstein & Preston, 2007.

9. Buss, 2000.

10. Laws & O'Donohue, 2008.

11. Greenfeld, 1997.

12. Bailey et al., 1994; Toro-Morn & Sprecher, 2003.

13. Bailey et al., 1994; Murnen & Stockton, 1997; Janssen et al., 2003.

14. Oliver & Hyde, 1993.

15. Buss, 1989, 2000; Schmitt, 2003; Herlitz & Kabir, 2006; Lippa, 2009; Lohman & Lakin, 2008; Schmitt et al., 2008.

16. Costa et al., 2001.

17. Williams & Meck, 1991.

18. Jozet-Alves et al., 2008.

19. Darmaillacq et al., 2005.

20. Lippa & Hershberger, 1999; Loehlin et al., 2005.

21. Zucker et al., 1996; Berenbaum, 1999; Berenbaum & Bailey, 2003; Hines et al., 2003b; Wisniewski et al., 2004; Cohen-Bendahan et al., 2005b; Meyer-Bahlburg et al., 2006.

22. Udry et al., 1995.

23. Kimura, 1994; Kimura & Carson, 1995; Loehlin & McFadden, 2003; Kraemer et al., 2006; Lippa, 2006; Kraemer et al., 2009; Hampson et al., 2008; Wallien et al., 2008.

24. Penton-Voak & Perrett, 2000; Johnston et al., 2001.

25. Gouchie & Kimura, 1991.

26. Halari et al., 2005.

27. McCormick & Witelson, 1991; Wegesin, 1998b; Loehlin & McFadden, 2003; Rahman & Wilson, 2003a; Peters et al., 2007.

28. Gladue & Bailey, 1995b.

29. Gladue & Bailey, 1995b; Peters et al., 2007.

30. Hall & Kimura, 1995.

31. Rahman et al., 2005.

32. Rahman & Wilson, 2003a; Collaer et al., 2007.

33. Rahman et al., 2003a.

34. Sanders & Wright, 1997

35. McCormick & Witelson, 1991

36. Wegesin, 1998b.

37. Neave et al., 1999.

38. Tuttle & Pillard, 1991.

39. Rahman et al., 2003c; Hassan & Rahman, 2007.

40. Medland et al., 2004.

41. Lalumière et al., 2000

42. Loehlin & McFadden, 2003

43. Mustanski et al., 2002.

44. Lippa, 2003b.

45. McCormick & Witelson, 1991.

46. Weinrich, 1978.

47. Lippa, 2008b.

48. Lippa, 2005b.

49. Schiller, 1986

50. Associated Press, 2009.

51. Bailey & Oberschneider, 1997.

52. Lippa, 2008b.

53. Lippa, 2008b.

54. Salais & Fischer, 1995; Sergeant et al., 2006

55. Nettle, 2007.

56. Nettle, 2007.

57. Nettle, 2007.

58. Ellis et al., 1990; Gladue & Bailey, 1995a; Sergeant et al., 2006.

59. Vanderlaan & Vasey, 2009b.

60. Lippa, 2005b; 2008b.

61. Bailey et al., 1997.

62. Kennedy, 1988; LeVay, 1996.

63. Faderman, 1991; Chauncey, 1994

64. Hart et al., 2003; Flores et al., 2009.

65. Weinrich et al., 1992.

66. Singh et al., 1999.

67. Bailey et al., 1994.

68. Bell & Weinberg, 1978; Laumann et al., 1994.

69. Bailey et al., 1994.

70. Vanderlaan & Vasey, 2008.

71. Harry & DeVall, 1978.

72. Spengler, 1977; Alison et al., 2001.

73. Tomassilli et al., 2009.

74. Hall & Kimura, 1995.

Chapter 6

1. LeVay, 1996.

2. LeVay, 1996.

3. Meyer-Bahlburg, 1984.

4. Pearcey et al., 1996; Singh et al., 1999.

5 van Anders & Watson, 2006; van Anders et al., 2007; van Anders & Watson, 2007.

6. Sperling, 2008.

7. Garagorri et al., 2008.

8. Quigley, 2002.

9. Garagorri et al., 2008.

10. Organisation Internationale des Intersexués, 2009.

11. Klein et al., 1994.

12. Meyer-Bahlburg et al., 2008

13. Hines et al., 2004.

14. Imperato-McGinley et al., 1991; Hines et al., 2003a.

15. Manning et al., 1998

16. Voracek, 2009

17. Lippa, 2003a; Manning et al., 2007; Loehlin et al., 2009.

18. Galis et al., 2010.

19. Lutchmaya et al., 2004.

20. Brown et al., 2002b; Ökten et al., 2002

21. Buck et al., 2003

22. Cattrall et al., 2005.

23. Berenbaum et al., 2009.

24 van Anders et al., 2006; Voracek & Dressler, 2007.

25. Talarovicova et al., 2009.

26. Williams et al., 2000; McFadden & Shubel, 2002; Rahman & Wilson, 2003b; Puts et al., 2004; Rahman, 2005b; Kraemer et al., 2006.

27. Hall & Schaeff, 2008; Lippa, 2003b; Manning et al., 2007.

28. Grimbos et al., 2010.

29. Brown et al., 2002a.

30. Tortorice, 2001.

31. McFadden & Shubel, 2002; Lippa, 2003a; Manning et al., 2007; Hall & Schaeff, 2008.

32. Robinson & Manning, 2000; Rahman & Wilson, 2003b; Puts et al., 2004; Rahman, 2005b.

33. Williams et al., 2000; Voracek et al., 2005; Kraemer et al., 2006.

34. Manning et al., 2007.

35. Bailey & Hurd, 2005; Collaer et al., 2007; McIntyre et al., 2007; Manning & Fink, 2008; Loehlin et al., 2009.

36. Puts et al., 2004; Lippa, 2006.

37. Wallen, 2009.

38. McFadden et al., 2005.

39. McFadden, 1998.

40. Bilger et al., 1990; McFadden, 1998.

41. McFadden et al., 2006; McFadden et al., 2009.

42. McFadden et al., 2009.

43. McFadden et al., 1996.

44. McFadden & Pasanen, 1998, 1999.

45. McFadden & Champlin, 2000.

46. Rahman et al., 2003b.

47. Grumbach & Auchus, 1999.

48. Auger & Jessen, 2009.

49. Jeong et al., 2008.

50. Obrietan & van den Pol, 1995; Mitchell & Redburn, 1996; Ikeda et al., 1997.

51. Auger et al., 2001.

52. Davis et al., 2000.

53. Ward & Weisz, 1984.

54. Chapman & Stern, 1978.

55. Dörner et al., 1980; Dörner et al., 1983.

56. Schmidt & Clement, 1990.

57. de Rooij et al., 2009.

58. Bailey et al., 1991.

59. Ellis et al., 1988.

Chapter 7

1. Taylor, 1992.

2. Pillard et al., 1981; LeVay, 1996

3. Pillard et al., 1982; Pillard & Weinrich, 1986; Pillard, 1990.

4. Bailey & Bell, 1993; Bailey & Benishay, 1993; Hamer et al., 1993; Bailey et al., 1999; Schwartz et al., 2009.

5. Bailey & Bell, 1993

6. Pillard et al., 1982; Pillard & Weinrich, 1986

7. Bailey & Benishay, 1993; Bailey et al., 1993; Hamer et al., 1993; Pattatucci & Hamer, 1995; Bailey et al., 1999; Schwartz et al., 2009.

8. Dawood et al., 2000.

9. Pattatucci & Hamer, 1995

10. Hamer et al., 1993; Bailey et al., 1995.

11. Bailey & Pillard, 1991; Bailey et al., 1993.

12. Bouchard et al., 1999

13. Bailey & Pillard, 1991; Bailey et al., 1993.

14. Whitam et al., 1993.

15. Kirk et al., 2000

16. Långström et al., 2010.

17. Alanko et al., 2010.

18. Hershberger, 1997.

19. Kendler et al., 2000.

20. Bailey & Pillard, 1991; Bailey et al., 2000; Alanko et al., 2010.

21 van Beijsterveldt et al., 2006.

22. Alanko et al., 2010.

23. Eckert et al., 1986.

24. Whitam et al., 1993.

25. Segal, 2000.

26. Hershberger, 1997.

27. Macke et al., 1993.

28. DuPree et al., 2004.

29. Hamer et al., 1993.

30. Camperio-Ciani et al., 2004; Rahman et al., 2008b

31. Bailey et al., 1999; McKnight & Malcolm, 2000.

32. Schwartz et al., 2009.

33. Hu et al., 1995.

34. Rice et al., 1999.

35. Hamer, 1999.

36. Mustanski et al., 2005.

37. Ramagopalan et al., 2010.

38. Sanders, n.d.

39. Butcher et al., 2008.

40. Bocklandt et al., 2006.

41. Gill, 1963.

42. Ryner et al., 1996.

43. Ito et al., 1996.

44. Demir & Dickson, 2005.

45. Yamamoto, 2007.

46. Kimura et al., 2008.

47. Finley et al., 1997; Grosjean et al., 2001; Svetec et al., 2005; Shirangi et al., 2006; Yamamoto, 2007; Grosjean et al., 2008; Liu et al., 2008.

48. Grosjean et al., 2008.

49. Liu et al., 2008.

50. Liu et al., 2009.

51. Ferveur et al., 1997.

52. Gatewood et al., 2006; Arnold, 2009a.

53. Bocklandt & Vilain, 2007.

54. National Library of Medicine, 2008.

55. Weinrich, 1987a.

56. Yankelovich Partners, 1994.

57. Iemmola & Camperio-Ciani, 2009

58. King et al., 2005.

59. King et al., 2005.

60. Rahman et al., 2008b.

61. Camperio-Ciani et al., 2004.

62. Wilson, 1975.

63. Vasey et al., 2007; Vasey & Vanderlaan, 2008, 2010.

64. Bobrow & Bailey, 2001; Rahman & Hull, 2005.

65. King et al., 2005.

66. Trivers, 1974; Hamer & Copeland, 1994.

67. Camperio-Ciani et al., 2004; Iemmola & Camperio-Ciani, 2009.

68. Rahman et al., 2008b.

69. Camperio Ciani et al., 2008.

70. Miller, 2000.

71. Zietsch et al., 2008.

72. Gavrilets & Rice, 2006.

Chapter 8

1. Swanson, 2003

2. Hooker et al., 2006.

3. Simerly, 2002; Shah et al., 2004; Choi et al., 2005.

4. Cooke & Woolley, 2005b.

5. Byne, 1998.

6. LeVay, 1991.

7. Byne et al., 2000; Byne et al., 2001.

8. Garcia-Falgueras & Swaab, 2008.

9. Swaab & Hofman, 1990.

10. Rahman & Silber, 2000.

11. Swaab & Fliers, 1985.

12. Swaab & Hofman, 1988; Hofman & Swaab, 1989; Swaab, 1995.

13. Swaab et al., 1992.

14. Allen et al., 1989; LeVay, 1991; Byne et al., 2001.

15. Swaab & Garcia-Falgueras, 2009.

16. Allen & Gorski, 1992.

17. Lasco et al., 2002.

18. Witelson et al., 2008.

19. Cowell et al., 1993; Tuncer et al., 2005.

20. Ponseti et al., 2007.

21. Savic & Lindstrom, 2008.

22. Kilpatrick et al., 2006.

23. Kranz & Ishai, 2006.

24. Ponseti et al., 2006; Ponseti et al., 2009.

25. Safron et al., 2007; Hu et al., 2008; Paul et al., 2008.

26. Chivers et al., 2004; Suschinsky et al., 2009.

27. Ponseti et al., 2006.

28. Safron et al., 2007.

29. Hu et al., 2008.

30. Stowers et al., 2002; Kimchi et al., 2007.

31. Trotier et al., 2000; Kouros-Mehr et al., 2001; Besli et al., 2004; Mast & Samuelsen, 2009.

32. Knecht et al., 2003; Savic et al., 2009.

33. Kohl et al., 2001; Preti et al., 2003.

34. Martins et al., 2005.

35. Kohl, 2007.

36. Spieth, 1974; Stockinger et al., 2005.

37. Gower et al., 1994.

38. Wysocki & Preti, 2009.

39. Bensafi et al., 2004.

40. Savic et al., 2001; Savic et al., 2005.

41. Berglund et al., 2006.

42. Perkins & Fitzgerald, 1992a.

43. Roselli et al., 2004a.

44. Roselli et al., 2004b.

45. Perkins et al., 1995.

46. Masek et al., 1999.

47. Roselli et al., 2006.

48. Roselli & Stormshak, 2009b, a.

49. Byne et al., 2001.

50. Paredes & Baum, 1995; Kindon et al., 1996; Paredes et al., 1998.

51. Kimchi et al., 2007.

52. Trimble et al., 1997.

53. Trimble et al., 1997; Wassersug, 2003.

54. Daskalos, 1998.

55. Gao & Moore, 1996.

Chapter 9

1. Blanchard & Bogaert, 1996a; Bogaert & Blanchard, 1996; Bogaert, 1998; Bogaert & Friesen, 2002; Bogaert, 2010.

2. Bogaert, 2010.

3. Bogaert, 1998; Tenhula & Bailey, 1998; Bogaert & Friesen, 2002; Bogaert, 2010.

4. Bogaert et al., 2002.

5. Savin-Williams & Ream, 2006.

6. Rogers, 2003.

7. Frisch & Zdravkovic, 2010.

8. Singh et al., 1999.

9. Maresh, 1955; Marshall & Tanner, 1974.

10. Martin & Nguyen, 2004.

11. Jansson et al., 1985.

12. Bogaert & Hershberger, 1999.

13. Harding & Golombok, 2002.

14. Ponseti et al., 2006.

15. Nedoma & Freund, 1961.

16. Savic & Lindstrom, 2008.

17. Basu & Brueckner, 2008.

18. Geschwind & Galaburda, 1985; McCormick et al., 1990.

19. Ludwig, 1932.

20. Fink et al., 2006.

21. Thornhill & Gangestad, 1999.

22. Shackelford & Larsen, 1997; Milne et al., 2003.

23. Hall & Schaeff, 2008.

24. Mustanski et al., 2002; Rahman & Wilson, 2003b; Rahman, 2005b.

25. Martin et al., 2008.

26. Lalumière et al., 2000.

27. McCormick & Witelson, 1994; Rahman et al., 2008a.

28. Sanders & Ross-Field, 1987; Sanders & Wright, 1997; Wegesin, 1998a.

29. Rahman et al., 2008a.

30. Savic & Lindstrom, 2008.

31. Sommer et al., 2004.

32. Klar, 2005.

33. Rahman et al., 2009; Schwartz et al., 2009.

34. Gaudio, 1994; Linville, 1998; Ambady et al., 1999; Smyth et al., 2003; Johnson et al., 2007; Rendall et al., 2008; Rieger et al., 2010; Smyth & Rogers, 2008.

35. Shelp, 2002, Woolery, 2007.

36. Rieger et al., 2008.

37. Rieger et al., 2010.

38. Martins et al., 2005.

39. Johnson & Tassinary, 2005; Johnson et al., 2007.

40. Rieger et al., 2010.

41. Smyth et al., 2003.

42. Smyth et al., 2003; Smyth & Rogers, 2008.

43. Pierrehumbert et al., 2004.

44. Smyth & Rogers, 2008.

45. Bouchard, 1984.

46. Eibl-Eibesfeldt, 2007.

Chapter 10

1. Blanchard, 2004.

2. Slater, 1962; Hare & Moran, 1979.

3. Blanchard & Zucker, 1994; Zucker & Blanchard, 1994; Blanchard & Bogaert, 1996a; Blanchard et al., 1998.

4. Blanchard & Bogaert, 1996b; Purcell et al., 2000; Ellis & Blanchard, 2001; Bogaert, 2003b; 2006; Blanchard & Lippa, 2007.

5. Blanchard & Lippa, 2007.

6. Bogaert, 2003b.

7. Bogaert, 2008.

8. Blanchard et al., 1995.

9. Blanchard & Sheridan, 1992; Zucker & Blanchard, 1994.

10. Bogaert et al., 1997; Blanchard & Bogaert, 1998; Blanchard et al., 2000.

11. Schwartz et al., 2009.

12. King et al., 2005.

13. Camperio-Ciani et al., 2004; Iemmola & Camperio-Ciani, 2009.

14. Rahman, 2005a.

15. Rahman, 2005a.

16. Vasey & VanderLaan, 2007.

17. Vanderlaan and Vasey, 2009a.

18. Frisch & Hviid, 2006.

19. Francis, 2008.

20. Green, 2000.

21. Blanchard, 2004; 2007a, b.

22. Blanchard & Bogaert, 1996b.

23. Schwartz et al., 2009.

24. Francis, 2008.

25. Cantor et al., 2002.

26. Cantor et al., 2002.

27. Blanchard & Bogaert, 2004.

28. Francis, 2008.

29. Haines, 2008.

30. Bogaert, 2004.

31. Marmor, 1980

32. Laumann et al., 1994.

33. Whitam, 1983.

34. Baca Zinn, 1994.

35. Laumann et al., 1994.

36. Blanchard et al., 2006; Bogaert et al., 2007; Blanchard & Lippa, 2008.

37. Blanchard & Lippa, 2007.

38. Sulloway, 1996.

39. Bogaert, 2006.

40. Blanchard & Bogaert, 1996b.

41. Blanchard & Ellis, 2001; Cote et al., 2003.

42. Nielsen et al., 2008.

43. Maccoby et al., 1979.

44. Green, 2000.

45. James et al., 2003; Piper et al., 2007.
46. Singer et al., 2009.
47. Miller, 2000.
48. Rahman, 2005a.
49. Bogaert, 2003a.
50. Blanchard et al., 2006.
51. Lippa, 2003b.

Chapter 11

1. Bouchard, 2004.
2. Alanko et al., 2010.
3. Auger et al., 2001.
4. Blanchard et al., 2006.
5. Rahman, 2005a.
6. Hall & Love, 2003.
7. Hall, 2000.
8. Searles et al., 2000.
9. Kimchi et al., 2007.
10. Paredes & Baum, 1995; Paredes et al., 1998.
11. Searles et al., 2000.
12. Petrulis, 2009
13. Simmons & Yahr, 2003.
14. Galor & Moav, 2002; Clark, 2007.
15. LeVay, 1996.
16. Bailey & Zucker, 1995; van Beijsterveldt et al., 2006.
17. Alanko et al., 2009.
18. Skidmore et al., 2006.
19. Alanko et al., 2009.
20. Hegarty, 2009.
21. Dennis, 2009.

22. Oosterhuis & Kennedy, 1991.
23. Bloomekatz, 2009.
24. Arcuri, 2009b.
25. Arcuri, 2009a.
26. Isay, 1989.

BIBLIOGRAPHY

Adkins-Regan, E. (2002). Development of sexual partner preference in the zebra finch: a socially monogamous, pair-bonding animal. *Arch Sex Behav.* 31, 27–33.

Adkins-Regan, E. (2005). *Hormones and animal social behavior.* Princeton University Press.

Ahmed, E. I., Zehr, J. L., Schulz, K. M., Lorenz, B. H., DonCarlos, L. L. & Sisk, C. L. (2008). Pubertal hormones modulate the addition of new cells to sexually dimorphic brain regions. *Nat Neurosci.* 11, 995–997.

Alanko, K., Santtila, P., Harlaar, N., Witting, K., Varjonen, M., Jern, P., Johansson, A., von der Pahlen, B. & Sandnabba, N. K. (2010). Common genetic effects of gender atypical behavior in childhood and sexual orientation in adulthood: A study of Finnish twins. *Arch Sex Behav.* 39, 81–92.

Alanko, K., Santtila, P., Witting, K., Varjonen, M., Jern, P., Johansson, A., von der Pahlen, B. & Kenneth Sandnabba, N. (2009). Psychiatric symptoms and same-sex sexual attraction and behavior in light of childhood gender atypical behavior and parental relationships. *J Sex Res.* 46, 494–504.

Alexander, G. M., Wilcox, T. & Woods, R. (2009). Sex differences in infants' visual interest in toys. *Arch Sex Behav.* 38, 427–433.

Alexander, M. A. & Hines, M. (2002). Sex differences in response to children's toys in nonhuman primates (*Cercopithecus aethiops sabaeus*). *Evolution and Human Behavior.* 23, 467–479.

Alison, L., Santtila, P., Sandnabba, N. K. & Nordling, N. (2001). Sadomasochistically oriented behavior: diversity in practice and meaning. *Arch Sex Behav.* 30, 1–12.

Allen, L. S. & Gorski, R. A. (1992). Sexual orientation and the size of the anterior commissure in the human brain. *Proc Natl Acad Sci U S A.* 89, 7199–7202.

Allen, L. S., Hines, M., Shryne, J. E. & Gorski, R. A. (1989). Two sexually dimorphic cell groups in the human brain. *J Neurosci.* 9, 497–506.

Ambady, N., Hallahan, M. & Conner, B. (1999). Accuracy of judgments of sexual orientation from thin slices of behavior. *J Pers Soc Psychol.* 77, 538–547.

American Psychiatric Association. (2007). *Just the facts about sexual orientation and youth.* Available at http://www.apa.org/pi/lgbc/publications/ justthefacts.html; accessed January 14, 2010.

Anderson, D. K., Rhees, R. W. & Fleming, D. E. (1985). Effects of prenatal stress on differentiation of the sexually dimorphic nucleus of the preoptic area (SDN-POA) of the rat brain. *Brain Res.* 332, 113–118.

Anderssen, N., Amlie, C. & Ytteroy, E. A. (2002). Outcomes for children with lesbian or gay parents. A review of studies from 1978 to 2000. *Scand J Psychol.* 43, 335–351.

Arai, Y., Sekine, Y. & Murakami, S. (1996). Estrogen and apoptosis in the developing sexually dimorphic preoptic area in female rats. *Neurosci Res.* 25, 403–407.

Arcuri, V. J., (2009a) *Channeling Laverne DeFazio.* Available at http://www. frontierspublishing.com/2726/columns/butch.html; accessed January 14, 2010.

Arcuri, V. J., (2009b) *Don't call me queen!* Available at http://www.frontier-spublishing.com/2804/columns/butch.html; accessed January 14, 2010.

Arnold, A. P. (2009a). Mouse models for evaluating sex chromo-some effects that cause sex differences in non-gonadal tissues. *J Neuroendocrinol.* 21, 377–386.

Arnold, A. P. (2009b). The organizational-activational hypothesis as the foundation for a unified theory of sexual differentiation of all mammalian tissues. *Horm Behav.* 55, 570–578.

Arnold, A. P. & Breedlove, S. M. (1985). Organizational and activational effects of sex steroids on brain and behavior: A reanalysis. *Horm Behav.* 19, 469–498.

Arnold, A. P., Xu, J., Grisham, W., Chen, X., Kim, Y. H. & Itoh, Y. (2004). Minireview: Sex chromosomes and brain sexual differen-tiation. *Endocrinology.* 145, 1057–1062.

Asby, D. J., Arlt, W. & Hanley, N. A. (2009). The adrenal cortex and sexual differentiation during early human development. *Rev Endocr Metab Disord.* 10, 43–49.

Associated Press. (2005). *Ellen DeGeneres molested as teen.* Available at http://www.cbsnews.com/stories/2005/05/18/entertainment/main696352.shtml; accessed January 14, 2010.

Associated Press. (2009). *Women more likely to be expelled under 'don't ask'.* Available at http://www.mercurynews.com/bay-area-news/ci_13523094?source=rss&nclick_check=1); accessed January 14, 2010.

Auger, A. P. & Jessen, H. M. (2009). Corepressors, nuclear receptors, and epigenetic factors on DNA: A tail of repression. *Psychoneuroendocrinology.* 34 (Suppl 1), S39–47.

Auger, A. P., Perrot-Sinal, T. S. & McCarthy, M. M. (2001). Excitatory versus inhibitory GABA as a divergence point in steroid-mediated sexual differentiation of the brain. *Proc Natl Acad Sci U S A.* 98, 8059–8064.

Auyeung, B., Baron-Cohen, S., Ashwin, E., Knickmeyer, R., Taylor, K., Hackett, G. & Hines, M. (2009). Fetal testosterone predicts sexually differentiated childhood behavior in girls and in boys. *Psychol Sci.* 20, 144–148.

Baca Zinn, M. (1994). Mexican-heritage families in the United States. In: Padilla, F. M. et al. (Eds.), *Handbook of Hispanic cultures in the United States.* Houston: Arte Publico Press.

Bagemihl, B. (1999). *Biological exuberance: Animal homosexuality and natural diversity.* New York: St. Martin's Press.

Bailey, J. M. (2009). What is sexual orientation and do women have one? In: Hope, D. A. (Ed.), *Contemporary perspectives on lesbian, gay, and bisexual identities.* Springer.

Bailey, A. A. & Hurd, P. L. (2005). Finger length ratio (2D:4D) correlates with physical aggression in men but not in women. *Biol Psychol.* 68, 215–222.

Bailey, J. M. & Bell, A. P. (1993). Familiality of female and male homosexuality. *Behav Genet.* 23, 313–322.

Bailey, J. M. & Benishay, D. S. (1993). Familial aggregation of female sexual orientation. *Am J Psychiatry.* 150, 272–277.

Bailey, J. M., Bobrow, D., Wolfe, M. & Mikach, S. (1995). Sexual orientation of adult sons of gay fathers. *Dev Psychol.* 31, 124–129.

Bailey, J. M., Dunne, M. P. & Martin, N. G. (2000). Genetic and environmental influences on sexual orientation and its correlates in an Australian twin sample. *J Pers Soc Psychol.* 78, 524–536.

Bailey, J. M., Gaulin, S., Agyei, Y. & Gladue, B. A. (1994). Effects of gender and sexual orientation on evolutionarily relevant aspects of human mating psychology. *J Pers Soc Psychol.* 66, 1081–1093.

Bailey, J. M., Kim, P. Y., Hills, A. & Linsenmeier, J. A. (1997). Butch, femme, or straight acting? Partner preferences of gay men and lesbians. *J Pers Soc Psychol.* 73, 960–973.

Bailey, J. M. & Oberschneider, M. (1997). Sexual orientation and professional dance. *Arch Sex Behav.* 26, 433–444.

Bailey, J. M. & Pillard, R. C. (1991). A genetic study of male sexual orientation. *Arch Gen Psychiatry.* 48, 1089–1096.

Bailey, J. M., Pillard, R. C., Dawood, K., Miller, M. B., Farrer, L. A., Trivedi, S. & Murphy, R. L. (1999). A family history study of male sexual orientation using three independent samples. *Behav Genet.* 29, 79–86.

Bailey, J. M., Pillard, R. C., Neale, M. C. & Agyei, Y. (1993). Heritable factors influence sexual orientation in women. *Arch Gen Psychiatry.* 50, 217–223.

Bailey, J. M., Willerman, L. & Parks, C. (1991). A test of the maternal stress theory of human male homosexuality. *Arch Sex Behav.* 20, 277–293.

Bailey, J. M. & Zucker, K. J. (1995). Childhood sex-typed behavior and sexual orientation: A conceptual analysis and quantitative review. *Dev Psychol.* 31, 43–55.

Baker, M. (1985). *Our three selves: The life of Radclyffe Hall.* London: Hamish Hamilton.

Bakker, J., Brand, T., van Ophemert, J. & Slob, A. K. (1993). Hormonal regulation of adult partner preference behavior in neonatally ATD-treated male rats. *Behav Neurosci.* 107, 480–487.

Bakwin, H. (1968). Deviant gender-role behavior in children: relation to homosexuality. *Pediatrics.* 41, 620–629.

Baron-Cohen, S. (2003). *The essential difference: Men, women, and the extreme male brain.* New York: Penguin.

Basu, B. & Brueckner, M. (2008). Cilia: multifunctional organelles at the center of vertebrate left-right asymmetry. *Curr Top Dev Biol.* 85, 151–174.

Becker, J. B., Breedlove, S. M., Crews, D. & McCarthy, M. M. (Eds.) (2002). *Behavioral endocrinology* (2nd. ed.). Boston: MIT Press.

Beer, J. & Fleming, P. (1989). Effects of eye color on the accuracy of ball throwing of elementary school children. *Percept Mot Skills.* 68, 163–166.

Bell, A. P. & Weinberg, M. S. (1978). *Homosexualities: A study of diversity in men and women.* New York: Simon and Schuster.

Bell, A. P., Weinberg, M. S. & Hammersmith, S. K. (1981). *Sexual preference: Its development in men and women.* Bloomington: Indiana University Press.

Bem, D. J. (1996). Exotic becomes erotic: A developmental theory of sexual orientation. *Psychol Rev.* 103, 320–335.

Bem, D. J. (2000). Exotic becomes erotic: interpreting the biological correlates of sexual orientation. *Arch Sex Behav.* 29, 531–548.

Bensafi, M., Brown, W. M., Khan, R., Levenson, B. & Sobel, N. (2004). Sniffing human sex-steroid derived compounds modulates mood, memory and autonomic nervous system function in specific behavioral contexts. *Behav Brain Res.* 152, 11–22.

Berenbaum, S. A. (1999). Effects of early androgens on sex-typed activities and interests in adolescents with congenital adrenal hyperplasia. *Horm Behav.* 35, 102–110.

Berenbaum, S. A. & Bailey, J. M. (2003). Effects on gender identity of prenatal androgens and genital appearance: evidence from girls with congenital adrenal hyperplasia. *J Clin Endocrinol Metab.* 88, 1102–1106.

Berenbaum, S. A., Bryk, K. K., Nowak, N., Quigley, C. A. & Moffat, S. (2009). Fingers as a marker of prenatal androgen exposure. *Endocrinology.* 150, 5119–5124.

Berenbaum, S. A., Duck, S. C. & Bryk, K. (2000). Behavioral effects of prenatal versus postnatal androgen excess in children with 21–hydroxylase-deficient congenital adrenal hyperplasia. *J Clin Endocrinol Metab.* 85, 727–733.

Berenbaum, S. A. & Snyder, E. (1995). Early hormonal influences on childhood sex-typed activity and playmate preferences: Implications for the development of sexual orientation. *Developmental Psychology.* 31, 31–42.

Bergen, S. E., Gardner, C. O. & Kendler, K. S. (2007). Age-related changes in heritability of behavioral phenotypes over adolescence and young adulthood: a meta-analysis. *Twin Res Hum Genet.* 10, 423–433.

Berglund, H., Lindstrom, P. & Savic, I. (2006). Brain response to putative pheromones in lesbian women. *Proc Natl Acad Sci U S A.* 103, 8269–8274.

Berman, P. W., Monda, L. C. & Myerscough, R. P. (1977). Sex differences in young children's responses to an infant: An observation within a day-care setting. *Child Dev.* 48, 711–715.

Besli, R., Saylam, C., Veral, A., Karl, B. & Ozek, C. (2004). The existence of the vomeronasal organ in human beings. *J Craniofac Surg.* 15, 730–735.

Bilger, R. C., Matthies, M. L., Hammel, D. R. & Demorest, M. E. (1990). Genetic implications of gender differences in the prevalence of spontaneous otoacoustic emissions. *J Speech Hear Res.* 33, 418–432.

Blanchard, R. (2004). Quantitative and theoretical analyses of the relation between older brothers and homosexuality in men. *J Theor Biol.* 230, 173–187.

Blanchard, R. (2007a). Older-sibling and younger-sibling sex ratios in Frisch and Hviid's (2006) national cohort study of two million Danes. *Arch Sex Behav.* 36, 860–863; discussion 864–867.

Blanchard, R. (2007b). Supplementary analyses regarding Langevin, Langevin, and Curnoe's (2007) findings on fraternal birth order in homosexual men. *Arch Sex Behav.* 36, 610–614; discussion 615–616.

Blanchard, R., Barbaree, H. E., Bogaert, A. F., Dickey, R., Klassen, P., Kuban, M. E. & Zucker, K. J. (2000). Fraternal birth order and sexual orientation in pedophiles. *Arch Sex Behav.* 29, 463–478.

Blanchard, R. & Bogaert, A. F. (1996a). Biodemographic comparisons of homosexual and heterosexual men in the Kinsey Interview Data. *Arch Sex Behav.* 25, 551–579.

Blanchard, R. & Bogaert, A. F. (1996b). Homosexuality in men and number of older brothers. *Am J Psychiatry.* 153, 27–31.

Blanchard, R. & Bogaert, A. F. (1998). Birth order in homosexual versus heterosexual sex offenders against children, pubescents, and adults. *Arch Sex Behav.* 27, 595–603.

Blanchard, R. & Bogaert, A. F. (2004). Proportion of homosexual men who owe their sexual orientation to fraternal birth order: An estimate based on two national probability samples. *Am J Hum Biol.* 16, 151–157.

Blanchard, R., Cantor, J. M., Bogaert, A. F., Breedlove, S. M. & Ellis, L. (2006). Interaction of fraternal birth order and handedness in the development of male homosexuality. *Horm Behav.* 49, 405–414.

Blanchard, R. & Ellis, L. (2001). Birth weight, sexual orientation and the sex of preceding siblings. *J Biosoc Sci.* 33, 451–467.

Blanchard, R. & Lippa, R. A. (2007). Birth order, sibling sex ratio, handedness, and sexual orientation of male and female partici-pants in a BBC internet research project. *Arch Sex Behav.* 36, 163–176.

Blanchard, R. & Lippa, R. A. (2008). The sex ratio of older siblings in non-right-handed homosexual men. *Arch Sex Behav.* 37, 970–976.

Blanchard, R., McConkey, J. G., Roper, V. & Steiner, B. W. (1983). Measuring physical aggressiveness in heterosexual, homosexual, and transsexual males. *Arch Sex Behav.* 12, 511–524.

Blanchard, R. & Sheridan, P. M. (1992). Sibship size, sibling sex ratio, birth order, and parental age in homosexual and nonhomosexual gender dysphorics. *J Nerv Ment Dis.* 180, 40–47.

Blanchard, R. & Zucker, K. J. (1994). Reanalysis of Bell, Weinberg, and Hammersmith's data on birth order, sibling sex ratio, and parental age in homosexual men. *Am J Psychiatry.* 151, 1375–1376.

Blanchard, R., Zucker, K. J., Bradley, S. J. & Hume, C. S. (1995). Birth order and sibling sex ratio in homosexual male adolescents and probably prehomosexual feminine boys. *Dev Psychol.* 31, 22–30.

Blanchard, R., Zucker, K. J., Siegelman, M., Dickey, R. & Klassen, P. (1998). The relation of birth order to sexual orientation in men and women. *J Biosoc Sci.* 30, 511–519.

Bloomekatz, A. B. (2009). Fairfax High's prom queen is a guy. *Los Angeles Times,* May 28.

Bobrow, D. & Bailey, J. M. (2001). Is male homosexuality maintained via kin selection? *Evolution Hum Behav.* 22, 361–368.

Bocklandt, S., Horvath, S., Vilain, E. & Hamer, D. H. (2006). Extreme skewing of X chromosome inactivation in mothers of homosexual men. *Hum Genet.* 118, 691–694.

Bocklandt, S. & Vilain, E. (2007). Sex differences in brain and behavior: hormones versus genes. *Adv Genet.* 59, 245–266.

Bodo, C. & Rissman, E. F. (2007). Androgen receptor is essential for sexual differentiation of responses to olfactory cues in mice. *Eur J Neurosci.* 25, 2182–2190.

Bogaert, A. F. (1998). Physical development and sexual orientation in women: Height, weight, and age of puberty comparisons. *Pers Individ Dif.* 24, 115–121.

Bogaert, A. F. (2003a). Interaction of older brothers and sex-typing in the prediction of sexual orientation in men. *Arch Sex Behav.* 32, 129–134.

Bogaert, A. F. (2003b). Number of older brothers and sexual orientation: new tests and the attraction/behavior distinction in two national probability samples. *J Pers Soc Psychol.* 84, 644–652.

Bogaert, A. F. (2004). The prevalence of male homosexuality: the effect of fraternal birth order and variations in family size. *J Theor Biol.* 230, 33–37.

Bogaert, A. F. (2006). Biological versus nonbiological older brothers and men's sexual orientation. *Proc Natl Acad Sci U S A.* 103, 10771–10774.

Bogaert, A. F. (2010). Physical development and sexual orientation in men and women: An analysis of NATSAL-2000. *Arch Sex Behav.* 39, 110–116.

Bogaert, A. F., Bezeau, S., Kuban, M. & Blanchard, R. (1997). Pedophilia, sexual orientation, and birth order. *J Abnorm Psychol.* 106, 331–335.

Bogaert, A. F. & Blanchard, R. (1996). Physical development and sexual orientation in men: Height, weight and age of puberty differences. *Pers Individ Dif.* 21, 77–84.

Bogaert, A. F., Blanchard, R. & Crosthwait, L. E. (2007). Interaction of birth order, handedness, and sexual orientation in the Kinsey interview data. *Behav Neurosci.* 121, 845–853.

Bogaert, A. F. & Friesen, C. (2002). Sexual orientation and height, weight, and age of puberty: new tests from a British national probability sample. *Biol Psychol.* 59, 135–145.

Bogaert, A. F., Friesen, C. & Klentrou, P. (2002). Age of puberty and sexual orientation in a national probability sample. *Arch Sex Behav.* 31, 73–81.

Bogaert, A. F. & Hershberger, S. (1999). The relation between sexual orientation and penile size. *Arch Sex Behav.* 28, 213–221.

Bouchard, J., Foulon, C., Storm, N., Nguyen, G. H. & Smith, C. L. (1999). Analyzing genomic DNA discordance between monozygotic twins. In: Crusio, W. E. and Gerlai, R. T. (Eds.), *Handbook of molecular-genetic techniques for brain and behavior research (Techniques in the behavioral and neural sciences, Vol. 13)*. Boston: Elsevier.

Bouchard, T. J. (2004). Genetic influence on human psychological traits: A survey. *Curr Direct Psychol Sci.* 13, 148–151.

Bouchard, T. J., Jr. (1984). Twins reared together and apart: What they tell us about human diversity. In: Fox, S. W. (Ed.), *Individuality and determinism*. New York: Plenum Press.

Bradley, S. J., Oliver, G. D., Chernick, A. B. & Zucker, K. J. (1998). Experiment of nurture: ablatio penis at 2 months, sex reassignment at 7 months, and a psychosexual follow-up in young adulthood. *Pediatrics.* 102, e9.

Braggio, J. T., Nadler, R. D., Lance, J. & Miseyko, D. (1978). Sex differences in apes and children. *Rec Adv Primatol.* 1, 529–532.

Brannock, J. C. & Chapman, B. E. (1990). Negative sexual experiences with men among heterosexual women and lesbians. *J Homosex.* 19, 105–110.

Brown, W. M., Finn, C. J., Cooke, B. M. & Breedlove, S. M. (2002a). Differences in finger length ratios between self-identified "butch" and "femme" lesbians. *Arch Sex Behav.* 31, 123–127.

Brown, W. M., Hines, M., Fane, B. A. & Breedlove, S. M. (2002b). Masculinized finger length patterns in human males and females with congenital adrenal hyperplasia. *Horm Behav.* 42, 380–386.

Buck, J. J., Williams, R. M., Hughes, I. A. & Acerini, C. L. (2003). In-utero androgen exposure and 2nd to 4th digit length ratio-comparisons between healthy controls and females with classical congenital adrenal hyperplasia. *Hum Reprod.* 18, 976–979.

Buss, D. M. (1989). Sex differences in human mate preference: Evolutionary hypothesis tested in 37 cultures. *Behav Brain Sci.* 12, 1–149.

Buss, D. M. (2000). *The dangerous passion: Why jealousy is as necessary as love and sex*. New York: The Free Press.

Buss, D. M. & Schmitt, D. P. (1993). Sexual strategies theory: A contextual evolutionary analysis of human mating. *Psychol Rev.* 100, 204–232.

Buss, R. R., Sun, W. & Oppenheim, R. W. (2006). Adaptive roles of programmed cell death during nervous system development. *Annu Rev Neurosci.* 29, 1–35.

Butcher, L. M., Davis, O. S., Craig, I. W. & Plomin, R. (2008). Genome-wide quantitative trait locus association scan of general cognitive ability using pooled DNA and 500K single nucleotide polymorphism microarrays. *Genes Brain Behav.* 7, 435–446.

Byne, W. (1998). The medial preoptic and anterior hypothalamic regions of the rhesus monkey: cytoarchitectonic comparison with the human and evidence for sexual dimorphism. *Brain Res.* 793, 346–350.

Byne, W., Lasco, M. S., Kemether, E., Shinwari, A., Edgar, M. A., Morgello, S., Jones, L. B. & Tobet, S. (2000). The interstitial nuclei of the human anterior hypothalamus: an investigation of sexual variation in volume and cell size, number and density. *Brain Res.* 856, 254–258.

Byne, W., Tobet, S., Mattiace, L. A., Lasco, M. S., Kemether, E., Edgar, M. A., Morgello, S., Buchsbaum, M. S. & Jones, L. B. (2001). The interstitial nuclei of the human anterior hypothalamus: an investigation of variation with sex, sexual orientation, and HIV status. *Horm Behav.* 40, 86–92.

Cahill, L. (2005). His brain, her brain. *Sci Amer.* 292 (5), 49–63.

Cameron, P. & Cameron, K. (1995). Does incest cause homosexuality? *Psychol Rep.* 76, 611–621.

Camperio-Ciani, A., Corna, F. & Capiluppi, C. (2004). Evidence for maternally inherited factors favouring male homosexuality and promoting female fecundity. *Proc RSL Series B: Biological Sciences.* 271, 2217–2221.

Camperio Ciani, A., Cermelli, P. & Zanzotto, G. (2008). Sexually antagonistic selection in human male homosexuality. *PLoS One.* 3, e2282.

Cantor, J. M., Blanchard, R., Paterson, A. D. & Bogaert, A. F. (2002). How many gay men owe their sexual orientation to fraternal birth order? *Arch Sex Behav.* 31, 63–71.

Cardoso, F. L. (2009). Recalled sex-typed behavior in childhood and sports' preferences in adulthood of heterosexual, bisexual, and homosexual men from Brazil, Turkey, and Thailand. *Arch Sex Behav.* 38, 726–736.

Cattrall, F. R., Vollenhoven, B. J. & Weston, G. C. (2005). Anatomical evidence for in utero androgen exposure in women with polycystic ovary syndrome. *Fertil Steril.* 84, 1689–1692.

Chapman, E., Baron-Cohen, S., Auyeung, B., Knickmeyer, R., Taylor, K. & Hackett, G. (2006). Fetal testosterone and empathy: evidence from the empathy quotient (EQ) and the "reading the mind in the eyes" test. *Soc Neurosci.* 1, 135–148.

Chapman, R. H. & Stern, J. M. (1978). Maternal stress and pituitary-adrenal manipulations during pregnancy in rats: effects on morphology and sexual behavior of male offspring. *J Comp Physiol Psychol.* 92, 1074–1083.

Chauncey, G. (1994). *Gay New York: Gender, urban culture and the making of the gay male world.* New York: Basic Books.

Chivers, M. L., Rieger, G., Latty, E. & Michael Bailey, J. (2004). A sex difference in the specificity of sexual arousal. *Psychol Sci.* 15, 736–744.

Chivers, M. L., Haberl, M., & Timmers, A. D., (2011). Sexual arousal patterns of bisexually attracted women: Specificity of sexual arousal increases with same-sex attractions. *Proceedings of the International Academy of Sex Research, 37th Annual Meeting,* p. 25.

Choi, G. B., Dong, H. W., Murphy, A. J., Valenzuela, D. M., Yancopoulos, G. D., Swanson, L. W. & Anderson, D. J. (2005). Lhx6 delineates a pathway mediating innate reproductive behaviors from the amygdala to the hypothalamus. *Neuron.* 46, 647–660.

Churchill, W. (1967). *Homosexual behavior among males: A cross-cultural and cross-species investigation.* Westerleight, UK: Hawthorn Books.

Clark, G. (2007). *A farewell to alms: A brief economic history of the world.* Princeton NJ: Princeton University Press.

Clemens, L. G., Gladue, B. A. & Coniglio, L. P. (1978). Prenatal endogenous androgenic influences on masculine sexual behavior and genital morphology in male and female rats. *Horm Behav.* 10, 40–53.

Cohen-Bendahan, C. C., Buitelaar, J. K., van Goozen, S. H., Orlebeke, J. F. & Cohen-Kettenis, P. T. (2005a). Is there an effect of prenatal testosterone on aggression and other behavioral traits? A study comparing same-sex and opposite-sex twin girls. *Horm Behav.* 47, 230–237.

Cohen-Bendahan, C. C., van de Beek, C. & Berenbaum, S. A. (2005b). Prenatal sex hormone effects on child and adult sex-typed behavior: methods and findings. *Neurosci Biobehav Rev.* 29, 353–384.

Colapinto, J. (2000). *As nature made him: The boy who was raised as a girl.* New York: HarperCollins.

Collaer, M. L., Reimers, S. & Manning, J. T. (2007). Visuospatial performance on an internet line judgment task and potential hormonal markers: sex, sexual orientation, and 2D:4D. *Arch Sex Behav.* 36, 177–192.

Commins, D. & Yahr, P. (1984). Adult testosterone levels influence the morphology of a sexually dimorphic area in the Mongolian gerbil brain. *J Comp Neurol.* 224, 132–140.

Compaan, J. C., Hutchison, J. B., Wozniak, A., de Ruiter, A. J. & Koolhaas, J. M. (1994). Brain aromatase activity and plasma testosterone levels are elevated in aggressive male mice during early ontogeny. *Brain Res Dev Brain Res.* 82, 185–192.

Connellan, J., Baron-Cohen, S., Wheelwright, S., Batki, A. & Ahluwalia, J. (2001). Sex differences in human neonatal social perception. *Infant Behav Dev.* 23, 113–118.

Cooke, B. M., Chowanadisai, W. & Breedlove, S. M. (2000). Post-weaning social isolation of male rats reduces the volume of the medial amygdala and leads to deficits in adult sexual behavior. *Behav Brain Res.* 117, 107–113.

Cooke, B. M., Tabibnia, G. & Breedlove, S. M. (1999). A brain sexual dimorphism controlled by adult circulating androgens. *Proc Natl Acad Sci U S A.* 96, 7538–7540.

Cooke, B. M. & Woolley, C. S. (2005a). Gonadal hormone modulation of dendrites in the mammalian CNS. *J Neurobiol.* 64, 34–46.

Cooke, B. M. & Woolley, C. S. (2005b). Sexually dimorphic synaptic organization of the medial amygdala. *J Neurosci.* 25, 10759–10767.

Costa, P. T., Jr., Terracciano, A. & McCrae, R. R. (2001). Gender differences in personality traits across cultures: robust and surprising findings. *J Pers Soc Psychol.* 81, 322–331.

Cote, K., Blanchard, R. & Lalumiere, M. L. (2003). The influence of birth order on birth weight: does the sex of preceding siblings matter? *J Biosoc Sci.* 35, 455–462.

Cowell, P. E., Kertesz, A. & Denenberg, V. H. (1993). Multiple dimensions of handedness and the human corpus callosum. *Neurology.* 43, 2353–2357.

Darmaillacq, A.-S., Chichery, R., Shashar, N. & Dickel, L. (2005). Early socialization overrides innate prey preference in newly hatched *Sepia officinalis* cuttlefish. *Animal Behav.* 71, 511–514.

Daskalos, C. T. (1998). Changes in the sexual orientation of six heterosexual male-to-female transsexuals. *Arch Sex Behav.* 27, 605–614.

Davenport, C. W. (1986). A follow-up study of 10 feminine boys. *Arch Sex Behav.* 15, 511–517.

Davis, A. M., Grattan, D. R. & McCarthy, M. M. (2000). Decreasing GAD neonatally attenuates steroid-induced sexual differentiation of the rat brain. *Behav Neurosci.* 114, 923–933.

Davis, E. C., Popper, P. & Gorski, R. A. (1996a). The role of apoptosis in sexual differentiation of the rat sexually dimorphic nucleus of the preoptic area. *Brain Res.* 734, 10–18.

Davis, E. C., Shryne, J. E. & Gorski, R. A. (1995). A revised critical period for the sexual differentiation of the sexually dimorphic nucleus of the preoptic area in the rat. *Neuroendocrinology.* 62, 579–585.

Davis, E. C., Shryne, J. E. & Gorski, R. A. (1996b). Structural sexual dimorphisms in the anteroventral periventricular nucleus of the rat hypothalamus are sensitive to gonadal steroids perinatally, but develop peripubertally. *Neuroendocrinology.* 63, 142–148.

Dawood, K., Pillard, R. C., Horvath, C., Revelle, W. & Bailey, J. M. (2000). Familial aspects of male homosexuality. *Arch Sex Behav.* 29, 155–163.

de Jonge, F. H., Muntjewerff, J. W., Louwerse, A. L. & van de Poll, N. E. (1988). Sexual behavior and sexual orientation of the female rat after hormonal treatment during various stages of development. *Horm Behav.* 22, 100–115.

de Rooij, S. R., Painter, R. C., Swaab, D. F. & Roseboom, T. J. (2009). Sexual orientation and gender identity after prenatal exposure to the Dutch famine. *Arch Sex Behav.* 38, 411–416.

de Waal, F. B. M. (1995). Bonobo sex and society. *Sci Amer.* 272 (March), 82–88.

Demir, E. & Dickson, B. J. (2005). fruitless splicing specifies male courtship behavior in *Drosophila. Cell.* 121, 785–794.

Dennis, W. (2009). When girls want to be boys and boys want to be girls. *Toronto Life,* August.

Diamond, L. M. (2003). Was it a phase? Young women's relinquishment of lesbian/bisexual identities over a 5–year period. *J Pers Soc Psychol.* 84, 352–364.

Diamond, L. M. (2008). *Sexual fluidity: Understanding women's love and desire.* Boston: Harvard University Press.

Diamond, M. & Sigmundson, H. K. (1997). Sex reassignment at birth. Long-term review and clinical implications. *Arch Pediatr Adolesc Med.* 151, 298–304.

Dickson, N., Paul, C. & Herbison, P. (2003). Same-sex attraction in a birth cohort: prevalence and persistence in early adulthood. *Soc Sci Med.* 56, 1607–1615.

Dominguez, R. C., Nelke, C. F. & Perry, B. D. (2002). Child sexual abuse. In: Levinson, D. (Ed.), *Encyclopedia of crime and punishment* (pp. 202–207). Newbury Park CA: Sage Publications.

Dörner, G. (1969). Zur Frage einer neuroendocrinen Pathogenese, Prophylaxe und Therapie angeborenen Sexualdeviationen. *Deutsche Medizinische Wochenschrift.* 94, 390–396.

Dörner, G. (1989/2001). Proposal for changing the status of homosexuality under the W.H.O.'s classification of diseases. *Neuroendocrinol Lett.* 22, 410.

Dörner, G., Geier, T., Ahrens, L., Krell, L., Munx, G., Sieler, H., Kittner, E. & Muller, H. (1980). Prenatal stress as possible aetiogenetic factor of homosexuality in human males. *Endokrinologie.* 75, 365–368.

Dörner, G., Poppe, I., Stahl, F., Kolzsch, J. & Uebelhack, R. (1991). Gene- and environment-dependent neuroendocrine etiogenesis of homosexuality and transsexualism. *Exp Clin Endocrinol.* 98, 141–150.

Dörner, G., Schenk, B., Schmiedel, B. & Ahrens, L. (1983). Stressful events in prenatal life of bi- and homosexual men. *Exp Clin Endocrinol.* 81.

Dover, K. J. (1978). *Greek homosexuality.* Boston: Harvard University Press.

Drummond, K. D., Bradley, S. J., Peterson-Badali, M. & Zucker, K. J. (2008). A follow-up study of girls with gender identity disorder. *Dev Psychol.* 44, 34–45.

Dugger, B. N., Morris, J. A., Jordan, C. L. & Breedlove, S. M. (2008). Gonadal steroids regulate neural plasticity in the sexually dimorphic nucleus of the preoptic area of adult male and female rats. *Neuroendocrinology*. 88, 17–24.

DuPree, M. G., Mustanski, B. S., Bocklandt, S., Nievergelt, C. & Hamer, D. H. (2004). A candidate gene study of CYP19 (aromatase) and male sexual orientation. *Behav Genet*. 34, 243–250.

Eaton, W. O. & Enns, R. (1986). Sex differences in human motor activity level. *Psychol Bull*. 100, 19–28.

Eckert, E. D., Bouchard, T. J., Bohlen, J. & Heston, L. L. (1986). Homosexuality in monozygotic twins reared apart. *Br J Psychiatry*. 148, 421–425.

Eckes, T. & Trautner, H. M. (Eds.). (2000). *The developmental social psychology of gender*. New York: Lawrence Erlbaum.

Eibl-Eibesfeldt, I. (2007). *Human Ethology*. New York: Aldine.

Ellis, L. & Ames, M. A. (1987). Neurohormonal functioning and sexual orientation: a theory of homosexuality-heterosexuality. *Psychol Bull*. 101, 233–258.

Ellis, L., Ames, M. A., Peckham, W. & Ahrens, L. (1988). Sexual orientation of human offspring may be altered by severe maternal stress during pregnancy. *J Sex Res*. 25, 152–157.

Ellis, L. & Blanchard, R. (2001). Birth order, sibling sex ratio, and maternal miscarriages in homosexual and heterosexual men and women. *Pers Individ Dif*. 30, 543–552.

Ellis, L., Hoffman, H. & Burke, D. M. (1990). Sex, sexual orientation and criminal and violent behavior. *Pers Individ Dif*. 11, 1207–1211.

Esquifino, A. I., Chacon, F., Jimenez, V., Reyes Toso, C. F. & Cardinali, D. P. (2004). 24-hour changes in circulating prolactin, follicle-stimulating hormone, luteinizing hormone and testosterone in male rats subjected to social isolation. *J Circadian Rhythms*. 2, 1.

Eysenck, H. J. (1985). *Decline and fall of the Freudian empire.* New York: Viking.

Faderman, L. (1991). *Odd girls and twilight lovers: A history of lesbian life in twentieth-century America.* Irvington NY: Columbia University Press.

Fagot, B. I., Leinbach, M. D. & O'Boyle, C. (1992). Gender labeling, gender stereotyping, and parenting behaviors. *Dev Psychol.* 28, 440–443.

Fenigstein, A. & Preston, M. (2007). The desired number of sexual partners as a function of gender, sexual risks, and the meaning of "ideal". *J Sex Res.* 44, 89–95.

Ferveur, J. F., Savarit, F., O'Kane, C. J., Sureau, G., Greenspan, R. J. & Jallon, J. M. (1997). Genetic feminization of pheromones and its behavioral consequences in *Drosophila* males. *Science.* 276, 1555–1558.

Fink, B., Brewer, G., Fehl, K. & Neave, N. (2007). Instrumentality and lifetime number of sexual partners. *Pers Individ Dif.* 43, 747–756.

Fink, B., Neave, N., Manning, J. T. & Grammer, K. (2006). Facial symmetry and judgements of attractiveness, health and personality. *Pers Individ Dif.* 41, 491–499.

Finley, K. D., Taylor, B. J., Milstein, M. & McKeown, M. (1997). dissatisfaction, a gene involved in sex-specific behavior and neural development of *Drosophila* melanogaster. *Proc Natl Acad Sci U S A.* 94, 913–918.

Flores, S. A., Mansergh, G., Marks, G., Guzman, R. & Colfax, G. (2009). Gay identity-related factors and sexual risk among men who have sex with men in San Francisco. *AIDS Educ Prev.* 21, 91–103.

Ford, J. J. (1983). Postnatal differentiation of sexual preference in male pigs. *Horm Behav.* 17, 152–162.

Forger, N. G. (2009). Control of cell number in the sexually dimorphic brain and spinal cord. *J Neuroendocrinol.* 21, 393–399.

Forger, N. G., Rosen, G. J., Waters, E. M., Jacob, D., Simerly, R. B. & de Vries, G. J. (2004). Deletion of Bax eliminates sex differences in the mouse forebrain. *Proc Natl Acad Sci U S A.* 101, 13666–13671.

Francis, A. M. (2008). Family and sexual orientation: the family-demographic correlates of homosexuality in men and women. *J Sex Res.* 45, 371–377.

Freud, S. (1905/1975). *Three essays on the theory of sexuality*. New York: Basic Books.

Freud, S. (1920/1955). The psychogenesis of a case of homosexuality in a woman. In: Strachey, J. (Ed.), *The standard edition of the complete works of Sigmund Freud*, vol. 18, pp. 147–172. London: Hogarth.

Frisch, M. & Hviid, A. (2006). Childhood family correlates of heterosexual and homosexual marriages: a national cohort study of two million Danes. *Arch Sex Behav.* 35, 533–547.

Frisch, M. & Zdravkovic, S. (2010). Body size at birth and same-sex marriage in young adulthood. *Arch Sex Behav.* 39, 17–123.

Fruth, B. & Hohmann, G. (2006). Social grease for females? Same-sex genital contacts in wild bonobos. In: Sommer, V. and Vasey, P. L. (Eds.), *Homosexual behavior in animals: An evolutionary perspective* (pp. 294–315). Cambridge NJ: Cambridge University Press.

Fry, M. (1993). The rest of the story. *The Living Bird*. Winter, 19.

Galis, F., Ten Broek, C. M., Van Dongen, S. & Wijnaendts, L. C. (2010). Sexual dimorphism in the prenatal digit ratio (2D:4D). *Arch Sex Behav.* 39, 57–62.

Galor, O. & Moav, O. (2002). Natural selection and the origin of economic growth. *Q J Econ.* 117, 1133–1191.

Gangestad, S. W., Bailey, J. M. & Martin, N. G. (2000). Taxometric analyses of sexual orientation and gender identity. *J Pers Soc Psychol.* 78, 1109–1121.

Gao, B. & Moore, R. Y. (1996). The sexually dimorphic nucleus of the hypothalamus contains GABA neurons in rat and man. *Brain Res.* 742, 163–171.

Garagorri, J. M., Rodriguez, G., Lario-Elboj, A. J., Olivares, J. L., Lario-Munoz, A. & Orden, I. (2008). Reference levels for 17–hydroxyprogesterone, 11–desoxycortisol, cortisol, testosterone, dehydroepiandrosterone sulfate and androstenedione in infants from birth to six months of age. *Eur J Pediatr.* 167, 647–653.

Garcia-Falgueras, A. & Swaab, D. F. (2008). A sex difference in the hypothalamic uncinate nucleus: relationship to gender identity. *Brain.* 131, 3132–3146.

Gatewood, J. D., Wills, A., Shetty, S., Xu, J., Arnold, A. P., Burgoyne, P. S. & Rissman, E. F. (2006). Sex chromosome complement and gonadal sex influence aggressive and parental behaviors in mice. *J Neurosci.* 26, 2335–2342.

Gaudio, R. (1994). Sounding gay: Pitch properties in the speech of gay and straight men. *Amer Speech.* 69, 30–57.

Gavrilets, S. & Rice, W. R. (2006). Genetic models of homosexuality: generating testable predictions. *Proc Biol Sci.* 273, 3031–3038.

Gazzaniga, M. S. (2008). *Human: The science behind what makes us unique.* New York: Ecco.

Geary, D. C., Saults, S. J., Liu, F. & Hoard, M. K. (2000). Sex differences in spatial cognition, computational fluency, and arithmetical reasoning. *J Exp Child Psychol.* 77, 337–353.

Geist, V. (1971). *Mountain sheep: A study in behavior and evolution.* Chicago: University of Chicago Press.

Geschwind, N. & Galaburda, A. M. (1985). Cerebral lateralization. Biological mechanisms, associations, and pathology: III. A hypothesis and a program for research. *Arch Neurol.* 42, 634–654.

Gill, K. S. (1963). A mutation causing abnormal courtship and mating behavior in males of *Drosophila melanogaster. Amer Zool.* 3, 507.

Gladue, B. A. & Bailey, J. M. (1995a). Aggressiveness, competitiveness, and human sexual orientation. *Psychoneuroendocrinology.* 20, 475–485.

Gladue, B. A. & Bailey, J. M. (1995b). Spatial ability, handedness, and human sexual orientation. *Psychoneuroendocrinology*. 20, 487–497.

Goldfoot, D. A., Wallen, K., Neff, D. A., McBrair, M. C. & Goy, R. W. (1984). Social influence on the display of sexually dimorphic behavior in rhesus monkeys: isosexual rearing. *Arch Sex Behav*. 13, 395–412.

Goldstein, J. M., Seidman, L. J., Horton, N. J., Makris, N., Kennedy, D. N., Caviness, V. S., Jr., Faraone, S. V. & Tsuang, M. T. (2001). Normal sexual dimorphism of the adult human brain assessed by in vivo magnetic resonance imaging. *Cereb Cortex*. 11, 490–497.

Goodenough, E. W. (1957). Interest in persons as an aspect of sex difference in the early years. *Genet Psychol Monogr*. 55, 287–323.

Gorski, R. A. (1985). Sexual dimorphisms of the brain. *J Anim Sci*. 61 Suppl 3, 38–61.

Gorski, R. A., Gordon, J. H., Shryne, J. E. & Southam, A. M. (1978). Evidence for a morphological sex difference within the medial preoptic area of the rat brain. *Brain Res*. 148, 333–346.

Goto, K., Koizumi, K., Ohta, Y., Hashi, M., Fujii, Y., Ohbo, N., Saika, O., Suzuki, H., Saito, K. & Suzuki, K. (2005). Evaluation of general behavior, memory, learning performance, and brain sexual differentiation in F1 offspring males of rats treated with flutamide during late gestation. *J Toxicol Sci*. 30, 249–259.

Gouchie, C. & Kimura, D. (1991). The relationship between testosterone levels and cognitive ability patterns. *Psychoneuroendocrinology*. 16, 323–334.

Gower, D. B., Holland, K. T., Mallet, A. I., Rennie, P. J. & Watkins, W. J. (1994). Comparison of 16–androstene steroid concentrations in sterile apocrine sweat and axillary secretions: interconversions of 16–androstenes by the axillary microflora--a mechanism for axillary odour production in man? *J Steroid Biochem Mol Biol*. 48, 409–418.

Goy, R. W., Bercovitch, F. B. & McBrair, M. C. (1988). Behavioral masculinization is independent of genital masculinization in prenatally androgenized female rhesus macaques. *Horm Behav.* 22, 552–571.

Green, R. (1987). *The "sissy-boy syndrome" and the development of homosexuality.* New Haven: Yale University Press.

Green, R. (2000). Birth order and ratio of brothers to sisters in transsexuals. *Psychol Med.* 30, 789–795.

Greenfeld, L. A. (1997). *Sex offenses and offenders: An analysis of data on rape and sexual assault.* Available at http://www.vaw.umn.edu/ FinalDocuments/sexoff.asp#; accessed January 14, 2010.

Grellert, E. A., Newcomb, M. D. & Bentler, P. M. (1982). Childhood play activities of male and female homosexuals and heterosexuals. *Arch Sex Behav.* 11, 451–478.

Grimbos, T., Dawood, K., Burriss, R. P., Zucker, K. J. & Puts, D. A. (2010). Sexual orientation and the second to fourth finger length ratio: A meta-analysis in men and women. *Behav Neurosci.* 124, 278–287.

Grimshaw, G. M., Sitarenios, G. & Finegan, J. A. (1995). Mental rotation at 7 years: relations with prenatal testosterone levels and spatial play experiences. *Brain Cogn.* 29, 85–100.

Grosjean, Y., Balakireva, M., Dartevelle, L. & Ferveur, J. F. (2001). PGal4 excision reveals the pleiotropic effects of Voila, a *Drosophila* locus that affects development and courtship behaviour. *Genet Res.* 77, 239–250.

Grosjean, Y., Grillet, M., Augustin, H., Ferveur, J. F. & Featherstone, D. E. (2008). A glial amino-acid transporter controls synapse strength and courtship in *Drosophila. Nat Neurosci.* 11, 54–61.

Grumbach, M. M. & Auchus, R. J. (1999). Estrogen: consequences and implications of human mutations in synthesis and action. *J Clin Endocrinol Metab.* 84, 4677–4694.

Habert, R. & Picon, R. (1984). Testosterone, dihydrotestosterone and estradiol-17 beta levels in maternal and fetal plasma and in fetal testes in the rat. *J Steroid Biochem.* 21, 193–198.

Haines, M. (2008). *Fertility and mortality in the United States.* Available at http://eh.net/encyclopedia/article/haines.demography; accessed January 14, 2010.

Halari, R., Hines, M., Kumari, V., Mehrotra, R., Wheeler, M., Ng, V. & Sharma, T. (2005). Sex differences and individual differences in cognitive performance and their relationship to endogenous gonadal hormones and gonadotropins. *Behav Neurosci.* 119, 104–117.

Haldeman, D. C. (1994). The practice and ethics of sexual orientation conversion therapy. *J Consult Clin Psychol.* 62, 221–227.

Hall, J. A. Y. & Kimura, D. (1995). Sexual orientation and performance on sexually dimorphic motor tasks. *Arch Sex Behav.* 24, 395–407.

Hall, L. S. (2000). Dermatoglyphic analysis of total finger ridge count of female monozygotic twins discordant for sexual orientation. *J Sex Res.* 37, 315–320.

Hall, L. S. & Love, C. T. (2003). Finger-length ratios in female monozygotic twins discordant for sexual orientation. *Arch Sex Behav.* 32, 23–28.

Hall, P. A. & Schaeff, C. M. (2008). Sexual orientation and fluctuating asymmetry in men and women. *Arch Sex Behav.* 37, 158–165.

Halpern, D. F. (2000). *Sex differences in cognitive abilities* (3rd. ed.). New York: Lawrence Erlbaum.

Hamer, D. & Copeland, P. (1994). *The science of desire: The search for the gay gene and the biology of behavior.* New York: Simon and Schuster.

Hamer, D. H. (1999). Genetics and male sexual orientation. *Science.* 285, 803.

Hamer, D. H., Hu, S., Magnuson, V. L., Hu, N. & Pattatucci, A. M. (1993). A linkage between DNA markers on the X chromosome and male sexual orientation. *Science.* 261, 321–327.

Hampson, E., Ellis, C. L. & Tenk, C. M. (2008). On the relation between 2D:4D and sex-dimorphic personality traits. *Arch Sex Behav.* 37, 133–144.

Harding, R. & Golombok, S. E. (2002). Test-retest reliability of the measurement of penile dimensions in a sample of gay men. *Arch Sex Behav.* 31, 351–357.

Hare, E. H. & Moran, P. A. (1979). Parental age and birth order in homosexual patients: a replication of Slater's study. *Br J Psychiatry.* 134, 178–182.

Harry, J. & DeVall, W. B. (1978). *The social organization of gay males.* New York: Praeger.

Hart, T. A., Wolitski, R. J., Purcell, D. W., Gomez, C. & Halkitis, P. (2003). Sexual behavior among HIV-positive men who have sex with men: what's in a label? *J Sex Res.* 40, 179–188.

Hassan, B. & Rahman, Q. (2007). Selective sexual orientation-related differences in object location memory. *Behav Neurosci.* 121, 625–633.

Hassett, J. M., Siebert, E. R. & Wallen, K. (2008). Sex differences in rhesus monkey toy preferences parallel those of children. *Horm Behav.* 54, 359–364.

Hegarty, P. (2009). Toward an LGBT-informed paradigm for children who break gender norms: Comment on Drummond et al. (2008) and Rieger et al. (2008). *Dev Psychol.* 45, 895–900.

Henderson, B. A. & Berenbaum, S. A. (1997). Sex-typed play in opposite-sex twins. *Dev Psychobiol.* 31, 115–123.

Herdt, G. H. (1981). *Guardians of the flutes: Idioms of masculinity.* New York: McGraw-Hill.

Herlitz, A. & Kabir, Z. N. (2006). Sex differences in cognition among illiterate Bangladeshis: a comparison with literate Bangladeshis and Swedes. *Scand J Psychol.* 47, 441–447.

Hershberger, S. L. (1997). A twin registry study of male and female sexual orientation. *J Sex Res.* 34, 212–222.

Hines, M., Ahmed, S. F. & Hughes, I. A. (2003a). Psychological outcomes and gender-related development in complete androgen insensitivity syndrome. *Arch Sex Behav.* 32, 93–101.

Hines, M., Allen, L. S. & Gorski, R. A. (1992). Sex differences in subregions of the medial nucleus of the amygdala and the bed nucleus of the stria terminalis of the rat. *Brain Res.* 579, 321–326.

Hines, M., Brook, C. & Conway, G. S. (2004). Androgen and psychosexual development: core gender identity, sexual orientation and recalled childhood gender role behavior in women and men with congenital adrenal hyperplasia (CAH). *J Sex Res.* 41, 75–81.

Hines, M., Fane, B. A., Pasterski, V. L., Mathews, G. A., Conway, G. S. & Brook, C. (2003b). Spatial abilities following prenatal androgen abnormality: targeting and mental rotations performance in individuals with congenital adrenal hyperplasia. *Psychoneuroendocrinology.* 28, 1010–1026.

Hines, M., Golombok, S., Rust, J., Johnston, K. J. & Golding, J. (2002). Testosterone during pregnancy and gender role behavior of preschool children: a longitudinal, population study. *Child Dev.* 73, 1678–1687.

Hofman, M. A. & Swaab, D. F. (1989). The sexually dimorphic nucleus of the preoptic area in the human brain: a comparative morphometric study. *J Anat.* 164, 55–72.

Hooker, C. I., Germine, L. T., Knight, R. T. & D'Esposito, M. (2006). Amygdala response to facial expressions reflects emotional learning. *J Neurosci.* 26, 8915–8922.

Hu, S., Pattatucci, A. M., Patterson, C., Li, L., Fulker, D. W., Cherny, S. S., Kruglyak, L. & Hamer, D. H. (1995). Linkage between sexual orientation and chromosome Xq28 in males but not in females. *Nat Genet.* 11, 248–256.

Hu, S. H., Wei, N., Wang, Q. D., Yan, L. Q., Wei, E. Q., Zhang, M. M., Hu, J. B., Huang, M. L., Zhou, W. H. & Xu, Y. (2008). Patterns of brain activation during visually evoked sexual arousal differ between homosexual and heterosexual men. *AJNR Am J Neuroradiol.* 29, 1890–1896.

Hunt, G. L., Jr., Newman, A. L., Warner, M. H., Wingfield, J. C. & Kaiwi, J. (1984). Comparative behavior of male-female and female-female pairs among western gulls prior to egg-laying. *The Condor.* 86, 157–162.

Hunt, G. L., Jr. & Warner Hunt, M. (1977). Female-female pairing in western gulls (*Larus occidentalis*) in Southern California. *Science.* 196, 1466–1467.

Hunt, G. L., Jr., Wingfield, J. C., Newman, A. & Farner, D. S. (1980). Sex ratios of gulls on Santa Barbara Island. *The Auk.* 97, 473–479.

Iemmola, F. & Camperio-Ciani, A. (2009). New evidence of genetic factors influencing sexual orientation in men: female fecundity increase in the maternal line. *Arch Sex Behav.* 38, 393–399.

Ikeda, Y., Nishiyama, N., Saito, H. & Katsuki, H. (1997). GABAA receptor stimulation promotes survival of embryonic rat striatal neurons in culture. *Brain Res Dev Brain Res.* 98, 253–258.

Imperato-McGinley, J., Pichardo, M., Gautier, T., Voyer, D. & Bryden, M. P. (1991). Cognitive abilities in androgen-insensitive subjects: comparison with control males and females from the same kindred. *Clin Endocrinol (Oxf).* 34, 341–347.

Isay, R. A. (1989). *Being homosexual: Gay men and their development.* New York: Farrar, Straus and Giroux.

Isay, R. A. (1999). Gender development in homosexual boys: Some developmental and clinical considerations. *Psychiatry.* 62, 187–194.

Isay, R. A. (2006). *Commitment and healing: Gay men and the need for romantic love.* New York: Wiley.

Ito, H., Fujitani, K., Usui, K., Shimizu-Nishikawa, K., Tanaka, S. & Yamamoto, D. (1996). Sexual orientation in *Drosophila* is altered by the satori mutation in the sex-determination gene fruitless that encodes a zinc finger protein with a BTB domain. *Proc Natl Acad Sci U S A.* 93, 9687–9692.

James, E., Chai, J. G., Dewchand, H., Macchiarulo, E., Dazzi, F. & Simpson, E. (2003). Multiparity induces priming to male-specific minor histocompatibility antigen, HY, in mice and humans. *Blood.* 102, 388–393.

Janssen, E., Carpenter, D. & Graham, C. A. (2003). Selecting films for sex research: gender differences in erotic film preference. *Arch Sex Behav.* 32, 243–251.

Jansson, J. O., Ekberg, S., Isaksson, O., Mode, A. & Gustafsson, J. A. (1985). Imprinting of growth hormone secretion, body growth, and hepatic steroid metabolism by neonatal testosterone. *Endocrinology.* 117, 1881–1889.

Jeong, J. K., Ryu, B. J., Choi, J., Kim, D. H., Choi, E. J., Park, J. W., Park, J. J. & Lee, B. J. (2008). NELL2 participates in formation of the sexually dimorphic nucleus of the pre-optic area in rats. *J Neurochem.* 106, 1604–1613.

Johnson, K. L., Gill, S., Reichman, V. & Tassinary, L. G. (2007). Swagger, sway, and sexuality: Judging sexual orientation from body motion and morphology. *J Pers Soc Psychol.* 93, 321–334.

Johnson, K. L. & Tassinary, L. G. (2005). Perceiving sex directly and indirectly: meaning in motion and morphology. *Psychol Sci.* 16, 890–897.

Johnston, V. S., Hagel, R., Franklin, M., Fink, B. & Grammer, K. (2001). Male facial attractiveness: Evidence for hormone mediated adaptive design. *Evol Hum Behav.* 22, 251–267.

Jozet-Alves, C., Moderan, J. & Dickel, L. (2008). Sex differences in spatial cognition in an invertebrate: the cuttlefish. *Proc Biol Sci.* 275, 2049–2054.

Kendler, K. S., Thornton, L. M., Gilman, S. E. & Kessler, R. C. (2000). Sexual orientation in a U.S. national sample of twin and nontwin sibling pairs. *Am J Psychiatry.* 157, 1843–1846.

Kennedy, E. L. & Davis, M. D. (1983). *Boots of leather, slippers of gold: The history of a lesbian community.* New York: Routledge.

Kennedy, H. (1988). *Ulrichs: The life and work of Karl Heinrich Ulrichs, pioneer of the modern gay movement.* New York: Alyson Publications.

Kerchner, M. & Ward, I. L. (1992). SDN-MPOA volume in male rats is decreased by prenatal stress, but is not related to ejaculatory behavior. *Brain Res.* 581, 244–251.

Kerns, K. A. & Berenbaum, S. A. (1991). Sex differences in spatial ability in children. *Behav Genet.* 21, 383–396.

Kilpatrick, L. A., Zald, D. H., Pardo, J. V. & Cahill, L. F. (2006). Sex-related differences in amygdala functional connectivity during resting conditions. *Neuroimage.* 30, 452–461.

Kimchi, T., Xu, J. & Dulac, C. (2007). A functional circuit underlying male sexual behaviour in the female mouse brain. *Nature.* 448, 1009–1014.

Kimura, D. (1994). Body asymmetry and intellectual pattern. *Pers Individ Dif.* 17, 53–60.

Kimura, D. (1999). *Sex and cognition.* Boston: MIT Press.

Kimura, D. & Carson, M. W. (1995). Dermatoglyphic asymmetry: Relation to sex, handedness and cognitive pattern. *Pers Individ Dif.* 19, 471–478.

Kimura, K., Hachiya, T., Koganezawa, M., Tazawa, T. & Yamamoto, D. (2008). Fruitless and doublesex coordinate to generate male-specific neurons that can initiate courtship. *Neuron.* 59, 759–769.

Kindon, H. A., Baum, M. J. & Paredes, R. J. (1996). Medial preoptic/anterior hypothalamic lesions induce a female-typical profile of sexual partner preference in male ferrets. *Horm Behav.* 30, 514–527.

King, M., Green, J., Osborn, D. P., Arkell, J., Hetherton, J. & Pereira, E. (2005). Family size in white gay and heterosexual men. *Arch Sex Behav.* 34, 117–122.

Kirk, K. M., Bailey, J. M., Dunne, M. P. & Martin, N. G. (2000). Measurement models for sexual orientation in a community twin sample. *Behav Genet.* 30, 345–356.

Kite, M. E. & Deaux, K. (1987). Gender belief systems: Homosexuality and the implicit inversion theory. *Psychol Women Q.* 11, 83–96.

Klar, A. J. S. (2005). Excess of counterclockwise scalp hair-whorl rotation in homosexual men. *J Genet.* 83 (3), 251–255.

Klein, K. O., Baron, J., Colli, M. J., McDonnell, D. P. & Cutler, G. B., Jr. (1994). Estrogen levels in childhood determined by an ultrasensitive recombinant cell bioassay. *J Clin Invest.* 94, 2475–2480.

Knecht, M., Lundstrom, J. N., Witt, M., Huttenbrink, K. B., Heilmann, S. & Hummel, T. (2003). Assessment of olfactory function and androstenone odor thresholds in humans with or without functional occlusion of the vomeronasal duct. *Behav Neurosci.* 117, 1135–1141.

Koerner, D. & LeVay, S. (2000). *Here be dragons: The scientific quest for extraterrestrial life.* New York: Oxford University Press.

Kohl, J. V. (2007). The mind's eye: Human pheromones, neuroscience, and male sexual preferences. *J Psychol Hum Sex.* 18, 313–369.

Kohl, J. V., Atzmueller, M., Fink, B. & Grammer, K. (2001). Human pheromones: integrating neuroendocrinology and ethology. *Neuro Endocrinol Lett.* 22, 309–321.

Koshibu, K., Levitt, P. & Ahrens, E. T. (2004). Sex-specific, postpuberty changes in mouse brain structures revealed by three-dimensional magnetic resonance microscopy. *Neuroimage.* 22, 1636–1645.

Kotrschal, K., Hemetsberger, J. & Weiss, B. M. (2006). Making the best of a bad situation: Homosociality in male greylag geese. In: Sommer, V. and Vasey, P. L. (Eds.), *Homosexual behavior in animals: An evolutionary perspective* (pp. 45–76). Cambridge NJ: Cambridge University Press.

Kouros-Mehr, H., Pintchovski, S., Melnyk, J., Chen, Y. J., Friedman, C., Trask, B. & Shizuya, H. (2001). Identification of non-functional human VNO receptor genes provides evidence for vestigiality of the human VNO. *Chem Senses.* 26, 1167–1174.

Kraemer, B., Noll, T., Delsignore, A., Milos, G., Schnyder, U. & Hepp, U. (2006). Finger length ratio (2D:4D) and dimensions of sexual orientation. *Neuropsychobiology.* 53, 210–214.

Kraemer, B., Noll, T., Delsignore, A., Milos, G., Schnyder, U. & Hepp, U. (2009). Finger length ratio (2D:4D) in adults with gender identity disorder. *Arch Sex Behav.* 38, 359–363.

Kranz, F. & Ishai, A. (2006). Face perception is modulated by sexual preference. *Curr Biol.* 16, 63–68.

Kudwa, A. E. & Rissman, E. F. (2003). Double oestrogen receptor alpha and beta knockout mice reveal differences in neural oestrogen-mediated progestin receptor induction and female sexual behaviour. *J Neuroendocrinol.* 15, 978–983.

Lalumière, M. L., Blanchard, R. & Zucker, K. J. (2000). Sexual orientation and handedness in men and women: a meta-analysis. *Psychol Bull.* 126, 575–592.

Laan, E., Sonderman, M. & Janssen, E. (1996). Straight and lesbian women's sexual responses to straight and lesbian erotica: No sexual orientation effects. Poster presentation at the 22nd Annual Meeting of the International Academy of Sex Research, Rotterdam, Netherlands.

Lame Deer, J. F. & Erdoes, R. (1972). *Lame Deer: Seeker of visions.* New York: Simon and Schuster.

Långström, N., Rahman, Q., Carlström, E. & Lichtenstein, P. (2010). Genetic and environmental effects on same-sex sexual behavior: A population study of twins in Sweden. *Arch Sex Behav.* 39, 75–80.

Lasco, M. S., Jordan, T. J., Edgar, M. A., Petito, C. K. & Byne, W. (2002). A lack of dimorphism of sex or sexual orientation in the human anterior commissure. *Brain Res.* 936, 95–98.

Laumann, E. O., Gagnon, J. H., Michael, R. T. & Michaels, S. (1994). *The social organization of sexuality: Sexual practices in the United States.* Chicago: University of Chicago Press.

Laws, D. R. & O'Donohue, W. T. (2008). *Sexual deviance: Theory, assessment, and treatment* (2nd ed.). New York: Guilford Press.

Lephart, E. D., Call, S. B., Rhees, R. W., Jacobson, N. A., Weber, K. S., Bledsoe, J. & Teuscher, C. (2001). Neuroendocrine regulation of sexually dimorphic brain structure and associated sexual behavior in male rats is genetically controlled. *Biol Reprod.* 64, 571–578.

LeVay, S. (1991). A difference in hypothalamic structure between heterosexual and homosexual men. *Science.* 253, 1034–1037.

LeVay, S. (1996). *Queer science: The use and abuse of research into homosexuality.* Boston: MIT Press.

Lever, J. (1994). Sexual revelations: The 1994 Advocate survey of sexuality and relationships: The men. *The Advocate*, August 23, 17–24.

Lever, J. (1995). Lesbian sex survey. *The Advocate*, August 22, 21–30.

Levitt, E. E. & Klassen, A. D. (1974). Public attitudes toward homosexuality: Part of the 1970 national survey by the Institute for Sex Research. *J Homosex.* 1, 29–43.

Lewontin, R. C. (1995). Sex, lies, and social science.*New York Review of Books*, 24–29.

Linville, S. E. (1998). Acoustic correlates of perceived versus actual sexual orientation in men's speech. *Folia Phoniatrica et Logopedica.* 50, 35–48.

Lippa, R. (1998). Gender-related individual differences and the structure of vocational interests: the importance of the people-things dimension. *J Pers Soc Psychol.* 74, 996–1009.

Lippa, R. & Hershberger, S. (1999). Genetic and environmental influences on individual differences in masculinity, femininity, and gender diagnosticity: analyzing data from a classic twin study. *J Pers.* 67, 127–155.

Lippa, R. & Patterson, T. M. (2010). Looking at and longing for male and female "swimsuit models": Men are much more category-specific than women. *Social Psychological and Personality Science* (in press).

Lippa, R. A. (2003a). Are 2D:4D finger-length ratios related to sexual orientation? Yes for men, no for women. *J Pers Soc Psychol.* 85, 179–188.

Lippa, R. A. (2003b). Handedness, sexual orientation, and gender-related personality traits in men and women. *Arch Sex Behav.* 32, 103–114.

Lippa, R. A. (2005a). *Gender, nature, and nurture* (2nd. ed.). New York: Lawrence Erlbaum.

Lippa, R. A. (2005b). Sexual orientation and personality. *Annu Rev Sex Res.* 16, 119–153.

Lippa, R. A. (2006). Finger lengths, 2D:4D ratios, and their relation to gender-related personality traits and the Big Five. *Biol Psychol.* 71, 116–121.

Lippa, R. A. (2009). Sex differences in sex drive, sociosexuality, and height across 53 nations: Testing evolutionary and social structural theories. *Arch Sex Behav.* 38, 631–651.

Lippa, R. A. (2008a). The relation between childhood gender nonconformity and adult masculinity-femininity and anxiety in heterosexual and homosexual men and women. *Sex Roles.* 59, 684–693.

Lippa, R. A. (2008b). Sex differences and sexual orientation differences in personality: findings from the BBC Internet survey. *Arch Sex Behav.* 37, 173–187.

Liu, T., Dartevelle, L., Yuan, C., Wei, H., Wang, Y., Ferveur, J. F. & Guo, A. (2008). Increased dopamine level enhances male-male courtship in *Drosophila*. *J Neurosci*. 28, 5539–5546.

Liu, T., Dartevelle, L., Yuan, C., Wei, H., Wang, Y., Ferveur, J. F. & Guo, A. (2009). Reduction of dopamine level enhances the attractiveness of male *Drosophila* to other males. *PLoS ONE*. 4, e4574.

Loehlin, J. C., Jonsson, E. G., Gustavsson, J. P., Stallings, M. C., Gillespie, N. A., Wright, M. J. & Martin, N. G. (2005). Psychological masculinity-femininity via the gender diagnosticity approach: heritability and consistency across ages and populations. *J Pers*. 73, 1295–1319.

Loehlin, J. C. & McFadden, D. (2003). Otoacoustic emissions, auditory evoked potentials, and traits related to sex and sexual orientation. *Arch Sex Behav*. 32, 115–127.

Loehlin, J. C., Medland, S. E. & Martin, N. G. (2009). Relative finger lengths, sex differences, and psychological traits. *Arch Sex Behav*. 38, 298–305.

Lohman, D. F. & Lakin, J. M. (2008). Consistencies in sex differences on the Cognitive Abilities Test across countries, grades, test forms, and cohorts. *Br J Educ Psychol*. 2009; 79(Part 2), 389–407. (Epub September 25, 2008).

Lovejoy, J. & Wallen, K. (1988). Sexually dimorphic behavior in group-housed rhesus monkeys (*Macaca mulatta*) at 1 year of age. *Psychobiology*. 16, 348–356.

Ludwig, W. (1932). *Das Rechts-links-Problem im Tierreich und beim Menschen*. Berlin: Springer.

Luine, V. & Dohanich, G. (2007). Sex differences in cognitive function in rodents. In: Becker, J. B. et al. (Eds.), *Sex differences in the brain: From genes to behavior* (pp. 217–251). New York: Oxford University Press.

Lutchmaya, S., Baron-Cohen, S., Raggatt, P., Knickmeyer, R. & Manning, J. T. (2004). 2nd to 4th digit ratios, fetal testosterone and estradiol. *Early Hum Dev.* 77, 23–28.

Maccoby, E. E. (1998). *The two sexes: Growing up apart, coming together.* Boston: Harvard University Press.

Maccoby, E. E., Doering, C. H., Jacklin, C. N. & Kraemer, H. (1979). Concentrations of sex hormones in umbilical-cord blood: their relation to sex and birth order of infants. *Child Dev.* 50, 632–642.

MacCulloch, M. J. & Waddington, J. L. (1981). Neuroendocrine mechanisms and the aetiology of male and female homosexuality. *Br J Psychiatry.* 139, 341–345.

Macke, J. P., Hu, N., Hu, S., Bailey, M., King, V. L., Brown, T., Hamer, D. & Nathans, J. (1993). Sequence variation in the androgen receptor gene is not a common determinant of male sexual orientation. *Am J Hum Genet.* 53, 844–852.

Madon, S. (1997). What do people believe about gay males? A study of stereotype content and strength. *Sex roles.* 37, 663–685.

Manning, J. T., Churchill, A. J. & Peters, M. (2007). The effects of sex, ethnicity, and sexual orientation on self-measured digit ratio (2D:4D). *Arch Sex Behav.* 36, 223–233.

Manning, J. T. & Fink, B. (2008). Digit ratio (2D:4D), dominance, reproductive success, asymmetry, and sociosexuality in the BBC Internet Study. *Am J Hum Biol.* 20, 451–461.

Manning, J. T., Scutt, D., Wilson, J. & Lewis-Jones, D. I. (1998). The ratio of 2nd to 4th digit length: a predictor of sperm numbers and concentrations of testosterone, luteinizing hormone and oestrogen. *Hum Reprod.* 13, 3000–3004.

Mansukhani, V., Adkins-Regan, E. & Yang, S. (1996). Sexual partner preference in female zebra finches: the role of early hormones and social environment. *Horm Behav.* 30, 506–513.

Marcus, E. (1992). *Making history: the struggle for gay and lesbian equal rights.* New York: HarperCollins.

Maresh, M. M. (1955). Linear growth of long bones of extremities from infancy through adolescence; continuing studies. *AMA Am J Dis Child.* 89, 725–742.

Marmor, J. (1980). The multiple roots of homosexual behavior. In: Marmor, J. (Ed.), *Homosexual behavior: A modern reappraisal.* New York: Basic Books.

Marshall, W. A. & Tanner, J. M. (1974). Puberty. In: Davis, J. A. and Dobbing, J. (Eds.), *Scientific foundations of paediatrics.* London: William Heinemann Medical Books.

Martin, J. T. & Nguyen, D. H. (2004). Anthropometric analysis of homosexuals and heterosexuals: implications for early hormone exposure. *Horm Behav.* 45, 31–39.

Martin, J. T., Puts, D. A. & Breedlove, S. M. (2008). Hand asymmetry in heterosexual and homosexual men and women: relationship to 2D:4D digit ratios and other sexually dimorphic anatomical traits. *Arch Sex Behav.* 37, 119–132.

Martins, Y., Preti, G., Crabtree, C. R., Runyan, T., Vainius, A. A. & Wysocki, C. J. (2005). Preference for human body odors is influenced by gender and sexual orientation. *Psychol Sci.* 16, 694–701.

Masek, K. S., Wood, R. I. & Foster, D. L. (1999). Prenatal dihydrotestosterone differentially masculinizes tonic and surge modes of luteinizing hormone secretion in sheep. *Endocrinology.* 140, 3459–3466.

Mast, T. G. & Samuelsen, C. L. (2009). Human pheromone detection by the vomeronasal organ: unnecessary for mate selection? *Chem Senses.* 34, 529–531.

McCarthy, M. M. & Konkle, A. T. (2005). When is a sex difference not a sex difference? *Front Neuroendocrinol.* 26, 85–102.

McCormick, C. M. & Witelson, S. F. (1991). A cognitive profile of homosexual men compared to heterosexual men and women. *Psychoneuroendocrinology.* 16, 459–473.

McCormick, C. M. & Witelson, S. F. (1994). Functional cerebral asymmetry and sexual orientation in men and women. *Behav Neurosci.* 108, 525–531.

McCormick, C. M., Witelson, S. F. & Kingstone, E. (1990). Left-handedness in homosexual men and women: neuroendocrine implications. *Psychoneuroendocrinology.* 15, 69–76.

McEwen, B. S. (1998). Multiple ovarian hormone effects on brain structure and function. *J Gend Specif Med.* 1, 33–41.

McEwen, B. S. (2008). Introduction: The end of sex as we once knew it. *Physiol Behav.*

McFadden, D. (1998). Sex differences in the auditory system. *Developmental Neuropsychology.* 14, 261–298.

McFadden, D. & Champlin, C. A. (2000). Comparison of auditory evoked potentials in heterosexual, homosexual, and bisexual males and females. *J Assoc Res Otolaryngol.* 1, 89–99.

McFadden, D., Loehlin, J. C., Breedlove, S. M., Lippa, R. A., Manning, J. T. & Rahman, Q. (2005). A reanalysis of five studies on sexual orientation and the relative length of the 2nd and 4th fingers (the 2D:4D ratio). *Arch Sex Behav.* 34, 341–356.

McFadden, D., Loehlin, J. C. & Pasanen, E. G. (1996). Additional findings on heritability and prenatal masculinization of cochlear mechanisms: click-evoked otoacoustic emissions. *Hear Res.* 97, 102–119.

McFadden, D. & Pasanen, E. G. (1998). Comparison of the auditory systems of heterosexuals and homosexuals: click-evoked otoacoustic emissions. *Proc Natl Acad Sci U S A.* 95, 2709–2713.

McFadden, D. & Pasanen, E. G. (1999). Spontaneous otoacoustic emissions in heterosexuals, homosexuals, and bisexuals. *J Acoust Soc Am.* 105, 2403–2413.

McFadden, D., Pasanen, E. G., Raper, J., Lange, H. S. & Wallen, K. (2006). Sex differences in otoacoustic emissions measured in rhesus monkeys (*Macaca mulatta*). *Horm Behav.* 50, 274–284.

McFadden, D., Pasanen, E. G., Valero, M. D., Roberts, E. K. & Lee, T. M. (2009). Effect of prenatal androgens on click-evoked otoacoustic emissions in male and female sheep (*Ovis aries*). *Horm Behav.* 55, 98–105.

McFadden, D. & Shubel, E. (2002). Relative lengths of fingers and toes in human males and females. *Horm Behav.* 42, 492–500.

McGuire, R. J., Carlisle, J. M. & Young, B. G. (1965). Sexual deviations as conditioned behavior: A hypothesis. *Behav Res Ther.* 2, 185–190.

McIntyre, M. H., Barrett, E. S., McDermott, R., Johnson, D. D. P., Cowden, J. & Rosen, S. P. (2007). Finger length ratio (2D:4D) and sex differences in aggression during a simulated war game. *Pers Individ Dif.* 42, 755–764.

McKnight, J. & Malcolm, J. (2000). Is male homosexuality maternally linked? *Psychology, Evolution and Gender.* 2, 229–252.

Medland, S. E., Perelle, I., De Monte, V. & Ehrman, L. (2004). Effects of culture, sex, and age on the distribution of handedness: an evaluation of the sensitivity of three measures of handedness. *Laterality.* 9, 287–297.

Meek, L. R., Schulz-Wilson, K. M. & Keith, C. A. (2006). Effects of prenatal stress on sexual partner preference in mice. *Physiol Behav.* 89, 133–138.

Mehren, E. (2004). Acceptance of gays rises among new generation. *Los Angeles Times,* April 11.

Meyer-Bahlburg, H. F., Dolezal, C., Baker, S. W., Carlson, A. D., Obeid, J. S. & New, M. I. (2004). Prenatal androgenization affects gender-related behavior but not gender identity in 5–12–year-old girls with congenital adrenal hyperplasia. *Arch Sex Behav.* 33, 97–104.

Meyer-Bahlburg, H. F., Dolezal, C., Baker, S. W., Ehrhardt, A. A. & New, M. I. (2006). Gender development in women with congenital adrenal hyperplasia as a function of disorder severity. *Arch Sex Behav.* 35, 667–684.

Meyer-Bahlburg, H. F., Dolezal, C., Baker, S. W. & New, M. I. (2008). Sexual orientation in women with classical or non-classical congenital adrenal hyperplasia as a function of degree of prenatal androgen excess. *Arch Sex Behav.* 37, 85–99.

Meyer-Bahlburg, H. F. L. (1984). Psychoendocrine research on sexual orientation: Current status and future options. *Prog Brain Res.* 61, 375–398.

Miller, E. M. (2000). Homosexuality, birth order, and evolution: toward an equilibrium reproductive economics of homosexuality. *Arch Sex Behav.* 29, 1–34.

Milne, B., Belsky, J., Poulton, R., Thompson, W., Caspi, A. & Kieser, J. (2003). Fluctuating asymmetry and physical health among young adults. *Evol Hum Behav.* 24, 53–63.

Mitchell, C. K. & Redburn, D. A. (1996). GABA and GABA-A receptors are maximally expressed in association with cone synaptogenesis in neonatal rabbit retina. *Brain Res Dev Brain Res.* 95, 63–71.

Money, J. & Ehrhardt, A. E. (1971). *Man and woman, boy and girl: The differentiation and dimorphism of gender identity from conception to maturity.* Baltimore: Johns Hopkins University Press.

Money, J., Hampson, J. G. & Hampson, J. L. (1957). Imprinting and the establishment of gender role. *Arch Neurol Psychiatry.* 77, 333–336.

Money, J. & Russo, A. J. (1979). Homosexual outcome of discordant gender identity/role: Longitudinal follow-up. *J Pediatr Psychol.* 4, 29–41.

Moore, C. L. (1984). Maternal contributions to the development of masculine sexual behavior in laboratory rats. *Dev Psychobiol.* 17, 347–356.

Moore, C. L. (1992). The role of maternal stimulation in the development of sexual behavior and its neural basis. *Ann N Y Acad Sci.* 662, 160–177.

Moore, C. L., Dou, H. & Juraska, J. M. (1992). Maternal stimulation affects the number of motor neurons in a sexually dimorphic nucleus of the lumbar spinal cord. *Brain Res.* 572, 52–56.

Moore, C. L. & Morelli, G. A. (1979). Mother rats interact differently with male and female offspring. *J Comp Physiol Psychol.* 93, 677–684.

Moore, D. S. & Johnson, S. P. (2008). Mental rotation in human infants: a sex difference. *Psychol Sci.* 19, 1063–1066.

Mori, H., Matsuda, K., Pfaff, D. W. & Kawata, M. (2008). A recently identified hypothalamic nucleus expressing estrogen receptor alpha. *Proc Natl Acad Sci U S A.* 105, 13632–13637.

Morris, J. A., Jordan, C. L. & Breedlove, S. M. (2008a). Sexual dimorphism in neuronal number of the posterodorsal medial amygdala is independent of circulating androgens and regional volume in adult rats. *J Comp Neurol.* 506, 851–859.

Morris, J. A., Jordan, C. L., King, Z. A., Northcutt, K. V. & Breedlove, S. M. (2008b). Sexual dimorphism and steroid responsiveness of the posterodorsal medial amygdala in adult mice. *Brain Res.* 1190, 115–121.

Murnen, S. K. & Stockton, M. (1997). Gender and self-reported sexual arousal in response to sexual stimuli: A meta-analytic review. *Sex Roles.* 37, 135–153.

Murray, S. O. (2000). *Homosexualities.* Chicago: University of Chicago Press.

Mustanski, B. S., Bailey, J. M. & Kaspar, S. (2002). Dermatoglyphics, handedness, sex, and sexual orientation. *Arch Sex Behav.* 31, 113–132.

Mustanski, B. S., Dupree, M. G., Nievergelt, C. M., Bocklandt, S., Schork, N. J. & Hamer, D. H. (2005). A genomewide scan of male sexual orientation. *Hum Genet.* 116, 272–278.

Nanda, S. (1990). *Neither man nor woman: The hijras of India.* New York: Wadsworth.

National Library of Medicine. (2008). *Androgen insensitivity syndrome.* Available at http://ghr.nlm.nih.gov/condition=androgeninsensi tivitysyndrome; accessed January 14, 2010.

Neave, N., Menaged, M. & Weightman, D. R. (1999). Sex differences in cognition: the role of testosterone and sexual orientation. *Brain Cogn.* 41, 245–262.

Nedoma, K. & Freund, K. (1961). Somatosexulni nalezy u homosexual-nich muzu. *Ceskoslovenska Psychiatrie.* 57, 100–103.

Neglia, A., (2009) *Comedian Carol Leifer on her mid-life change.* Available at http://www.aolhealth.com/healthy-living/relationships/carol-l eifer?icid=main | welcome | dl3 | link3 | http%3A%2F%2Fwww. aolhealth.com%2Fhealthy-living%2Frelationships%2Fcarol-leifer; accessed January 14, 2010.

Nettle, D. (2007). Empathizing and systemizing: What are they, and what do they contribute to our understanding of psychological sex differences? *Brit J Psychol.* 98, 237–255.

Nicolosi, J. & Nicolosi, L. A. (2002). *A parent's guide to preventing homosexuality.* Downers Grove IL: InterVarsity Press.

Nielsen, H. S., Mortensen, L., Nygaard, U., Schnor, O., Christiansen, O. B. & Andersen, A. M. (2008). Brothers and reduction of the birth weight of later-born siblings. *Am J Epidemiol.* 167, 480–484.

Norton, R. (1999). *Mother Clap's molly house: The gay subculture in England,* 1700–1830. Kalispell MT: Heretic Books.

Obrietan, K. & van den Pol, A. N. (1995). GABA neurotransmission in the hypothalamus: developmental reversal from Ca2+ elevating to depressing. *J Neurosci.* 15, 5065–5077.

Ökten, A., Kalyoncu, M. & Yaris, N. (2002). The ratio of second- and fourth-digit lengths and congenital adrenal hyperplasia due to 21–hydroxylase deficiency. *Early Hum Dev.* 70, 47–54.

Oliver, M. B. & Hyde, J. S. (1993). Gender differences in sexuality: A meta-analysis. *Psychol Bull.* 114, 29–51.

Oosterhuis, H. (1991). Homosexual emancipation in Germany: Two traditions. In: Oosterhuis, H. and Kennedy, H. (Eds.), *Homosexuality and male bonding in pre-Nazi Germany* (pp. 1–27). Binghamton NY: Harrington Park Press.

Oosterhuis, H. & Kennedy, H. (1991). *Homosexuality and male bonding in pre-Nazi Germany.* Binghamton NY: Harrington Park Press.

Organisation Internationale des Intersexués. (2009). *Androgen insensitivity syndrome.* Available at http://www.intersexualite.org/AIS.html; accessed January 14, 2010.

Pallone, D. & Steinberg, A. (1990). *Behind the mask: My double life in baseball.* New York: Viking.

Papadatou-Pastou, M., Martin, M., Munafo, M. R. & Jones, G. V. (2008). Sex differences in left-handedness: a meta-analysis of 144 studies. *Psychol Bull.* 134, 677–699.

Paredes, R. G. & Baum, M. J. (1995). Altered sexual partner preference in male ferrets given excitotoxic lesions of the preoptic area/anterior hypothalamus. *J Neurosci.* 15, 6619–6630.

Paredes, R. G., Tzschentke, T. & Nakach, N. (1998). Lesions of the medial preoptic area/anterior hypothalamus (MPOA/AH) modify partner preference in male rats. *Brain Res.* 813, 1–8.

Pasterski, V., Hindmarsh, P., Geffner, M., Brook, C., Brain, C. & Hines, M. (2007). Increased aggression and activity level in 3– to 11–year-old girls with congenital adrenal hyperplasia (CAH). *Horm Behav.* 52, 368–374.

Pattatucci, A. M. & Hamer, D. H. (1995). Development and familiality of sexual orientation in females. *Behav Genet.* 25, 407–420.

Paul, T., Schiffer, B., Zwarg, T., Kruger, T. H., Karama, S., Schedlowski, M., Forsting, M. & Gizewski, E. R. (2008). Brain response to visual sexual stimuli in heterosexual and homosexual males. *Hum Brain Mapp.* 29, 726–735.

Pearcey, S. M., Docherty, K. J. & Dabbs, J. M., Jr. (1996). Testosterone and sex role identification in lesbian couples. *Physiol Behav.* 60, 1033–1035.

Pei, M., Matsuda, K., Sakamoto, H. & Kawata, M. (2006). Intrauterine proximity to male fetuses affects the morphology of the sexually dimorphic nucleus of the preoptic area in the adult rat brain. *Eur J Neurosci.* 23, 1234–1240.

Penton-Voak, I. S. & Perrett, D. I. (2000). Female preference for male faces change cyclically: Further evidence. *Evol Hum Behav.* 21, 39–48.

Perkins, A. & Fitzgerald, J. A. (1992a). Luteinizing hormone, testosterone, and behavioral response of male-oriented rams to estrous ewes and rams. *J Anim Sci.* 70, 1787–1794.

Perkins, A. & Fitzgerald, J. A. (1992b). Luteinizing hormone, testosterone, and behavioral response of male-oriented rams to estrous ewes and rams. *J Anim Sci.* 70, 1787–1794.

Perkins, A., Fitzgerald, J. A. & Moss, G. E. (1995). A comparison of LH secretion and brain estradiol receptors in heterosexual and homosexual rams and female sheep. *Horm Behav.* 29, 31–41.

Peters, M., Manning, J. T. & Reimers, S. (2007). The effects of sex, sexual orientation, and digit ratio (2D:4D) on mental rotation performance. *Arch Sex Behav.* 36, 251–260.

Petrulis, A. (2009). Neural mechanisms of individual and sexual recognition in Syrian hamsters (*Mesocricetus auratus*). *Behav Brain Res.* 200, 260–267.

Phoenix, C. H., Goy, R. W., Gerall, A. A. & Young, W. C. (1959). Organizing action of prenatally administered testosterone propionate on the tissues mediating mating behavior in the female guinea pig. *Endocrinology.* 65, 369–382.

Pierrehumbert, J. B., Bent, T., Munson, B., Bradlow, A. R. & Bailey, J. M. (2004). The influence of sexual orientation on vowel production. *J Acoustical Soc Amer.* 116, 1905–1908.

Pillard, R. C. (1990). The Kinsey scale: Is it familial? In: McWhirter, D. P. et al. (Eds.), *Homosexuality/heterosexuality: Concepts of sexual orientation.* New York: Oxford University Press.

Pillard, R. C., Poumadere, J. & Carretta, R. A. (1981). Is homosexuality familial? A review, some data, and a suggestion. *Arch Sex Behav.* 10, 465–475.

Pillard, R. C., Poumadere, J. & Carretta, R. A. (1982). A family study of sexual orientation. *Arch Sex Behav.* 11, 511–520.

Pillard, R. C. & Weinrich, J. D. (1986). Evidence of familial nature of male homosexuality. *Arch Gen Psychiatry.* 43, 808–812.

Piper, K. P., McLarnon, A., Arrazi, J., Horlock, C., Ainsworth, J., Kilby, M. D., Martin, W. L. & Moss, P. A. (2007). Functional HY-specific CD8+ T cells are found in a high proportion of women following pregnancy with a male fetus. *Biol Reprod.* 76, 96–101.

Plöderl, M. & Fartacek, R. (2008). Childhood gender nonconformity and harassment as predictors of suicidality among gay, lesbian, bisexual, and heterosexual Austrians. *Arch Sex Behav.* 38, 400–410.

Ponseti, J., Bosinski, H. A., Wolff, S., Peller, M., Jansen, O., Mehdorn, H. M., Buchel, C. & Siebner, H. R. (2006). A functional endophenotype for sexual orientation in humans. *Neuroimage.* 33, 825–833.

Ponseti, J., Granert, O., Jansen, O., Wolff, S., Mehdorn, H., Bosinski, H. & Siebner, H. (2009). Assessment of sexual orientation using the hemodynamic brain response to visual sexual stimuli. *J Sex Med.* 6, 1628–1634. (Epub March 17, 2009).

Ponseti, J., Siebner, H. R., Kloppel, S., Wolff, S., Granert, O., Jansen, O., Mehdorn, H. M. & Bosinski, H. A. (2007). Homosexual women have less grey matter in perirhinal cortex than heterosexual women. *PLoS ONE.* 2, e762.

Preti, G., Wysocki, C. J., Barnhart, K. T., Sondheimer, S. J. & Leyden, J. J. (2003). Male axillary extracts contain pheromones that affect pulsatile secretion of luteinizing hormone and mood in women recipients. *Biol Reprod.* 68, 2107–2113.

Purcell, D. W., Blanchard, R. & Zucker, K. J. (2000). Birth order in a contemporary sample of gay men. *Arch Sex Behav.* 29, 349–356.

Puts, D. A., Gaulin, S. J. C., Sporter, R. J. & McBurney, D. H. (2004). Sex hormones and finger length: What does 2D:4D indicate? *Evol Hum Behav.* 25, 182–199.

Quigley, C. A. (2002). The postnatal gonadotropin and sex steroid surge: Insights from the androgen insensitivity syndrome. *J Clin Endocrinol Metab.* 87, 24–28.

Quinn, P. C. & Liben, L. S. (2008). A sex difference in mental rotation in young infants. *Psychol Sci.* 19, 1067–1070.

Rafanello, D. (2004). *Can't touch my soul: A guide for lesbian survivors of child sexual abuse.* New York: Alyson Publications.

Rahman, Q. (2005a). The association between the fraternal birth order effect in male homosexuality and other markers of human sexual orientation. *Biol Lett.* 1, 393–395.

Rahman, Q. (2005b). Fluctuating asymmetry, second to fourth finger length ratios and human sexual orientation. *Psychoneuroendocrinology.* 30, 382–391.

Rahman, Q., Abrahams, S. & Wilson, G. D. (2003a). Sexual-orientation-related differences in verbal fluency. *Neuropsychology.* 17, 240–246.

Rahman, Q., Andersson, D. & Govier, E. (2005). A specific sexual orientation-related difference in navigation strategy. *Behav Neurosci.* 119, 311–316.

Rahman, Q., Clarke, K. & Morera, T. (2009). Hair whorl direction and sexual orientation in human males. *Behav Neurosci.* 123, 252–256.

Rahman, Q., Cockburn, A. & Govier, E. (2008a). A comparative analysis of functional cerebral asymmetry in lesbian women, heterosexual women, and heterosexual men. *Arch Sex Behav.* 37, 566–571.

Rahman, Q., Collins, A., Morrison, M., Orrells, J. C., Cadinouche, K., Greenfield, S. & Begum, S. (2008b). Maternal inheritance and familial fecundity factors in male homosexuality. *Arch Sex Behav.* 37, 962–969.

Rahman, Q. & Hull, M. S. (2005). An empirical test of the kin selection hypothesis for male homosexuality. *Arch Sex Behav.* 34, 461–467.

Rahman, Q., Kumari, V. & Wilson, G. D. (2003b). Sexual orientation-related differences in prepulse inhibition of the human startle response. *Behav Neurosci.* 117, 1096–1102.

Rahman, Q. & Silber, K. (2000). Sexual orientation and the sleep-wake cycle: a preliminary investigation. *Arch Sex Behav.* 29, 127–134.

Rahman, Q. & Wilson, G. D. (2003a). Large sexual-orientation-related differences in performance on mental rotation and judgment of line orientation tasks. *Neuropsychology.* 17, 25–31.

Rahman, Q. & Wilson, G. D. (2003b). Sexual orientation and the 2nd to 4th finger length ratio: evidence for organising effects of sex hormones or developmental instability? *Psychoneuroendocrinology.* 28, 288–303.

Rahman, Q., Wilson, G. D. & Abrahams, S. (2003c). Sexual orientation related differences in spatial memory. *J Int Neuropsychol Soc.* 9, 376–383.

Ramagopalan, S. V., Dyment, D. A., Handunnetthi, L., Rice, G. P. & Ebers, G. C. (2010). A genome-wide scan of male sexual orientation. *J Hum Genet.* (Epub ahead of print January 8).

Reiner, W. G. & Gearhart, J. P. (2004). Discordant sexual identity in some genetic males with cloacal exstrophy assigned to female sex at birth. *N Engl J Med.* 350, 333–341.

Rendall, D., Vasey, P. L. & McKenzie, J. (2008). The Queen's English: an alternative, biosocial hypothesis for the distinctive features of "gay speech". *Arch Sex Behav.* 37, 188–204.

Reynolds, M. (2002). Kandahar's lightly veiled homosexual habits. *Los Angeles Times,* April 3.

Rhees, R. W., Shryne, J. E. & Gorski, R. A. (1990a). Onset of the hormone-sensitive perinatal period for sexual differentiation of the sexually dimorphic nucleus of the preoptic area in female rats. *J Neurobiol.* 21, 781–786.

Rhees, R. W., Shryne, J. E. & Gorski, R. A. (1990b). Termination of the hormone-sensitive period for differentiation of the sexually dimorphic nucleus of the preoptic area in male and female rats. *Brain Res Dev Brain Res.* 52, 17–23.

Rice, G., Anderson, C., Risch, N. & Ebers, G. (1999). Male homosexuality: absence of linkage to microsatellite markers at Xq28. *Science.* 284, 665–667.

Rieger, G., Chivers, M. L. & Bailey, J. M. (2005). Sexual arousal patterns of bisexual men. *Psychol Sci.* 16, 579–584.

Rieger, G., Linsenmeier, J. A., Gygax, L. & Bailey, J. M. (2008). Sexual orientation and childhood gender nonconformity: evidence from home videos. *Dev Psychol.* 44, 46–58.

Rieger, G., Linsenmeier, J. A., Gygax, L., Garcia, S. & Bailey, J. M. (2010). Dissecting "gaydar": Accuracy and the role of masculinity-femininity. *Arch Sex Behav.* 39, 124–140.

Roberts, E. K., Flak, J. N., Ye, W., Padmanabhan, V. & Lee, T. M. (2009). Juvenile rank can predict male-typical adult mating behavior in female sheep treated prenatally with testosterone. *Biol Reprod.* 80, 737–742.

Robinson, S. J. & Manning, J. T. (2000). The ratio of 2nd to 4th digit length and male homosexuality. *Evol Hum Behav.* 21, 333–345.

Rodeck, C. H., Gill, D., Rosenberg, D. A. & Collins, W. P. (1985). Testosterone levels in midtrimester maternal and fetal plasma and amniotic fluid. *Prenat Diagn.* 5, 175–181.

Rogers, I. (2003). The influence of birthweight and intrauterine environment on adiposity and fat distribution in later life. *Int J Obes Relat Metab Disord.* 27, 755–777.

Romeo, R. D. (2003). Puberty: a period of both organizational and activational effects of steroid hormones on neurobehavioural development. *J Neuroendocrinol.* 15, 1185–1192.

Roselli, C. E., Larkin, K., Resko, J. A., Stellflug, J. N. & Stormshak, F. (2004a). The volume of a sexually dimorphic nucleus in the ovine medial preoptic area/anterior hypothalamus varies with sexual partner preference. *Endocrinology.* 145, 478–483.

Roselli, C. E., Larkin, K., Schrunk, J. M. & Stormshak, F. (2004b). Sexual partner preference, hypothalamic morphology and aromatase in rams. *Physiol Behav.* 83, 233–245.

Roselli, C. E., Schrunk, J. M., Stadelman, H. L., Resko, J. A. & Stormshak, F. (2006). The effect of aromatase inhibition on the sexual differentiation of the sheep brain. *Endocrine.* 29, 501–511.

Roselli, C. E. & Stormshak, F. (2009a). The neurobiology of sexual partner preferences in rams. *Horm Behav.* 55, 611–620.

Roselli, C. E. & Stormshak, F. (2009b). Prenatal programming of sexual partner preference: the ram model. *J Neuroendocrinol.* 21, 359–364.

Rosenthal, A. M., Sylva, D., Safron, A. & Bailey, J. M. (2011). Sexual arousal patterns of bisexual men revisited. *Biological Psychology*, online ahead of print, http://dx.doi.org/10.1016/j.biopsycho.2011.06.015.

Rust, J., Golombok, S., Hines, M., Johnston, K. & Golding, J. (2000). The role of brothers and sisters in the gender development of preschool children. *J Exp Child Psychol.* 77, 292–303.

Ryner, L. C., Goodwin, S. F., Castrillon, D. H., Anand, A., Villella, A., Baker, B. S., Hall, J. C., Taylor, B. J. & Wasserman, S. A. (1996). Control of male sexual behavior and sexual orientation in *Drosophila* by the fruitless gene. *Cell.* 87, 1079–1089.

Sachs, J., Lieberman, P. & Erickson, D. (1973). Anatomical and cultural determinants of male and female speech. In: Shuy, W. and Fasold, R. W. (Eds.), *Language attitudes: Current trends and prospects.* Washington DC: Georgetown University Press.

Safron, A., Barch, B., Bailey, J. M., Gitelman, D. R., Parrish, T. B. & Reber, P. J. (2007). Neural correlates of sexual arousal in homosexual and heterosexual men. *Behav Neurosci.* 121, 237–248.

Sakuma, Y. (2009). Gonadal steroid action and brain sex differentiation in the rat. *J Neuroendocrinol.* 21(4), 410–414.

Salais, D. & Fischer, R. B. (1995). Sexual preference and altruism. *J Homosex.* 28, 185–196.

Sanders, A. R. (n.d.). *Molecular genetic study of sexual orientation.* Available at http://www.gaybros.com/index.html; accessed January 14, 2010.

Sanders, G. & Ross-Field, L. (1987). Neuropsychological development of cognitive abilities: a new research strategy and some preliminary evidence for a sexual orientation model. *Int J Neurosci.* 36, 1–16.

Sanders, G. & Wright, M. (1997). Sexual orientation differences in cerebral asymmetry and in the performance of sexually dimorphic cognitive and motor tasks. *Arch Sex Behav.* 26, 463–480.

Savic, I., Berglund, H., Gulyas, B. & Roland, P. (2001). Smelling of odorous sex hormone-like compounds causes sex-differentiated hypothalamic activations in humans. *Neuron.* 31, 661–668.

Savic, I., Berglund, H. & Lindstrom, P. (2005). Brain response to putative pheromones in homosexual men. *Proc Natl Acad Sci U S A.* 102, 7356–7361.

Savic, I., Heden-Blomqvist, E. & Berglund, H. (2009). Pheromone signal transduction in humans: What can be learned from olfactory loss. *Hum Brain Mapp.* 30(9), 3057–3065.

Savic, I. & Lindstrom, P. (2008). PET and MRI show differences in cerebral asymmetry and functional connectivity between homo- and heterosexual subjects. *PNAS.* 105, 9403–9408.

Savin-Williams, R. C. & Ream, G. L. (2006). Pubertal onset and sexual orientation in an adolescent national probability sample. *Arch Sex Behav.* 35, 279–286.

Schiller, G., director (1986). Before Stonewall: The making of a gay and lesbian community (documentary film).

Schmalz, J. (1993). Poll finds an even split on homosexuality's cause. *New York Times,* March 5.

Schmidt, G. & Clement, U. (1990). Does peace prevent homosexuality? *Arch Sex Behav.* 19, 183–187.

Schmitt, D. P. (2003). Universal sex differences in the desire for sexual variety: tests from 52 nations, 6 continents, and 13 islands. *J Pers Soc Psychol.* 85, 85–104.

Schmitt, D. P., Realo, A., Voracek, M. & Allik, J. (2008). Why can't a man be more like a woman? Sex differences in Big Five personality traits across 55 cultures. *J Pers Soc Psychol.* 94, 168–182.

Schwartz, G., Kim, R. M., Kolundzija, A. B., Rieger, G. & Sanders, A. R. (2010). Biodemographic and physical correlates of sexual orientation in men. *Arch Sex Behav.* 39, 83–109.

Searles, R. V., Yoo, M. J., He, J. R., Shen, W. B. & Selmanoff, M. (2000). Sex differences in GABA turnover and glutamic acid decarboxylase

(GAD(65) and GAD(67)) mRNA in the rat hypothalamus. *Brain Res.* 878, 11–19.

Segal, N. (2000). *Entwined lives: Twins and what they tell us about human behavior.* New York: Plume.

Serbin, L. A., Poulin-Dubois, D., Colburne, K. A., Sen, M. G. & Eichstedt, J. A. (2001). Gender stereotyping in infancy: Visual preferences for and knowledge of gender-stereotyped toys in the second year. *Intern J Behav Dev.* 25, 7–15.

Sergeant, M. J. T., Dickins, T. E., Davies, M. N. O. & Griffiths, M. D. (2006). Aggression, empathy and sexual orientation in males. *Pers Individ Dif.* 40, 475–486.

Shackelford, T. K. & Larsen, R. J. (1997). Facial asymmetry as an indicator of psychological, emotional, and physiological distress. *J Pers Soc Psychol.* 72, 456–466.

Shah, N. M., Pisapia, D. J., Maniatis, S., Mendelsohn, M. M., Nemes, A. & Axel, R. (2004). Visualizing sexual dimorphism in the brain. *Neuron.* 43, 313–319.

Shelp, S. G. (2002). Gaydar: visual detection of sexual orientation among gay and straight men. *J Homosex.* 44, 1–14.

Shirangi, T. R., Taylor, B. J. & McKeown, M. (2006). A double-switch system regulates male courtship behavior in male and female *Drosophila melanogaster. Nat Genet.* 38, 1435–1439.

Signoret, J. P. (1970). Reproductive behaviour of pigs. *J Reprod Fertil Suppl.* 11, Suppl 11:105+.

Simerly, R. B. (2002). Wired for reproduction: organization and development of sexually dimorphic circuits in the mammalian forebrain. *Annu Rev Neurosci.* 25, 507–536.

Simmons, D. A. & Yahr, P. (2003). GABA and glutamate in mating-activated cells in the preoptic area and medial amygdala of male gerbils. *J Comp Neurol.* 459, 290–300.

Simmons, J. L. (1965). Public stereotypes of deviants. *Social Problems.* 13, 223–232.

Singer, H. S., Morris, C., Gause, C., Pollard, M., Zimmerman, A. W. & Pletnikov, M. (2009). Prenatal exposure to antibodies from mothers of children with autism produces neurobehavioral alterations: A pregnant dam mouse model. *J Neuroimmunol.* 211, 39–48.

Singh, D., Vidaurri, M., Zambarano, R. J. & Dabbs, J. M., Jr. (1999). Lesbian erotic role identification: behavioral, morphological, and hormonal correlates. *J Pers Soc Psychol.* 76, 1035–1049.

Skidmore, W. C., Linsenmeier, J. A. & Bailey, J. M. (2006). Gender non-conformity and psychological distress in lesbians and gay men. *Arch Sex Behav.* 35, 685–697.

Slater, E. (1962). Birth order and maternal age of homosexuals. *Lancet.* 1, 69–71.

Smith, A. M., Rissel, C. E., Richters, J., Grulich, A. E. & de Visser, R. O. (2003). Sex in Australia: sexual identity, sexual attraction and sexual experience among a representative sample of adults. *Aust N Z J Public Health.* 27, 138–145.

Smyth, R., Jacobs, G. & Rogers, H. (2003). Male voices and perceived sexual orientation: An experimental and theoretical approach. *Lang Soc.* 32, 329–350.

Smyth, R. & Rogers, H. (2008). Do gay-sounding men speak like women? *Toronto Working Papers in Linguistics.* 27, 129–144.

Socarides, C. W. (1978). *Homosexuality.* Northvale NJ: J. Aronson.

Sommer, I. E., Aleman, A., Bouma, A. & Kahn, R. S. (2004). Do women really have more bilateral language representation than men? A meta-analysis of functional imaging studies. *Brain.* 127, 1845–1852.

Sommer, I. E., Aleman, A., Somers, M., Boks, M. P. & Kahn, R. S. (2008). Sex differences in handedness, asymmetry of the planum temporale and functional language lateralization. *Brain Res.* 1206, 76–88.

Sommer, V. & Vasey, P. L. (Eds.). (2006). *Homosexual behaviour in animals: An evolutionary perspective.* Cambridge NJ: Cambridge University Press.

Spengler, A. (1977). Manifest sadomasochism of males: results of an empirical study. *Arch Sex Behav.* 6, 441–456.

Sperling, M. A. (2008). *Pediatric endocrinology* (3rd ed.). New York: Saunders.

Spieth, H. T. (1974). Courtship behavior in *Drosophila. Ann Rev Entomol.* 19, 385–405.

Spitzer, R. L. (2003). Can some gay men and lesbians change their sexual orientation? 200 participants reporting a change from homosexual to heterosexual orientation. *Arch Sex Behav.* 32, 403–417; discussion 419–472.

Statistics Canada, (2004) *Canadian Community Health Survey* 2003. Available at http://www.statcan.ca/Daily/English/040615/d040615b.htm; accessed January 14, 2010.

Stockinger, P., Kvitsiani, D., Rotkopf, S., Tirian, L. & Dickson, B. J. (2005). Neural circuitry that governs *Drosophila* male courtship behavior. *Cell.* 121, 795–807.

Stowers, L., Holy, T. E., Meister, M., Dulac, C. & Koentges, G. (2002). Loss of sex discrimination and male-male aggression in mice deficient for TRP2. *Science.* 295, 1493–1500.

Su, R., Rounds, J. & Armstrong, P.I. (2009). Men and things, women and people: A meta-analysis of sex differences in interests. *Psychol Bull.* 135, 859–884.

Sulloway, F. J. (1996). *Born to rebel: Birth order, family dynamics, and creative lives.* New York: Pantheon Books.

Suschinsky, K. D., Lalumiere, M. L. & Chivers, M. L. (2009). Sex differences in patterns of genital sexual arousal: Measurement artifacts or true phenomena? *Arch Sex Behav.* 38, 559–573.

Svetec, N., Houot, B. & Ferveur, J. F. (2005). Effect of genes, social experience, and their interaction on the courtship behaviour of transgenic *Drosophila* males. *Genet Res.* 85, 183–193.

Swaab, D. F. (1995). Development of the human hypothalamus. *Neurochem Res.* 20, 509–519.

Swaab, D. F. & Fliers, E. (1985). A sexually dimorphic nucleus in the human brain. *Science.* 228, 1112–1115.

Swaab, D. F. & Garcia-Falgueras, A. (2009). Sexual differentiation of the human brain in relation to gender identity and sexual orientation. *Funct Neurol.* 24, 17–28.

Swaab, D. F., Gooren, L. J. & Hofman, M. A. (1992). Gender and sexual orientation in relation to hypothalamic structures. *Horm Res.* 38 Suppl 2, 51–61.

Swaab, D. F. & Hofman, M. A. (1988). Sexual differentiation of the human hypothalamus: ontogeny of the sexually dimorphic nucleus of the preoptic area. *Brain Res Dev Brain Res.* 44, 314–318.

Swaab, D. F. & Hofman, M. A. (1990). An enlarged suprachiasmatic nucleus in homosexual men. *Brain Res.* 537, 141–148.

Swanson, L. W. (2003). The amygdala and its place in the cerebral hemisphere. *Ann NY Acad Sci.* 985, 174–184.

Talarovicova, A., Krskova, L. & Blazekova, J. (2009). Testosterone enhancement during pregnancy influences the 2D:4D ratio and open field motor activity of rat siblings in adulthood. *Horm Behav.* 55, 235–239.

Taylor, A. (1983). Conceptions of masculinity and femininity as a basis for stereotypes of male and female homosexuals. *J Homosex.* 9, 37–53.

Taylor, J. (1992). *Born that way?* (documentary film). Windfall Films, London.

Tenhula, W. N. & Bailey, J. M. (1998). Female sexual orientation and pubertal onset. *Dev Neuropsychol.* 14, 369–383.

The National Children's Study. (2009). *What is the National Children's Study?* Available at http://www.nationalchildrensstudy.gov/Pages/default. aspx; accessed January 14, 2010.

Thornhill, R. & Gangestad, S. W. (1999). Facial attractiveness. *Trends Cogn Sci.* 3, 452–460.

Tobet, S. A., Zahniser, D. J. & Baum, M. J. (1986). Differentiation in male ferrets of a sexually dimorphic nucleus of the preoptic/anterior hypothalamic area requires prenatal estrogen. *Neuroendocrinology.* 44, 299–308.

Tomassilli, J. C., Golub, S. A., Bimbi, D. S. & Parsons, J. T. (2009). Behind closed doors: An exploration of kinky sexual behaviors in urban lesbian and bisexual women. *J Sex Res.* 1–8.

Tomeo, M. E., Templer, D. I., Anderson, S. & Kotler, D. (2001). Comparative data of childhood and adolescence molestation in heterosexual and homosexual persons. *Arch Sex Behav.* 30, 535–541.

Tooby, J. & Cosmides, L. (1992). The psychological foundations of culture. In: Barkow, J. H. et al. (Eds.), *The adapted mind* (pp. 19–136). New York: Oxford University Press.

Toro-Morn, M. & Sprecher, S. (2003). A cross-cultural comparison of mate preferences among university students: The United States vs. the People's Republic of China (PRC). *J Comparative Fam Studies.* 34, 151–174.

Tortorice, J. (2001). Gender identity, sexual orientation, and second-to-fourth digit ratio in females. *Hum Behav Evol Soc Abstr.* 13, 35.

Trimble, M. R., Mendez, M. F. & Cummings, J. L. (1997). Neuropsychiatric symptoms from the temporolimbic lobes. In: Salloway, S. et al. (Eds.), *The neuropsychiatry of limbic and subcortical disorders.* Washington DC: American Psychiatric Publishing.

Trivers, R. L. (1974). Parent-offspring conflict. *Amer Zool.* 14, 249–264.

Trotier, D., Eloit, C., Wassef, M., Talmain, G., Bensimon, J. L., Doving, K. B. & Ferrand, J. (2000). The vomeronasal cavity in adult humans. *Chem Senses.* 25, 369–380.

Tuncer, M. C., Hatipoglu, E. S. & Ozates, M. (2005). Sexual dimorphism and handedness in the human corpus callosum based on magnetic resonance imaging. *Surg Radiol Anat.* 27, 254–259.

Tuttle, G. E. & Pillard, R. C. (1991). Sexual orientation and cognitive abilities. *Arch Sex Behav.* 20, 307–318.

Udry, J. R., Morris, N. M. & Kovenock, J. (1995). Androgen effects on women's gendered behaviour. *J Biosoc Sci.* 27, 359–368.

van Anders, S. M., Hamilton, L. D., Schmidt, N. & Watson, N. V. (2007). Associations between testosterone secretion and sexual activity in women. *Horm Behav.* 51, 477–482.

van Anders, S. M., Vernon, P. A. & Wilbur, C. J. (2006). Finger-length ratios show evidence of prenatal hormone-transfer between opposite-sex twins. *Horm Behav.* 49, 315–319.

van Anders, S. M. & Watson, N. V. (2006). Relationship status and testosterone in North American heterosexual and non-heterosexual men and women: cross-sectional and longitudinal data. *Psychoneuroendocrinology.* 31, 715–723.

van Anders, S. M. & Watson, N. V. (2007). Testosterone levels in women and men who are single, in long-distance relationships, or same-city relationships. *Horm Behav.* 51, 286–291.

van Beijsterveldt, C. E., Hudziak, J. J. & Boomsma, D. I. (2006). Genetic and environmental influences on cross-gender behavior and relation to behavior problems: a study of Dutch twins at ages 7 and 10 years. *Arch Sex Behav.* 35, 647–658.

Vanderlaan, D. P. & Vasey, P. L. (2008). Mate retention behavior of men and women in heterosexual and homosexual relationships. *Arch Sex Behav.* 37, 572–585.

Vanderlaan, D. P. & Vasey, P.L. (2009a). Male sexual orientation in Independent Samoa: Evidence for fraternal birth order and maternal fecundity effects. *Arch Sex Behav.* (Epub ahead of print December 29).

Vanderlaan, D. P. & Vasey, P. L. (2009b). Patterns of sexual coercion in heterosexual and non-heterosexual men and women. *Arch Sex Behav.* 38, 987–999.

Vasey, P. L. (2006). The pursuit of pleasure: An evolutionary history of female homosexual behavior in Japanese macaques. In: Sommer, V. and Vasey, P. L. (Eds.), *Homosexual behavior in animals: An evolutionary perspective* (pp. 191–219). Cambridge NJ: Cambridge University Press.

Vasey, P. L. & Bartlett, N. H. (2007). What can the Samoan "Fa'afafine" teach us about the Western concept of gender identity disorder in childhood? *Perspect Biol Med.* 50, 481–490.

Vasey, P. L. & Jiskoot, H. (2009). The biogeography and evolution of female homosexual behavior in Japanese macaques. *Arch Sex Behav.* (Epub ahead of print August 18).

Vasey, P. L. & Pfaus, J. G. (2005). A sexually dimorphic hypothalamic nucleus in a macaque species with frequent female-female mounting and same-sex sexual partner preference. *Behav Brain Res.* 157, 265–272.

Vasey, P. L., Pocock, D. S. & Vanderlaan, D. P. (2007). Kin selection and male androphilia in Samoan *fa'afafine*. *Evol Hum Behav.* 28, 159–167.

Vasey, P. L. & VanderLaan, D. P. (2007). Birth order and male androphilia in Samoan fa'afafine. *Proc Biol Sci.* 274, 1437–1442.

Vasey, P. L. & Vanderlaan, D. P. (2008). Avuncular tendencies and the evolution of male androphilia in Samoan *Fa'afafine*. *Arch Sex Behav.* September 23 (Epub ahead of print).

Vasey, P. L. & Vanderlaan, D. P. (2010). An adaptive cognitive dissociation between willingness to help kin and non-kin in Samoan *fa'fafine*. *Psychol Sci.* (Epub ahead of print January 14).

Vega Matuszczyk, J., Fernandez-Guasti, A. & Larsson, K. (1988). Sexual orientation, proceptivity, and receptivity in the male rat as a function of neonatal hormonal manipulation. *Horm Behav.* 22, 362–378.

vom Saal, F. S. & Bronson, F. H. (1980). Sexual characteristics of adult female mice are correlated with their blood testosterone levels during prenatal development. *Science.* 208, 597–599.

Voracek, M. (2009). Comparative study of digit ratios (2D:4D and other) and novel measures of relative finger length: testing magnitude and consistency of sex differences across samples. *Percept Mot Skills.* 108, 83–93.

Voracek, M. & Dressler, S. G. (2007). Digit ratio (2D:4D) in twins: heritability estimates and evidence for a masculinized trait expression in women from opposite-sex pairs. *Psychol Rep.* 100, 115–126.

Voracek, M., Manning, J. T. & Ponocny, I. (2005). Digit ratio (2D:4D) in homosexual and heterosexual men from Austria. *Arch Sex Behav.* 34, 335–340.

Wallen, K. (1996). Nature needs nurture: The interaction of hormonal and social influences on the development of behavioral sex differences in rhesus monkeys. *Horm Behav.* 30, 364–378.

Wallen, K. (2009). Does finger fat produce sex differences in second to fourth digit ratios? *Endocrinology.* 150, 4819–4822.

Wallien, M. S. & Cohen-Kettenis, P. T. (2008). Psychosexual outcome of gender-dysphoric children. *J Am Acad Child Adolesc Psychiatry.* 47, 1413–1423.

Wallien, M. S., Zucker, K. J., Steensma, T. D. & Cohen-Kettenis, P. T. (2008). 2D:4D finger-length ratios in children and adults with gender identity disorder. *Horm Behav.* 54, 450–454.

Wang, P. Y., Protheroe, A., Clarkson, A. N., Imhoff, F., Koishi, K. & McLennan, I. S. (2009). Mullerian inhibiting substance contributes to sex-linked biases in the brain and behavior. *Proc Natl Acad Sci U S A.* 106, 7203–7208.

Ward, I. L. (1972). Prenatal stress feminizes and demasculinizes the behavior of males. *Science.* 175, 82–84.

Ward, I. L. & Stehm, K. E. (1991). Prenatal stress feminizes juvenile play patterns in male rats. *Physiol Behav.* 50, 601–605.

Ward, I. L. & Weisz, J. (1984). Differential effects of maternal stress on circulating levels of corticosterone, progesterone, and testosterone in male and female rat fetuses and their mothers. *Endocrinology.* 114, 1635–1644.

Wassersug, R. (2003). *Castration anxiety article from OUT magazine.* Available at http://www.eunuch.org/Alpha/C/ea_195222castrati.htm; accessed January 14, 2010.

Wegesin, D. J. (1998a). Event-related potentials in homosexual and heterosexual men and women: sex-dimorphic patterns in verbal asymmetries and mental rotation. *Brain Cogn.* 36, 73–92.

Wegesin, D. J. (1998b). A neuropsychologic profile of homosexual and heterosexual men and women. *Arch Sex Behav.* 27, 91–108.

Weinrich, J. D. (1978). Nonreproduction, homosexuality, transsexualism, and intelligence: I. A systematic literature search. *J Homosex.* 3, 275–289.

Weinrich, J. D. (1987a). A new sociobiological theory of homosexuality applicable to societies with universal marriage. *Behav Ecol Sociobiol.* 8, 37–47.

Weinrich, J. D. (1987b). *Sexual landscapes: Why we are what we are, why we love whom we love.* New York: Scribners.

Weinrich, J. D., Grant, I., Jacobson, D. L., Robinson, S. R. & McCutchan, J. A. (1992). Effects of recalled childhood gender nonconformity on adult genitoerotic role and AIDS exposure. HNRC Group. *Arch Sex Behav.* 21, 559–585.

Wellings, K., Field, J., Johnson, A. M. & Wadsworth, J. (1994). *Sexual Behavior in Britain: The National Survey of Sexual Attitudes and Lifestyles.* New York: Penguin Books.

Whitam, F. L. (1983). Culturally invariant properties of male homosexuality: Tentative conclusions from cross-cultural research. *Arch Sex Behav.* 12, 207–226.

Whitam, F. L., Diamond, M. & Martin, J. (1993). Homosexual orientation in twins: a report on 61 pairs and three triplet sets. *Arch Sex Behav.* 22, 187–206.

White, M. (1994). *Stranger at the gate: To be gay and Christian in America.* New York: Simon and Schuster.

Wilhelm, D., Palmer, S. & Koopman, P. (2007). Sex determination and gonadal development in mammals. *Physiol Rev.* 87, 1–28.

Williams, C. L. & Meck, W. H. (1991). The organizational effects of gonadal steroids on sexually dimorphic spatial ability. *Psychoneuroendocrinology.* 16, 155–176.

Williams, T. J., Pepitone, M. E., Christensen, S. E., Cooke, B. M., Huberman, A. D., Breedlove, N. J., Breedlove, T. J., Jordan, C. L. & Breedlove, S. M. (2000). Finger-length ratios and sexual orientation. *Nature.* 404, 455–456.

Williams, W. L. (1986). *The spirit and the flesh: Sexual diversity in American Indian culture.* New York: Beacon Press.

Wilson, E. O. (1975). *Sociobiology: The new synthesis.* Boston: Harvard University Press.

Wilson, H. W. & Widom, C. S. (2009). Does physical abuse, sexual abuse, or neglect in childhood Increase the likelihood of same-sex sexual relationships and cohabitation? A prospective 30–year follow-up. *Arch Sex Behav.* 39, 63–74

Wisniewski, A. B., Migeon, C. J., Malouf, M. A. & Gearhart, J. P. (2004). Psychosexual outcome in women affected by congenital adrenal hyperplasia due to 21–hydroxylase deficiency. *J Urol.* 171, 2497–2501.

Witelson, S. F., Kigar, D. L., Scamvougeras, A., Kideckel, D. M., Buck, B., Stanchev, P. L., Bronskill, M. & Black, S. (2008). Corpus callosum anatomy in right-handed homosexual and heterosexual men. *Arch Sex Behav.* 37, 857–863.

Woolery, L. M. (2007). Gaydar: a social-cognitive analysis. *J Homosex.* 53, 9–17.

Wysocki, C. J. & Preti, G. (2009). *Human pheromones: What's purported, what's supported.* Available at http://senseofsmell.org/papers/ Human_Pheromones_Final%207–15–09.pdf; accessed January 14, 2010.

Yamamoto, D. (2007). The neural and genetic substrates of sexual behavior in *Drosophila. Adv Genet.* 59, 39–66.

Yang, S. L., Chen, Y. Y., Hsieh, Y. L., Jin, S. H., Hsu, H. K. & Hsu, C. (2004). Perinatal androgenization prevents age-related neuron loss in the sexually dimorphic nucleus of the preoptic area in female rats. *Dev Neurosci.* 26, 54–60.

Yankelovich Partners (1994). *A Yankelovich MONITOR perspective on gays/ lesbians.* Chapel Hill NC: Yankelovich Partners.

Zietsch, B. P., Morley, K. I., Shekar, S. N., Verweij, K. H., Keller, M. C., Macgregor, S., Wright, M. J., Bailey, J. M. & Martin, N. G. (2008). Genetic factors predisposing to homosexuality may increase mating success in heterosexuals. *Evol Hum Behav.* 29, 424–433.

Zucker, K. J. & Blanchard, R. (1994). Reanalysis of Bieber et al.'s 1962 data on sibling sex ratio and birth order in male homosexuals. *J Nerv Ment Dis.* 182, 528–530.

Zucker, K. J., Bradley, S. J., Oliver, G., Blake, J., Fleming, S. & Hood, J. (1996). Psychosexual development of women with congenital adrenal hyperplasia. *Horm Behav.* 30, 300–318.

Zuger, B. (1984). Early effeminate behavior in boys: Outcome and significance for homosexuality. *J Nerv Mental Dis.* 172, 90–97.

Zuloaga, D. G., Puts, D. A., Jordan, C. L. & Breedlove, S. M. (2008). The role of androgen receptors in the masculinization of brain and behavior: what we've learned from the testicular feminization mutation. *Horm Behav.* 53, 613–626.

AUTHOR INDEX

SUBJECT INDEX